Gender Stereotyping

PENNSYLVANIA STUDIES
IN HUMAN RIGHTS

Bert B. Lockwood, Jr., Series Editor

A complete list of books in the series is available from the publisher.

Gender Stereotyping

Transnational Legal Perspectives

Rebecca J. Cook and Simone Cusack

PENN

University of Pennsylvania Press

Philadelphia

Published by
University of Pennsylvania Press
Philadelphia, Pennsylvania 19104-4112

Printed in the United States of America on acid-free paper
10 9 8 7 6 5 4 3 2 1

Library of Congress Cataloging-in-Publication Data

Cook, Rebecca J.
    Gender stereotyping : transnational legal perspectives / Rebecca J. Cook and Simone Cusack.
        p.   cm. — (Pennsylvania studies in human rights)
    ISBN: 978-0-8122-4214-0 (alk. paper)
    Includes bibliographical references and index.
    1. Convention on the Elimination of All Forms of Discrimination against Women (1980).
2. Sex discrimination against women—Law and legislation.   3. Stereotypes (Social psychology).   I. Title.   II. Cusack, Simone.
    K3243 .C68   2010
    342.08/78—dc22   2009029477

Contents

Foreword

LOUISE ARBOUR

Striking about this book is its demonstration of how common the phenomenon of repressive stereotyping of women is in all parts of the world. Within a country, stereotyping is liable to pervade different sectors of national life, whether it be in the education, employment or health sectors, marriage or family relations or other areas of national life. The pervasiveness of gender stereotypes that determine women's value in life or direct or restrict their "proper" role in their communities combines with the persistence of the conceptions of women's roles, qualities and attributes over time. While the content of stereotypes might vary according to countries and sectors, they generally function to contribute to systemic beliefs that justify women's subordination in society.

If countries are going to benefit from the knowledge, capacity, ingenuity, and leadership of their female populations, they will need to take seriously the importance of eliminating restrictive stereotypes of women. Countries will need to ensure that women are considered in terms of their actual characteristics and competence, not in terms of stereotypical generalizations about their inherent value as human beings or the roles that they should perform in the various dimensions of their families, communities, and wider societies.

Societies cannot wait for extraordinary individuals to break stereotypes, although such individuals are to be supported and celebrated. They need to refine their own strategic methodology, informed by the methodology presented in this book, of identifying each stereotype, diagnosing its harm and determining how the law perpetuates its use. They will need to take account of its historical origins and its political, economic and social contexts, to inspire individuals and institutions to eliminate its harms to women and society at large.

This book is an important step in advancing understanding of how the law can be applied to achieve real equality for women. It will help to foster transnational conversations about how the law, including international human rights treaties, can be used to eliminate restrictive stereotypes of women. It will raise the consciousness of those working to advance the equality of men and women, especially those working in the executive, legislative and judicial branches of government and at international levels, about how their thinking might be biased by stereotypical assumptions about the inherent value, and proper role, of women in society. It will illuminate thinking about how the law can be used to expose impoverished patterns of presumption and propriety about women that deny women and their families, communities and nations, opportunities to benefit from the full contributions women are capable of making.

Table of Cases

This and the following table have been designed to complement but not repeat the index at the back of the book. For page references to concepts and subjects, please see the index. The Convention on the Elimination of All Forms of Discrimination against Women and the Optional Protocol to the Convention on the Elimination of All Forms of Discrimination against Women are briefly referenced in these tables; due to the necessity for sub-entries, detailed references are in the index.

Page references to cases mentioned in the endnotes, but not in the text, are included here.

DOMESTIC JURISPRUDENCE

REGIONAL JURISPRUDENCE

INTERNATIONAL JURISPRUDENCE

Table of Treaties, Legislation, and Other Relevant Instruments

DOMESTIC LEGISLATION

REGIONAL HUMAN RIGHTS TREATIES

INTERNATIONAL HUMAN RIGHTS TREATIES AND INSTRUMENTS

Introduction

Stereotyping is part of human nature. It is the way we categorize individuals, often unconsciously, into particular groups or types, in part to simplify the world around us. It is the process of ascribing to an individual general attributes, characteristics, or roles by reason only of his or her apparent membership in a particular group. Stereotyping produces generalizations or preconceptions concerning attributes, characteristics, or roles of members of a particular social group, which renders unnecessary consideration of any particular individual members' abilities, needs, wishes, and circumstances.

Stereotypes affect both men and women. However, they often have a particularly egregious effect on women. As one commentator has explained, a "useful way of examining the continued disadvantage of women is to identify the assumptions and stereotypes which have been central to the perpetuation and legitimation of women's legal and social subordination. Such assumptions have roots which stretch deep into the history of ideas, yet continue to influence the legal and social structure of modern society. Indeed, the continuity is startling, given the extent and fundamental nature of change in the political and economic context."[1]

Stereotypes degrade women when they assign them to subservient roles in society, and devalue their attributes and characteristics. Prejudices about women's inferiority and their stereotyped roles generate disrespect and devaluation of women in all sectors of society. Women themselves may be socially conditioned to absorb negative stereotypes about themselves, and to fulfill the subordinate, passive role they consider appropriate to their status. When societies fail to recognize and eliminate such prejudices and their associated stereotypes, that failure exacerbates a climate of impunity with respect to violations of women's rights. The climate of impunity enables prejudices and wrongful gender stereotypes to fester, causing further devaluation of women.

Gender stereotypes are concerned with the social and cultural construction or understanding of men and women, due to their different physical, biological, sexual, and social functions. The term "gender stereotype" is an overarching generic term that includes stereotypes of women and subgroups of women, and stereotypes of men and subgroups of men. Its meaning reflects different social and cultural constructions of men and women. As a result, its meaning is fluid, and changes over time and across cultures and societies. This book focuses primarily on stereotypes of women, but addresses stereotypes of men at various points because it recognizes that stereotypes of both men and women need to be changed in order to liberate both men and women to be all that they can be.

Achieving the emancipation of women through the elimination of gender stereotyping is based on the thesis that women are socially constructed into subservient roles and as having inferior attributes and characteristics, by gender stereotypes. The social construction thesis is one explanation of how societies devalue and subordinate women. It has been explained that "the structure and organization of society is built on gender stereotypes, hence ensuring that existing unequal power relations between the sexes are sustained."[2] Subordination and exclusion of women take place through the uncritical application of "stereotyped (often traditional and implicit) ideas, symbols, and roles."[3] Analysis of how such stereotypical assumptions are socially constructed and shaped by gender-based judgments regarding women's attributes, characteristics, and roles is critical, regardless of whether they are accurate. These assumptions are important sources of social meanings, norms, and values on which social structures are built and perpetuated.[4]

Eliminating some of the most hidden, yet pervasive, forms of discrimination against women requires the dismantling of gender stereotypes.[5] Such gender stereotypes are remarkably resilient and resistant to eradication or reform. Some gender stereotypes, such as the stereotype of women as primarily caregivers, seem constant. Other stereotypes might fade for a time, but they might reemerge in other forms. An example of the application of the stereotype of women as the property of men has enabled husbands to beat their wives, so long as the stick they use is not bigger than their thumb. This has led to the use of the expression "the rule of thumb," as a norm by which we are guided. Another example of the application of the property stereotype is fathers "giving away" their daughters in marriage. These and other examples of the application of the stereotype of women as property under men's control persists in some contexts, and enables, for example, the violent treatment of women in many forms, such as domestic and sexual violence, in that legal rights of ownership include redesign or destruction of the object owned.

The thesis of this book is that, in order to eliminate all forms of discrimination against women, and indeed to eliminate other violations of women's rights whether or not they constitute a form of discrimination, greater priority and thought need to be given to the elimination of wrongful gender stereotyping. Naming a gender stereotype and identifying its harm is critical to its eradication. An analogy to diagnoses of medical diseases might be helpful.[6] A medical diagnosis of a disease is required in order to proceed with its treatment. A difficulty with a diagnosis of a gender stereotype as a disease is that often it is not considered a disease at all, because it is part and parcel of a natural way of functioning, and of unconscious gendered modes of thinking. As a result, a concerted effort needs to be made to diagnose a wrongful gender stereotype as a disease, identify its harms, and determine its treatment.

The harms of gender stereotyping can be thought about in terms of degrading women or diminishing their dignity, and in many cases denying them justified benefits or imposing unjust burdens. For example, stereotypes of women as lacking capacities to learn not only degrade them, but also often deny them access to education, and impose burdens of submissive gender roles, such as caretaking.

While there are many ways to dismantle gender stereotypes, such as through humorous films that show women's equality with men or mock the stereotypical assumptions of women's inabilities,[7] this book concentrates on the role of domestic, regional, and international law in dismantling wrongful gender stereotypes. A challenge is to explore which gender stereotypes the law should dismantle, in what contexts, in what ways, and for what reasons.[8] How willing should a court or human rights treaty body be to reshape stereotypes that reflect gender norms? Should a court be reluctant to disturb gender norms where they are considered fundamental or of prominent significance to a society or its stability?[9] One must ask what gender practices are salient and meaningful to the identity of members of a society. There will inevitably be tensions among different groups regarding what gender stereotypes need to be eliminated to achieve women's equality, and which are important to preserve for maintenance of individuals' identities.

Examples of this tension are debates around the ordination of women as ministers of religion,[10] or around dress and appearance standards.[11] Some consider the obligation of dress to wear jewelry or high heeled shoes as prescribing or scripting women's identity in ways that oppress or subordinate them. Others consider the ability to wear jewelry or high heeled shoes as a liberating way of articulating or expressing one's own identity. Debates around prescriptive stereotypes concerning dress and appearance standards might center on whether women's identities are oppressively imposed on them, or freely chosen as preference of fashion.

A leading international framework for such debates is provided by the international Convention on the Elimination of All Forms of Discrimination against Women ("Women's Convention" or "Convention"; see Appendix A).[12] By the Women's Convention, member states, known as States Parties,[13] accept the obligation to eliminate all forms of discrimination against women and ensure substantive equality. "Discrimination against women" is defined as "any distinction, exclusion or restriction made on the basis of sex which has the effect or purpose of impairing or nullifying the recognition, enjoyment or exercise by women, irrespective of their marital status, on a basis of equality of men and women, of human rights and fundamental freedoms in the political, economic, social, cultural, civil or any other field."[14]

This definition needs to be considered and given effect in light of the Convention's overall object and purpose, which is discernible from its title, preamble, foundational articles 1 to 5 and 24, and subsequent practice and application, especially by the Committee on the Elimination of Discrimination against Women ("the Women's Committee" or "the Committee"). This Committee, created under the Convention, is composed of 23 members, elected by States Parties, to serve in their expert capacity to monitor the implementation of the Convention.[15] The Committee has explained that States Parties are required "to eliminate all forms of discrimination against women with a view to achieving women's de jure and de facto equality with men in the enjoyment of their human rights and fundamental freedoms."[16] The Committee has further explained that, in order to fulfil this overarching purpose, States Parties have three core obligations:

Firstly, States parties' obligation is to ensure that there is no direct or indirect discrimination against women in their laws and that women are protected against discrimination—committed by public authorities, the judiciary, organizations, enterprises or private individuals—in the public as well as the private spheres by competent tribunals as well as sanctions and other remedies. Secondly, States parties' obligation is to improve the de facto position of women through concrete and effective policies and programmes. Thirdly, States parties' obligation is to address prevailing gender relations and the persistence of gender-based stereotypes that affect women not only through individual acts by individuals but also in law, and legal and societal structures and institutions.[17]

The primary focus of this book is the examination of the third obligation, "to address . . . the persistence of gender-based stereotypes that affect women not only through individual acts but also in law, and legal and societal structures and institutions." While it is necessary to eliminate direct and indirect discrimination and to improve the de facto position of women, it is not sufficient to achieve substantive equality. The Women's Convention requires States Parties to go farther, to reformulate laws, policies, and practices in order to ensure that they do not devalue women or reflect the patriarchal attitudes that attribute particular subservient characteristics and roles to women through gender stereotypes. The Preamble to the Women's Convention recognizes that "a change in the traditional role of men as well as the role of women in society and in the family is needed to achieve full equality between men and women."[18]

The Women's Committee explains that the Convention requires States Parties to adopt measures "towards a *real transformation* of opportunities, institutions and systems so that they are no longer grounded in historically determined male paradigms of power and life patterns."[19] The Committee thus has made clear not only that the Convention requires States Parties to eliminate wrongful gender stereotyping, but also that this obligation is central to eliminating all forms of discrimination against women.

Article 5(a) of the Women's Convention requires States Parties to transform patriarchal norms by taking all appropriate measures to "modify the social and cultural patterns of conduct of men and women, with a view to achieving the elimination of prejudices and customary and all other practices which are based on the idea of the inferiority or the superiority of either of the sexes or on stereotyped roles for men and women." Article 5(a) critically emphasizes the obligation to achieve the modification of social and cultural patterns of conduct to eliminate prejudices and customary and all other practices grounded in stereotypes about the inferiority or superiority of, or appropriate sex roles for men and women.

Article 2 lays out the basic obligations that States Parties undertake when they ratify, accede to, or succeed to the Convention. Subsection (f) of article 2 requires States Parties to "take all appropriate measures, including legislation, to modify or abolish existing laws, regulations, customs and practices which constitute discrimination against women." Article 5(a) is applicable upon just a showing that a prejudice or practice was based on a stereotype concerning "the inferiority or superiority of either of the sexes" or on "stereotyped roles for men and women." In contrast, article 2(f) is applicable upon showing that a law, regulation, custom, or practice, including gender stereotyping, constitutes discrimination against women.

The Women's Convention is one of the international human rights treaties that require the elimination of wrongful gender stereotyping. It requires such elimination in order to "ensure the full development and advancement of women, for the purpose of guaranteeing them the exercise and enjoyment of human rights and fundamental freedoms on a basis of equality with men," as mandated by article 3 of the Convention. This means that States Parties must make available to women the institutions appropriate to their needs where those needs differ from those of men. An obvious example is respectful access to gynecological care. It also means that women must have equality of access to institutions where their needs are the same as men's, such as educational institutions. Article 3 is reinforced by article 24, which requires States Parties to "adopt all necessary measures at the national level aimed at achieving the full realization of the rights recognized" in the Convention.

On the basis of this transformative view of equality, States Parties are required to undertake measures that lead to a social reordering of stereotypical views of men and women in the political economy (i.e., the division of labor and resources), and in the cultural valuations ascribed to men and women (i.e., the privileging of masculinity and devaluing of femininity). States Parties must seek to eliminate wrongful, often patronizing, treatment of women grounded in gender stereotypes. States Parties will need to take appropriate measures to ensure that their laws, policies, and practices reflect emancipatory norms, not stereotypical ones, which will enable women to create their own roles and identities and be all that they can be, irrespective of male standards.

Applying the Women's Convention as the primary framework for analysis, the book is structured in the following sequence.

Chapter 1 explores different understandings of stereotypes and the different reasons why people might stereotype, examining the specific nature of gender stereotypes, what forms they might take, in what contexts, and why. This chapter considers how the law is and might be used as a means of perpetuation and elimination of gender stereotypes. Stereotypes of both men and women are examined, because both have to be changed in order to "modify the social and cultural patterns of conduct of men and women," as required by article 5(a) of the Women's Convention.

Chapter 2 considers the importance of identifying, naming, and exposing gender stereotypes in different contexts. It continues by exploring how their application, enforcement, or perpetuation harms women through the denial of a benefit, imposition of a burden, or otherwise degrading treatment. Consideration is given to how stereotypes of men may harm both men and women. For example, limiting men to their stereotypical role as primary breadwinners has denied them the opportunity to share equally in the care of their children. The breadwinner stereotype of men harms women, because it denies women the help they need in caretaking and the ability to move beyond their nurturing role.

Chapter 3 analyzes the nature and scope of the obligations under the Women's Convention to eliminate wrongful gender stereotypes by state and non-state actors. It continues by determining the appropriateness of measures to remedy their harmful effects on the individual or their comparably harmful effects of a structural or systemic nature. The chapter ends by examining the responsibilities of States Parties to withdraw any reservations to their acceptance of the Women's Convention by which they try to exempt their obligations to eliminate wrongful gender stereotypes.

Chapter 4 explores the specific nature of the obligation to eliminate gender stereotypes that operate as a form of discrimination against women. In so doing, it examines the different ways that states have tried to justify gender stereotyping, and explores whether those justifications are valid in the circumstances.

Chapter 5 illustrates and assesses the role of the Women's Committee in eliminating wrongful gender stereotypes through the Convention's reporting procedure, and the communication and inquiry procedures of the Optional Protocol to the Convention on the Elimination of All Forms of Discrimination against Women[20] ("Optional Protocol"; see Appendix B). Emphasis is given to how the Committee might provide guidance to ensure improved use of the reporting procedure to eliminate wrongful gender stereotyping, and how the reasoning in particular decisions and reports under the Optional Protocol might have been strengthened.

Chapter 6 concludes by reviewing some of the reasons why gender stereotypes have proved so resistant to change, what might be some of the obstacles to the elimination of wrongful gender stereotypes in the years ahead, and what role the Women's Committee might play in addressing these obstacles.

Throughout the book, judgments given by courts and human rights treaty bodies were selected because of their reasoning about gender stereotypes. In most instances judgments are chosen because of the powerful and insightful nature of the reasoning. In other instances, judgments are chosen because of the uncritical reasoning. This selection follows extensive research into decisions addressing gender stereotypes made in domestic, regional, and international courts and human rights treaty bodies. Judgments that cover stereotyping issues that are common to several countries are identified and chosen for analysis. Where possible, judgments are selected that apply the Women's Convention. Attempts are also made to choose decisions from the various regions of the world, but not all are represented, in part because of language barriers and difficulties in finding the actual texts of judgments.

In that challenges of dismantling wrongful gender stereotypes involve international human rights law and comparative law, especially comparative constitutional law,[21] the challenges have a transnational character. It has been explained that transnational legal process has four distinctive features.

First, it is nontraditional: it breaks down two traditional dichotomies that have historically dominated the study of international law: between domestic and international, public and private. Second, it is nonstatist; the actors in this process are not just, or even primarily, nation states, but include nonstate actors as well. Third, transnational legal process is dynamic, not static. Transnational law transforms, mutates, and percolates up and down, from the public to the private, from the domestic to the international level and back down again. Fourth and finally, it is normative. From this process of interaction, new rules of law emerge, which are interpreted, internalized, and enforced, thus beginning the process all over again.[22]

The methodology used in this book is transnational: it draws on both domestic and international law, and it builds on the work of state and non-state actors. The book is designed to instigate readers' reflection on their own experiences with how they stereotype and how they have been stereotyped, and to facilitate learning across national and disciplinary boundaries about the harms caused by the application, enforcement, or perpetuation of gender stereotypes. The book is intended to provide perspectives into how wrongful gender stereotypes might be effectively eliminated through the transnational legal process in order to develop the meaning and application of transformative equality.

Chapter 1
Understanding Gender Stereotyping

What Is a Stereotype?

What precisely do we mean by the term "stereotype"? As understood in this book, a stereotype is a generalized view or preconception of attributes or characteristics possessed by, or the roles that are or should be performed by, members of a particular group (e.g., women, lesbians, adolescents).[1] In this view, a stereotype presumes that all members of a certain social group possess particular attributes or characteristics (e.g., adolescents are irresponsible), or perform specified roles (e.g., women are caregivers). It does not matter for purposes of characterizing a generalization as a stereotype that attributes or characteristics are or are not common to individual members of that group, or whether members perform those roles or do not. The key consideration is that, because a particular group is presumed to possess those attributes or characteristics or perform those roles, an individual, simply by virtue of membership in that group, is believed to conform to the generalized view or preconception. All the dimensions of personality that make that individual unique are consequently filtered through the lens of a generalized view or preconception of the group with which the individual is identified.[2]

Stereotypes have long been the subject of inquiry. Coined in 1798 by the French printer Fermin Didot, the term *stereotype* was first used to describe a method or process of printing whereby a cast-metal plate, or mold, was used to duplicate original material.[3] The term itself derives from the Greek words *stereos* and *typos*, roughly translated to mean "solid" and "mold" respectively.[4]

In 1922, the usage of the term stereotype in printing was adapted metaphorically as a social science concept to explain how people preconceive others only as reprints from a mold.[5] The "perfect stereotype" was described as follows: "Its hallmark is that it precedes the use of reason; is a form of perception, imposes a certain character on the data of our senses before the data reach the intelligence."[6] A stereotype tells us:

about the world before we see it. We imagine most things before we experience them. And those preconceptions, unless education has made us acutely aware, govern deeply the whole process of perception. They mark out certain objects as familiar or strange, emphasizing the difference, so that the slightly familiar is seen as very familiar, and the somewhat strange as sharply alien. They are aroused by small signs, which may vary from a true index to a vague analogy. Aroused, they flood fresh vision with older images, and project into the world what has been resurrected in memory.[7]

In this view, we human beings do not see the "world outside" exactly as it is; rather, we preconceive "pictures in our heads,"[8] or stereotypes, that we rely upon to give meaning to the world we perceive. Simply put, stereotypes help us to understand, simplify, and process the infinitely variable personal attributes, characteristics, and roles in the world in which we live. Individuals can be placed in categories, or stereotyped, according to various criteria, such as their gender, pigmentation, age, language, religion, sexual orientation, and racial or ethnic origin.

The purpose of this chapter is to explore the meaning of stereotypes as they are applied to women. What is a stereotype? What does it mean to say that someone is stereotyping? Why do people stereotype? What purpose or purposes do stereotypes serve? Why do people conform to stereotypes, or break them? Are all stereotypes the same? Are there different forms of gender stereotypes? What is meant by the term "sex stereotype"? How does that term differ from "sexual stereotype," or "sex role stereotype"? What is meant by the term "compounded stereotype"? How do these various forms interact to formulate the overarching notion of a gender stereotype? What are the consequences to individuals, groups, or societies of gender stereotyping? How do their contexts matter? How do stereotypes evolve, and what is the role of the law in their evolution, perpetuation, and elimination?

We do not claim to have answers to every one of these questions. Rather, the purpose of this chapter is to explore these questions. Readers are encouraged to consider the various questions in light of their own experiences of stereotyping. It is hoped that these questions are helpful in illuminating the readers' personal experiences of how they, or their family and friends, have been stereotyped, or how they themselves stereotype others.

Consider, as an example, the stereotypical belief that "men are physically powerful." In this example, the social group in question is "men," while the generalized view concerns their physical strength. According to this stereotype, all men, by virtue of their membership in the social group of men, are considered physically powerful. When we stereotype, we do not consider the characteristics of a particular individual. For example, even though an individual man, say Tom, may be physically weak or at least weaker than other men, and an individual woman may be stronger than he is, he will be stereotyped as physically powerful, because he is a man. The generalized, impersonal view or preconception of him renders unnecessary consideration of his particular physical capabilities.

Consider also the stereotypical belief that "motherhood is women's natural role and destiny." In this example, there is a generalized view that all women should become mothers, irrespective of their distinctive reproductive health capacity and physical and emotional circumstances, or their individual priorities. It does not matter for purposes of defining the stereotype that an individual woman, say Mary, may not wish, for whatever reason, to become a mother. Precisely because Mary is categorized as a woman, it is believed that motherhood is her natural role and destiny.

Conversely, it is irrelevant for the purpose of characterizing a generalization as a stereotype whether it is in fact an accurate reflection of an individual's needs, wishes, abilities, and/or circumstances. Assume for the purpose of the present discussion that Tom is indeed physically strong. His actual strength does not in any way render less true the fact that the generalization concerning his physical capabilities is a stereotype. While the stereotype coincides with his particular situation, no regard was paid to the latter when determining the existence of the stereotype. Rather, the fact that this stereotype does reflect Tom's individual situation bears only on the accuracy of the stereotype for him. The same could be said of Mary, whose reproductive goals and/or choices may in fact bear out the stereotypical belief that "motherhood is women's natural role and destiny."

To the extent that stereotypes ignore particular individuals' needs, wishes, abilities, and circumstances, they significantly impact their ability to create and/or shape their individual identities according to their own values and wishes. They also limit the full and diverse expressions of human character.[9] Put differently, stereotypes infringe unduly on the capacity of individuals to construct and make decisions about their own life plans. For example, men, painted with the broad brush of stereotype, are often preconceived to be ill-suited to, or unwilling, or unable to fulfill caregiving roles, notwithstanding that men can and do fulfill such roles. Yet, owing to the embeddedness of these impersonal generalizations in popular culture, men face considerable obstacles in carving out identities as primary caregivers; instead, they frequently find themselves forced into breadwinning roles with limited opportunities for active caregiving. As Justice Mokgoro of the Constitutional Court of South Africa has observed, through reliance upon stereotypes regarding childcare responsibilities, society has "denied fathers the opportunity to participate in child rearing, which is detrimental both to fathers and their children."[10] Such stereotyping has also served to constrict women's identities, as, at the same time, women have been forced into caregiving roles without regard to their individual aptitudes, willingness, or preferences.[11]

A stereotypical characterization is not necessarily negative.[12] Many generalizations based on statistical evidence, for instance, do not carry negative connotations, but nonetheless still qualify as stereotypes.[13] Returning to the example of Tom, we see that the underpinning generalization in his case is concerned not with a negative assumption about men, but rather a statistical correlation between physical strength and being a man.

Yet, although negative connotations need not be present for a generalization to be a stereotype, many stereotypes do carry such connotations, such as where women are stereotyped as inferior to men. Take, as a further example, the generalization that women are incapable of making health care decisions in their own best interests, a stereotypical belief sometimes found in policies requiring nonmedical third parties (e.g., husbands) to authorize medical services for women.[14] At the heart of that stereotype is the negative and false belief that women are unable to make sound medical decisions, a belief that fundamentally denies women's moral agency and reflects women's subordinate status in their marriages, families, and societies.[15]

If the term "stereotype" is applied to refer to a generalized view or preconception concerning attributes, characteristics, or roles of members of a particular social group, which renders unnecessary consideration of any particular individual members' needs, wishes, abilities, and circumstances, what does it mean to say that someone is stereotyping? The term "stereotyping" is employed in this book to refer to the process of ascribing to an individual specific attributes, characteristics, or roles by reason only of her or his membership in a particular group.[16] Returning once more to the example of Mary, we see that the operative stereotypical belief about her concerns women's role as mothers; therefore, attributing maternal dedication to Mary as her natural role and destiny, because she is a woman, is stereotyping. In the case of Tom, the operative stereotypical belief about him concerns men's physical strength; therefore, ascribing the characteristic of physical strength to Tom, because he is a man, is stereotyping.

The Vanuatu case of *Public Prosecutor v. Kota*,[17] concerning the kidnapping and forcible return of Marie Kota to her abusive husband, Walter Kota, provides a further example of stereotyping. Upon learning of the separation of Marie and Walter, two local Pacific Island chiefs organized a community meeting in an attempt to facilitate the couple's reconciliation. The defendants (including Walter and four police officers) forcibly took Marie to the meeting, where she expressed a clear intention to divorce her husband. Against her express wishes, the chiefs ordered that Marie be returned to the family home. A week after her forcible return, she fled the family home, seeking assistance from local authorities and the Women Against Violence Against Women Association.

The Supreme Court of Vanuatu found a violation of Marie Kota's constitutional right to liberty and freedom of movement by the local chiefs' stereotyping of Marie Kota as her husband's property and ordering her forcible return to the family home. According to Justice Downing, "Article 5 of the [Vanuatu] Constitution makes it quite clear that men are to be treated the same as women, and women are to be treated the same as men. All people in Vanuatu are equal and whilst the custom may have been that women were to be treated as property, and could be directed to do things by men, whether those men are their husbands or chiefs, they cannot be discriminated against under the Constitution."[18] What is significant about this decision is that the Supreme Court was unwilling to allow a customary stereotype of women as men's property to restrict Marie Kota's right to liberty and freedom of movement, including making decisions about her own life and relationships.

Why Do People Stereotype?

Stereotypes are invoked for complex, varied and, sometimes, contradictory reasons. We stereotype to define a category of people. We create categories to maximize ease of understanding and predictability. We stereotype to know what people we are dealing with, and to anticipate how people we do not personally know will behave. We stereotype to differentiate among subcategories of people. We differentiate among subcategories to assign difference to people, to label and compartmentalize them in their subcategories. Sometimes, we stereotype to malign or subjugate people, and sometimes we stereotype people to protect or justify deferring to them. We stereotype "to script identities,"[19] to assign norms and codes by which men and women can be preconceived and expected to live their lives. It is through the understanding of these and other reasons for stereotyping that we can uncover and dismantle the unstated assumptions behind stereotypes.[20] In so doing, we may hope to prevent their perpetuation when that is unjust to those preconceived through stereotypes, and prevent people from making inaccurate and unjust assessments of those seen only through stereotypes.

People might stereotype for one or a combination of reasons. It may not always be clear exactly why stereotypes have been invoked. Take the example of the stereotype of women as primarily caregivers. It can often be difficult to determine whether women are being stereotyped into motherhood because they are, on average, more likely than men to care for children (statistical/descriptive stereotyping), or because social norms dictate that women, and not men, ought to perform the mothering role (normative/prescriptive stereotyping). Furthermore, as one commentator has illustrated, "Often when it is said that women are 'weak' or that they lack 'aggression,' . . . it is not clear whether the assertions signify empirical, statistical claims, or whether they signify instead normative claims about what it means to be a woman."[21] Rather than viewing those claims as problematic, we need to embrace the fluidity of reasons, acknowledging that "Stereotypes not infrequently hover ambiguously between these meanings."[22]

Sometimes we are unaware, or only partially aware, that we might be thinking in stereotypes. Stereotyping can be so much part of our perceptive fabric, our mode of thinking and categorizing, that we are unaware of it. That is, we have not diagnosed it as a problem in need of legal and other forms of redress. A challenge in combating sexism, which is often perpetuated through stereotypes, is that many of our attitudes are unconsciously formed. We are not always fully aware, or aware at all, of our sexism. To the extent that we are aware, we might have developed ways or rationalizations to conceal our prejudicial attitudes.[23]

Whether consciously or unconsciously, we stereotype for different reasons. Those reasons can operate in different ways to reduce stereotyped subjects' enjoyment of their human rights and fundamental freedoms.[24] These different reasons affect the ways in which stereotypes should be approached, as well as the kind of remedial response that should be pursued.[25]

To Maximize Simplicity and Predictability

In 1922, the idea was introduced that stereotypes serve the functional purpose of efficiently reducing, or reducing for the sake of simplicity, the challenge of comprehending the social complexity of the surrounding world. It was argued that "the real environment is altogether too big, too complex, and too fleeting for direct acquaintance. We are not equipped to deal with so much subtlety, so much variety, so many permutations and combinations. And although we have to act in that environment, we have to reconstruct it on a simpler model before we can manage with it."[26]

As human beings, we are not able, for instance, to process and articulate the distinctive features of every individual we pass on the street or encounter in casual social or work-related settings. Instead, we conserve our resources, relying on generalized views or preconceptions to help distill the outside world's complexity. It is for that reason that we classify passers-by on the street and in social and work encounters into generalized categories of human beings. On this view, there is economy of effort in stereotypes: "For the attempt to see all things freshly and in detail, rather than as types and generalities, is exhausting, and among busy affairs practically out of the question."[27]

In addition to reducing the outside world's complexity, stereotypes help people to order and defend their positions within society.[28] It has been explained that stereotypes "are an ordered, more or less consistent picture of the world, to which our habits, our tastes, our capacities, our comforts and our hopes have adjusted themselves. They may not be a complete picture of the world, but they are a picture of a possible world to which we are adapted."[29] Understood thus, stereotypes provide predictability and security. One can feel comforted and confident in the familiarity that results from their repeated use: "In that world people and things have their well-known places, and do certain expected things. We feel at home there. We fit in. We are members. We know the way around. There we find the charm of the familiar, the normal, the dependable; its grooves and shapes are where we are accustomed to find them."[30]

Sometimes people stereotype because they believe a particular attribute, characteristic, or role is constitutive of a certain social group. Phrased differently, they stereotype in order to describe "beliefs about the attributes, roles, and behaviors that characterize men and women,"[31] and to describe how individuals typically are or typically behave.[32] Examples of statistical or descriptive stereotypes include generalized preconceptions that "women are shorter than men," "women live longer than men," and "women assume primary responsibility for childcare." In the first and second examples, the stereotypes are based on a statistical reality that women are typically shorter and, on average, live longer than men. In the final example, the underpinning generalization derives from the fact that women, by common observation, are statistically more likely to assume primary responsibility for childcare.

Statistical or descriptive stereotypes can be problematic when relied upon to impose a burden on or deny a benefit to an individual who is atypical of the social group to which the generalization is applied. Consider the example of Mary, the female firefighter applicant who is denied employment on the basis of a stereotypical belief that women are physically weak and therefore lack the strength needed to be a firefighter, even though she herself is physically able to perform that role.[33] Here, there is a general preconception about the social group concerned—namely, women—that is pertinent to the employment decision: "Strength, let us suppose, really is a bona fide occupational qualification for a firefighter, and women really are, on average, weaker than men. But this general fact does not bear on the question of Mary's suitability for the job if she is in fact stronger than most men—stronger, in fact, than the weakest male fireman."[34]

Sometimes, statistical or descriptive stereotyping misunderstands the relevance of the facts.[35] Although we may accept as fact that women are, on average, weaker than men, that fact should not matter in determining whether to hire Mary as a firefighter, when she is physically strong enough to perform the duties required of a firefighter. The statistical fact that women in general are weaker than men has no relevance to whether or not she in particular is a suitable candidate for the job of firefighter, and should not be allowed to influence the employer's decision whether to employ her.

To Assign Difference

We stereotype to define difference, to label people as being other than the norm with which we are familiar, particularly ourselves. We label people so that we do not have to take the time or make the effort to understand their differences, to know them as individuals. People stereotype by falsely ascribing an attribute, characteristic, or role to an individual because they believe that all members of the social group with which that individual identifies are likely to have those attributes, or characteristics, or fulfill those roles.[36] One such example is that of ethnic stereotypes, which might, for instance, lead some employers to not hire, or to fire an ethnic foreign female worker because of stereotypical preconceptions of higher absenteeism among those with dependent children.[37] Assigning difference to an individual often reflects prejudice or bias about the group of which that individual is perceived to be a member. In addition to marginalizing an individual, a stereotype can exacerbate the subordination of the social group to which the stereotyped individual belongs.

There is a long history in the law of stereotypes of female witnesses as "inherently untruthful" or as "intrinsically unreliable," and therefore more likely to lie about cases involving sexual assault.[38] Such false beliefs have often caused women as a group to be considered noncredible witnesses, and their testimonies to be viewed with suspicion. For example, in *R. v. Henry and Manning*,[39] Lord Justice Salmon commented that it was "really dangerous to convict [an accused of sexual assault] on the evidence of the woman or girl alone. This is dangerous because human experience has shown that in these courts, girls and women do sometimes tell an entirely false story which is very easy to fabricate, but extremely difficult to refute. Such stories are fabricated for all sorts of reasons, which I need not now enumerate, and sometimes for no reason at all."[40] The preconceived unreliability of women as witnesses is a stereotype institutionalized in some applications of Islamic law, where a man's testimony can be equaled or countered only by that of two or more women.[41]

We often stereotype to assign difference to people for a variety of malign or hostile purposes, including to make ourselves feel special or superior, or as a way to distinguish the targets of our stereotyping as other than what we are, often called "otherizing." We do this in part because we do not want to identify with their characteristics and practices, even when we sense that we share those characteristics or engage in those practices. Paradigmatic examples include invoking harmful stereotypes with the intent to minimize another's enjoyment of their human capacities, or to acquire or maintain our social power. Male hierarchies in religious institutions, professions or, for instance, academic occupations, may accordingly stereotype women as incapable or unworthy of membership. The false stereotypical view of some religious hierarchies that women as such are incapable of spiritual inspiration and leadership, results in all women being precluded from religious ordination and ministry, without regard to their individual capacity and suitability.[42]

False stereotypes can devalue the dignity or worth of individual members of the subject group on the basis of an attribute or characteristic that is wrongly ascribed to them. False stereotypes can treat particular social groups as something that they are not and, in so doing, devalue them as a group. For example, many false ethnic stereotypes are disparaging, even when presented as a form of humor.

We may also stereotype to assign difference or label people for protective or benign purposes. Protective policies are found in many sectors of the economy and life. Sometimes they are referred to as benevolent paternalism, such as the attitude of the kindly uncle who does not want his niece to have to "worry her pretty little head" about the business conducted by men. It has been explained that

the paternalistic person believes he or she is acting for the best, for the benefit of the person on the receiving end of the paternalism. They do not consciously "discriminate." Yet some of the most . . . sexist behaviour is expressed through paternalism.

The head of a . . . department who believes women are not physically, physiologically or mentally able to accept responsibility may hold that belief convinced of his very real concern for the well-being of women. . . . He may believe women should not be appointed to positions of responsibility because a senior post means late nights back at work, corporate meetings at odd hours or weekend work. He may consider this will upset the woman worker. He may think women employees will have to give up activities they prefer, such as meeting the children after school, cooking the evening meal or attending school meetings. . . . [H]e may accept a general notion of women appropriately filling the role of nurse rather than doctor, because women "prefer" the "service role." [43]

The holder of such beliefs may not be conscious of them, and be outraged, devastated, or bewildered by any suggestions that he or she is sexist.[44] "In contrast to hostile stereotyping, benevolent stereotyping entails employers who may see themselves as 'just being thoughtful' or 'considerate' of, for example, a new mother's responsibilities."[45]

Protective stereotypes preclude consideration of individuals' needs, capacities, wishes, and interests because of the paternalistic instincts of the "protector." It reduces expectations one has of individuals because they belong to a certain group, without taking account of their actual interests. As one commentator has explained with regard to stereotyping of women and men as parents,

> Regardless of whether stereotyping is hostile or benevolent, it strips the decision-making power about how to interpret the responsibilities of motherhood away from the mother herself, in favor of an assumption that she will (or should) follow traditionalist patterns. In one instance, after a husband and wife who worked for the same employer had a baby, the wife was sent home at 5:30 P.M., with the solicitous sentiment that she should be at home with the child. In sharp contrast, the husband was given extra work and was expected to stay late. The additional work was meant to be helpful, for the husband now had a family to support. The employer effectively created workplace pressures that pushed the family into traditionalist gender roles; the decision about how to distribute family caretaking responsibilities was taken out of the hands of the family itself.[46]

To Script Identities

A further reason people stereotype is to script identities,[47] to prescribe attributes, roles, and behaviors to which men and women are expected to conform.[48] That is, we script identities to describe how members of a group "*ought* to behave in order to conform appropriately to the norms associated with membership in their group."[49] Stereotypes that seek to prescribe identities are often called normative or prescriptive stereotypes.

An example of prescriptive stereotyping is the expectation that women conform to prevailing concepts of beauty, sexuality, and modesty. The phenomenon of surgical breast enhancement and the rise of slenderness-directed eating disorders, such as anorexia nervosa and bulimia, especially among Western women, echo stereotypical notions about what it means to be beautiful, and suggest that women are only valued for their beauty, sexual attractiveness, and submissive natures.[50] Such prescriptive norms require women, and not men, to wear makeup,[51] or to wear sexually revealing work uniforms.[52] Foot binding of Chinese women, for example, was associated with stereotypical notions that women should be submissive, obedient, and petite. As a result, foot binding was justified as a means to limit women's freedom of movement, and ensure their obedience.[53] As article 5(a) of the Convention on the Elimination of All Forms of Discrimination against Women ("Women's Convention" or "Convention"; see Appendix A) explains, when social norms or practices are centered on the idea of inferiority or superiority of either men or women, they become cause for concern. Dress and behavioral standards that objectify and construct women as inferior, submissive, incompetent or sexually provocative, are based on the idea of inferiority of women.

The case of *Price Waterhouse v. Hopkins* is illustrative of prescriptive stereotyping.[54] The issue in that case concerned behavioral expectations imposed by the accounting firm, Price Waterhouse, on its female employees. In 1982, Ann Hopkins, then a senior manager and key employee at Price Waterhouse, was passed over for partnership for displaying "unfeminine" attributes in the workplace. Although clients and some partners praised Hopkins for her accomplishments, others criticized her for failure to conform to norms of femininity. In particular, one partner informed Hopkins that she should walk, talk, and dress more femininely, "wear make-up, have her hair styled, and wear jewelry."[55] Other partners described Hopkins as "macho" and in need of "a course at charm school."[56] Still others objected to what they perceived to be Hopkins' "unfeminine" use of profanity.[57] When Price Waterhouse refused to repropose Hopkins for partnership the following year, she sued, alleging unlawful discrimination on the basis of sex.

The U.S. Supreme Court held Price Waterhouse's decision not to promote Ann Hopkins to partnership had been motivated by impermissible stereotyping, in violation of Title VII of the Civil Rights Act of 1964.[58] Justice Brennan, delivering the opinion of the Court, explained that, "In the specific context of sex stereotyping, an employer who acts on the basis of a belief that a *woman cannot be aggressive, or that she must not be*, has acted on the basis of gender."[59] In other words, the Supreme Court found that it was unlawful for an employer to deny a benefit to an employee, in this case promotion, because she (or he) failed to adhere to social norms of femininity (or masculinity). What was unjust about Price Waterhouse's failure to promote Hopkins was that it penalized her for being insufficiently feminine (e.g., she did not wear makeup, have her hair styled, or wear jewelry); that is, for being too masculine (e.g., she was too "macho" and regularly used profanity). According to Justice Brennan, such discriminatory behavior by an employer was no longer acceptable as "we are beyond the day when an employer could evaluate employees by assuming or insisting that they matched the stereotype associated with their group."[60]

What Are Gender Stereotypes?

Gender stereotypes are concerned with the social and cultural construction of men and women, due to their different physical, biological, sexual, and social functions. More broadly, they can be thought of as the "conventions that underwrite the social practice of gender."[61] "Gender stereotype" is an overarching term that refers to a "structured set of beliefs about the personal attributes of women and men."[62] Beliefs can cover a range of components, including personality traits, behaviors and roles, physical characteristics and appearance, occupations, and assumptions about sexual orientation.[63] A personal stereotype reflects an individual's personal beliefs about a subject group or the subject of the stereotype, while a cultural or collective stereotype reflects a widely shared belief about a subject group or the subject of the stereotype.[64] The components of gender stereotypes evolve and vary according to different contexts.

The process of gender stereotyping refers to the use of gender stereotypic knowledge in forming an impression of an individual man or woman.[65] Like gender stereotypes, gender stereotyping evolves, in part, due to how gender is understood. Gender stereotyping is not necessarily problematic. It becomes problematic when it operates to ignore individuals' characteristics, abilities, needs, wishes, and circumstances in ways that deny individuals their human rights and fundamental freedoms, and when it creates gender hierarchies. Understanding how the law embodies, and contributes to, gender stereotyping is part of understanding women's gendered experiences of inequality. For instance, legislation historically made by men considered women as incapable of civil capacity and, therefore, women could not be elected or appointed as members of legislatures,[66] or join learned professions such as law or medicine.[67]

In understanding gender stereotypes, it helps to be clear about the different components of gender to which stereotypic generalizations are referring. For example, gender stereotypes might refer to intellectual or cognitive abilities, a psychosocial profile or biological differences, which render unnecessary any consideration of the attributes or characteristics of particular individuals in these three regards. Stereotypes of women's intellectual or cognitive abilities, as being weaker than those of men's, are often used to deny women positions in educational or professional arenas. Stereotypes of women's psychosocial abilities emphasize their skills for cooperation, while stereotypes of men value their aggressive and assertive attributes. As a result, women usually are not hired in jobs that value aggressiveness and assertiveness, such as leadership positions. Women's biological ability to become pregnant and their hormonal differences with men have been used to promote gender classification of women. For example, gender stereotypes based on biological differences have been used to deny women jobs as flight attendants on airlines,[68] and promote stereotypes of girls as weak and therefore in need of protection through abstinence-only sex education programs.[69]

Gender is at the core of understanding "gender stereotypes." The meaning of the term "gender" is fluid, its use is ambiguous, and it varies according to ideologies about women's proper role and behavior in society. The meaning of gender evolves over time, across nations and cultures, across decision-making bodies, and from judge to judge. Biological sex is "the raw material that cultures mold into genders and sexualities."[70] Some commentators use the terms "sex" and "gender" interchangeably because they want "to disavow the idea that either of these categories might be natural and thus immutable."[71] Distinctions between men and women, whether based on constructions of sex or gender, change over time, and thus are not tied to the immutability of sex in the biological sense.

Gender can describe a sense of identity, elaborating those "characteristics of individuals, the meanings of sex differences ingrained on bodies, minds and identities."[72] Because of the complexity, variability, and multidimensional nature of gender, "gendered identities" might be a more appropriate term: "Not only are there numerous forms of identity explicitly related to gender, such as mother, feminist or Barbie doll, but also gender infuses and influences many other identities, including those of ethnicity, class, and occupation."[73]

Gendered identities are often thought about in terms of what it means to be feminine or masculine. Masculinity and femininity vary according to time and place.[74] This is due in part to the fact that people do not share the same meanings of these terms because "the various gendered domains of life, such as personality traits, physical attributes, recreational interests, and occupational preferences, have different developmental histories and complex interactions."[75] In many cultures, for instance, being a physician is masculine in part because they are seen to treat disease and save lives, and being a nurse is feminine since it involves rendering tender loving care. As more women become physicians, and more men become nurses, the masculine and feminine connotations of the terms "physician" and "nurse" respectively will change over time.

The Committee on the Elimination of Discrimination against Women ("the Women's Committee" or "the Committee"), established under the Women's Convention[76] to monitor its implementation, adopted the definition of gender as the "socially and culturally constructed differences between women and men."[77] The definition explains that the term refers to "the social meanings given to biological sex differences. It is an ideological and cultural construct, but is also reproduced within the realm of material practices; in turn it influences the outcomes of such practices. It affects the distribution of resources, wealth, work, decision-making and political power, and enjoyment of rights and entitlements within the family as well as public life." [78] This definition explains that "gender is a social stratifier, and in this sense it is similar to other stratifiers such as race, class, ethnicity, sexuality, and age. It helps us understand the social construction of gender identities and the unequal structure of power that underlies the relationship between the sexes."[79]

A particular characteristic of gender stereotypes is that they are resilient; they are pervasive and persistent. They are *socially pervasive* when they are articulated across social sectors and cultures, and they are *socially persistent* where they are articulated over time.[80] Conditions for social stratification and subordination of women exist when practices, including stereotypes, are both socially pervasive and socially persistent.[81] These conditions for social stratification or subordination are exacerbated when the stereotypes are reflected or embedded in the law, such as in the implicit premises of legislation and the implications of judges' reasoning and language.

The prescriptive stereotypes that women should be mothers, housewives, and caregivers are both pervasive and persistent. A former member of the Women's Committee, Frances Raday, has explained: "The most globally pervasive of the harmful cultural practices . . . is the stereotyping of women exclusively as mothers and housewives in a way that limits their opportunities to participate in public life, whether political or economic."[82] She explains that the "stereotypical assignment of sole or major responsibility for childcare to women"[83] disadvantages women across cultures. The stereotypes that women should be mothers and homemakers, and therefore be "the center of home and family life" have had a long history of use to justify women's exclusion from public life, such as their ability to hold or stand for public office[84] and to serve on juries.[85]

In Ireland, for example, the stereotype of women as mothers and homemakers is reflected in the Constitution. Article 41(2) provides:

(1) In particular, the State recognises that by her life within the home, woman gives to the State a support without which the common good cannot be achieved.
(2) The State shall, therefore, endeavour to ensure that mothers shall not be obliged by economic necessity to engage in labour to the neglect of their duties in the home.[86]

The Women's Committee has expressed its concern at "the persistence of traditional stereotypical views of the social roles and responsibilities of women and men in the family and in society at large which are reflected in article 41.2 of the Constitution and its male-oriented language . . . in women's educational choices and employment patterns, and in women's low participation in political and public life."[87] Taking into account this concern, the Committee has urged the Irish Government to eliminate traditional stereotypical attitudes, including the stereotype of women as mothers and homemakers found in article 41(2) of its Constitution.[88]

The distinctive kinds of stereotypes and biases against women, once they become mothers, is known as the "maternal wall" in the employment discrimination context. The maternal wall phenomenon shows that negative assumptions about decreased competence are attributed to mothers, and not fathers, or other women who are not mothers.[89] It has been explained that "both hostile and benevolent sexism affect working mothers. Hostile stereotyping involves strident criticism of women who do not adhere to traditionalist norms of selfless, stay-at-home motherhood. Benevolent stereotyping involves assumptions about mothers' availability or suitability for particular tasks. For example, employers may fail to consider a mother for a promotion because the higher-level job requires travel, but without asking the woman in question about her preferences."[90]

The United Nations Special Rapporteur on Violence against Women, Yakin Ertürk, has explained that "the persistence of cultural and social norms, traditional beliefs and negative gender stereotypes were the obstacles most frequently cited by governments to the achievement of gender equality in all regions. . . . Even in countries where basic indicators of women's advancement show considerable progress and a 'critical mass' in decision-making positions ha[s] been achieved, gender roles and identities continue to be shaped by patriarchal notions of 'femininity' and 'masculinity' (albeit in modernized forms)."[91] A Women's Committee member observed that she found it surprising that in all the countries the Committee had considered, including the apparently progressive Scandinavian countries, gender stereotypes had proved extremely persistent. While the Committee member noted that there was greater equality in some countries than others, "stereotypes about men and women persisted, particularly those that focused on women as caregivers."[92]

These observations about the pervasiveness and persistence of gender stereotypes comport with observations in the psychological literature examining gender stereotypes: "the overall stereotype of women has remained remarkably stable, despite sweeping changes in gender relations. . . . We believe that stereotypes of women still contain significant prescriptive content as well (e.g., that women ought to be nurturant and supportive of others). This is not to say that stereotypes of women have been unresponsive to social change. Changes, such as the movement of women into the paid workforce, are reflected in images of subtypes of women (e.g., career women), which are quite different than the general stereotype of women as a group."[93]

Understanding why gender stereotypes are so resilient to change requires insight into the causes of gender injustice. Explanations for gender injustice vary, and they include political-economic, cultural, and ideological dimensions.[94] As has been explained, "On the one hand, gender structures the fundamental division between paid 'productive' labor and unpaid 'reproductive' and domestic labor, assigning women primary responsibility for the latter. On the other hand, gender also structures the division within paid labor between higher-paid, male dominated, manufacturing and professional occupations and lower-paid, female-dominated 'pink-collar' and domestic service occupations. The result is a political-economic structure that generates gender-specific modes of exploitation, marginalization, and deprivation. . . . Much like class, gender justice requires transforming the political economy so as to eliminate its gender structuring."[95]

Barriers to valuing women and recognizing their worth are rooted in androcentrism and sexism: "a major feature of gender injustice is androcentrism: the authoritative construction of norms that privilege traits associated with masculinity. Along with this goes cultural sexism: the pervasive devaluation and disparagement of things coded as 'feminine,' paradigmatically-but not only-women."[96] Gender devaluation and disparagement happen in many ways, including

- the different modes of sexual exploitation;
- devaluation in all spheres of public life, including denial of human rights;
- imposition of androcentric norms that privilege male superiority and emphasize female inferiority; and,
- attitudinal discrimination.[97]

These injustices are buttressed by the many different forms of gender stereotypes, discussed immediately below. Dismantling stereotypes is difficult because they contribute to, and result from, the many different modes of patriarchy, power structures, and gender injustices embedded in societies.[98] In order to overcome them, androcentric norms need to be decentered, and sexism needs to be replaced with positive valuation of those attributes, characteristics, and behaviors that are coded as feminine.[99]

THEIR FORMS: SEX, SEXUAL, SEX ROLE, AND COMPOUNDED

In this book, we have chosen to address sex, sexual, sex role, and compounded stereotypes, because they are implicit or explicit in the reasoning of courts and human rights treaty bodies. This is not to say that other forms of stereotypes, or variants of these forms, have not or will not emerge in laws, policies and practices, or decisions of courts and regional and international human rights bodies. Gender stereotypes, whatever their form, refer to women's intellectual or cognitive abilities, their psychosocial profile or their biological characteristics.[100]

Sex stereotypes focus on the physical and biological differences between men and women (e.g., men's and women's comparative strength). Sexual stereotypes center on the sexual interaction of men and women. Sex role stereotypes are the roles and behavior that are ascribed to and expected of men and women because of their physical, social and cultural constructions. Compounded stereotypes are gender stereotypes that interact with other stereotypes, which ascribe attributes, characteristics or roles to different subgroups of women. For example, gender and age-based stereotypes might compound to produce specific stereotypes relating to adolescent girls, women of childbearing years, or elderly women. The forms that are discussed below are by no means the only forms of gender stereotypes. Readers are encouraged to think about which forms of gender stereotypes are more pervasive and persistent, which forms trigger descriptive, false or prescriptive stereotyping, and what are the consequential harms of each form.

(a) *Sex Stereotypes.* The term "sex stereotype" is taken to describe a generalized view or preconception concerning physical, including biological, attributes or characteristics possessed by men or women.[101] Sex stereotypes include generalized views that men and women have distinct physical characteristics. For example, there is a generalized view that "men are physically stronger than women." This generalization can be a statistical description insofar as men are, on average, stronger than women. The generalization can also be false when it is applied to a woman who is stronger than a man, and it can be prescriptive when it is applied to suggest that a woman should not be stronger than a man.

International law has perpetuated sex stereotypes of women as weak, vulnerable, and fragile, and as a result, has a strong protective streak that has produced a subjugated category of persons in need of protection in such areas as employment and trafficking.[102] For example, in 1932, the Permanent Court of International Justice reinforced stereotypes of women as vulnerable and therefore in need of protection through international labor standards. In an Advisory Opinion, that Court interpreted the Convention of 1919 Concerning Employment of Women during the Night to prevent women in supervisory positions from working at night.[103] The Court did not examine the effects of such protective policies, such as precluding women from accessing higher paying jobs,[104] and reinforcing "stereotypes of women's inadequacies, including assumptions about their physical weakness and their susceptibility to corruption in male dominated workplaces."[105]

The Permanent Court of International Justice was not explicit about the reasons for such protective policies, as some domestic courts had been. For example, in 1908 the U.S. Supreme Court upheld a protective labor law that prevented women from working more than ten hours in a day, despite their right to freedom of contract. The Supreme Court explained regarding a woman that "Though limitations upon personal and contractual rights may be removed by legislation, there is that in her disposition and habits of life which will operate against a full assertion of those rights. . . . [Woman's] physical structure and a proper discharge of her maternal functions—having in view not merely her own health, but the well-being of the race—justify legislation to protect her from the greed, as well as the passion, of man. . . . The two sexes differ in structure of body, [and] in the functions to be performed by each. . . . This difference justifies a difference in legislation, and upholds that which is designed to compensate for some of the burdens which rest upon her."[106]

International and domestic courts are beginning to dismantle sex stereotypes of women as weak, vulnerable and fragile as justifications for protective laws and policies. For example, the European Court of Justice in its decision in *Tanja Kreil v. Federal Republic of Germany* interpreted European Community Law to require the Federal Republic of Germany to allow a woman, Tanja Kreil, who was trained in electronics, to work in positions involving the use of armaments, specifically on weapon electronics.[107] It decided that the European Community's Equal Treatment Directive did not allow women to be excluded from certain types of employment. It reasoned that women should not be given greater protection than men against risks. In so doing, the European Court of Justice broke part of the false stereotype that women, as opposed to men, are vulnerable, and therefore require laws to protect them against physical dangers.[108]

Examples of domestic court decisions that have similarly dismantled sex stereotypes by permitting women to engage in certain forms of employment include an Indian decision permitting women to work in bars,[109] and an Israeli decision permitting women to be trained to pilot Air Force jets.[110]

(b) *Sexual Stereotypes.* Sexual stereotypes endow men and/or women with specific sexual characteristics or qualities that play a role in sexual attraction and desire, sexual initiation and intercourse, sexual intimacy, sexual possession, sexual assault, transactional sex (sexual intimacy in exchange for gifts, opportunities or money) and sexual objectification and exploitation. One form of sexual stereotype applies the characterization of: "women's sexuality as part of procreation: there are women whose sexuality is reserved for 'relationships', 'marriage or family' and for the purpose of 'nurturing' or 'taking life affirming decisions about birth, marriage or family.' They have sex not because they want to, but to procreate or to 'nurture' their partners; sex, it seems is a form of housekeeping or self-sacrifice."[111] This kind of sexual stereotype is prescriptive because it prescribes reasons for acceptable sexual partnerships and types of sexual behavior. Sexual stereotypes operate to demarcate acceptable forms of male and female sexuality, often privileging heterosexuality over homosexuality through stigmatizing lesbian relationships and prohibiting lesbian marriage and family formation, such as through artificial insemination or adoption.

There are many other ways of understanding sexual stereotypes. The way that societies prescribe sexual attributes to women, treating them as the sexual property of men, and condemning them for promiscuous sexual behavior when men have no responsibility for such behavior, allows societies to deny women their dignity and their rights.[112] Examples of the way societies script chaste sexual identities for women but not men are criminal codes that make adultery a crime for married women and not married men. Such a provision of the Ugandan Penal Code was held by the Constitutional Court of Uganda to violate the Constitution, including provisions on the right to equality and the right to dignity and protection from inhuman treatment.[113]

When women are stereotyped as men's sexual property, the stereotype operates to privilege male sexuality and to enable sexual exploitation of women through sexual assault and violence,[114] and, for example, trafficking.[115] Sexual stereotypes have, for instance, long been used to regulate women's sexuality, and to justify and immunize male power for their sexual gratification. Consider the assertion made by Justice Bollen of the Supreme Court of South Australia that it is acceptable for a husband to use "rougher than usual handling" when attempting to persuade his wife to engage in sexual intercourse.[116] Comments prejudicial to women based on stereotypes of women as sexual property of their husbands enable the rough treatment of wives in order that they submit to sexual intercourse. Such an attitude operates not only to minimize women's agency and their right to bodily integrity, but also to entrench stereotypical notions of male sexual power over women.

In contrast, an English Court of Appeal judge, Lord Lane, in over-turning the judicially created common law rule that a husband could not "rape" his wife, explained that: "This is not the creation of a new offence, it is the removal of a common law fiction which has become anachronistic and offensive and we consider that it is our duty having reached that conclusion to act upon it."[117] Magistrate Nadakuitavuki, in the Fijian case *State v. Filipe Bechu*,[118] was more explicit in identifying that when women are stereotyped as a form of property, that preconception enables sexual assault. In finding the defendant guilty of rape, the Magistrate stated: "The old school of thoughts, that women were infe-rior to men; or part of your personal property, that can be discarded or treated unfairly at will, is now obsolete and no longer accepted by our society."[119]

(c) *Sex Role Stereotypes.* In contrast to a sex and a sexual stereotype, a "sex role stereotype" is understood to describe a normative or statistical view regarding appropriate roles or behavior for men and women.[120] Inasmuch as sex role stereotypes rely on biological sex differences to determine socially and culturally appropriate roles and/or behavior for men and women, they can be said to build on sex stereotypes.[121] Social roles themselves create stereotypes. Social role theory explains "how the relative positions and roles of men and women in society generate shared gender stereotypes and prescriptive gender ideologies. Social role theory focuses on the effects of the traditional division of labor, with women confined more to domestic tasks and men engaging in paid work outside the home. These roles divisions by themselves are suffi-cient to produce stereotypes that members of each sex have the traits suited to their respective roles."[122]

Common sex role stereotypes concerning appropriate roles for men and women are the generalized views that men should be primary breadwinners for families, and women should be mothers and home-makers. In the Australian case of *Haines v. Leves*,[123] the Court of Appeal of New South Wales affirmed a decision of the Equal Opportunity Tri-bunal, holding that it was discriminatory to segregate students in single sex schools in order to ensure curricula differences that reflected sex role stereotypes of men as breadwinners and women as homemakers, because this limited girls' future choices of education, vocations, and careers.

The applicant in this case was Melinda Leves, a female student at Canterbury Girls High School. Melinda's twin brother, Rhys, attended nearby Canterbury Boys High School. Both schools required students to complete a range of elective subjects. However, the choice of electives differed between the schools, reflecting sex role stereotypes. While Ms.

Leves was offered a choice of home economics subjects, her brother had access to industrial arts subjects. On account of these differences, students who attended Canterbury Boys High School were more qualified to pursue tertiary education and had better employment prospects than female students at Canterbury Girls High School. Ms. Leves initiated a complaint alleging that the denial of industrial arts subjects and the provision of home economic subjects to her and her classmates unlawfully discriminated against her on the ground of sex.

In its decision, the Equal Opportunity Tribunal found that the choice of subjects available to Ms. Leves and her classmates had been limited because of a "domestic" characteristic that had been imputed to females; that is, a wrongful sex role stereotype of women as primarily homemakers.[124] The Court of Appeal agreed, noting that girls' restricted choice of electives was "founded in a stereotype of post-education roles for male and female students."[125] It was further elaborated that industrial arts and home economics are "sex stereotyped" subjects: "The industrial arts have traditionally been seen as appropriate for males, whereas the home economics subjects have been seen as appropriate for females. . . . This stereotyping assumes girls are more likely to spend the larger and more important part of their adult lives in the home. Therefore they will be interested in home economic subjects and will benefit more from them. The career-oriented subjects of industrial arts fall outside this 'domestic' image. Those subjects are appropriate for boys, who will be the future breadwinners, rather than for girls, who will be the future homekeepers."[126]

The Court of Appeal and the Equal Opportunity Tribunal both explained that reliance on sex role stereotypes of women as homemakers and men as breadwinners harmed Ms. Leves and her classmates, in that it provided an unequal and inferior basis for future educational choices and employment prospects. It was explained, for instance, that there were declining employment opportunities for women who followed traditional female-oriented occupations.[127] As well, it was cautioned that limiting girls' educational choices because of sex role stereotypes would likely become a self-fulfilling prophecy, since it would entrench girls' "domestic" aspirations and, in turn, affect expectations of girls.[128]

(d) *Compounded Stereotypes.* Gender intersects with other traits in a wide variety of ways to create compounded stereotypes that impede the elimination of all forms of discrimination against women and the realization of substantive equality. Traits include, but are not limited to: age, race or ethnicity, ability or disability, sexual orientation, and class or group status, including national or immigrant status. The challenge is to identify the different stereotypes that operate to discriminate against a woman because of each one of her traits, not just her gender. A further challenge is to understand why and how gendered traits interact with other traits in compounded ways to cause hostile or false stereotyping. Compounded stereotypes often reflect false preconceptions about different subcategories of women, and evolve according to different articulations of patriarchy and power structures.[129]

Compounded stereotypes of subgroups of women often contain certain ideological messages about that subgroup's proper role in society. The case of *Yilmaz-Dogan v. The Netherlands*[130] provides an example of a compounded stereotype, albeit not directly recognized in the decision itself. That case concerned the racially motivated termination of the employment of Ms. Yilmaz, a female Turkish national residing and working in the Netherlands. Information before the Committee on the Elimination of Racial Discrimination ("the Race Committee") suggested that Yilmaz was terminated because of her employer's stereotypical belief that there was higher absenteeism among foreign female workers with dependent children. Specifically, the employer believed that, while Dutch women cease work on the birth of their child, "foreign women workers . . . take the child to neighbours or family and at the slightest setback disappear on sick leave under the terms of the Sickness Act. They repeat that endlessly. Since we all must do our utmost to avoid going under, we cannot afford such goings-on."[131] Female Turkish workers with dependent children were, thus, wrongly believed to be more likely to be absent from work.

Having unsuccessfully pursued her case in domestic courts, Yilmaz initiated a complaint before the Race Committee, alleging a violation of her rights to gainful employment and protection from unemployment under the International Convention on the Elimination of All Forms of Racial Discrimination ("the Race Convention").[132] Specifically, she submitted that, in failing to address allegations of racial discrimination, the Dutch authorities had endorsed her employer's racially motivated sexist behavior. It had also, she submitted, violated her rights to adequate protection against racial discrimination, the provision of legal remedies, and due process of law.[133]

In its views, the Race Committee concluded that the Dutch authorities had failed to protect Yilmaz's right to work, in violation of state obligations under the Race Convention. The Race Committee found that, in reviewing the complainant's dismissal, the Dutch authorities had failed to address allegations of racial discrimination.[134] Consequently, it recommended that the authorities ascertain whether Yilmaz was gainfully employed and, in the event that she was not, assist in the securing of alternative employment and/or provide equitable relief.[135] The Race Committee might have strengthened its reasoning in the *Yilmaz-Dogan* case, for instance, had it identified and directed the state to investigate how the stereotype concerning higher absenteeism among female foreign workers with dependent children was used to deny them jobs.

Sometimes compounded stereotypes are recognized in a particular international treaty. For example, the Convention on the Rights of Persons with Disabilities[136] recognizes the importance of eliminating compounded stereotypes by requiring States Parties "to combat stereotypes, prejudices and harmful practices relating to persons with disabilities, including those based on sex."[137] In the case of women with disabilities, it is important to consider how gendered stereotypes coincide with stereotypes of persons with disabilities to harm and discriminate against them in compounded ways.

Where compounded stereotypes are not specifically identified in a treaty, their exposure might arise in a court case. For example, a French lesbian, Ms. E.B., had to appeal her case to the European Court of Human Rights in order to obtain state authorization to adopt a child, because of a false stereotype that lesbian women could not be good mothers. The Grand Chamber of the European Court of Human Rights, in *E.B. v France*, held that the state agency's refusal to authorize E.B. for adoptive parenthood on the basis of her sexuality amounted to a violation of her equal right to enjoy her private and family life, protected by articles 14 and 8 respectively of the European Convention on Human Rights.[138]

The Grand Chamber did not explicitly address how the reasons the government offered as justifications for sex-based classifications relied on a compounded stereotype. The traits of E.B. as a single, lesbian woman were compounded in a way that denied her the authorization to adopt. Had she been a single heterosexual woman, her authorization to adopt might well have been accepted. A prescriptive stereotype also operated to deny E.B. authorization to adopt, because she did not fit the sex role stereotype of mothers as heterosexual women fulfilling gender-differentiated family roles.[139]

THEIR CONTEXTS

Gender stereotypes, whatever their form, reflect and gain meaning from the contexts in which they are found. Theories of social psychology "illuminate how the structure of male-female relations within society creates complex and polarized, but predictable, patterns of discrimination. This approach links the sociological level of analysis with the thoughts, emotions, and (consequent) behavior of individuals. Further, it explains how and why discriminatory treatment of women depends not only on an individual's personal traits (e.g., sexist beliefs), but also on the situational (e.g., organization) context."[140] For this book, the purpose of analyzing the context of a gender stereotype is to determine how a stereotype is harmful or discriminatory, and how it is perpetuated or eliminated. There are many contextual factors that explain how stereotypes contribute to social stratification and subordination. One approach to context is to think about it in terms of

- the individual factors, such as cognitive and behavioral considerations;
- the situational factors, such as predisposing conditions, found in different sectors, including the employment, family, and health sectors; and
- the broader factors, such as cultural, religious, economic and legal considerations,

any of which may be relevant to the application, enforcement, or perpetuation of different gender stereotypes.

As *individuals,* we absorb stereotypes through our everyday interactions with family, friends, neighbors, and, for example, colleagues, and also through exposure to our cultural heritage comprised of, among other influences, politics, art, literature, media, sport, and religion.[141] Over time, through these daily encounters, stereotypes become "deeply embedded in our unconscious"[142] such that we come to accept them uncritically as a normal or inevitable understanding of life. That is to say, our everyday encounters with stereotypes are often rendered invisible. Where stereotypes have been socially ingrained for generations, or where they are pervasive across sectors and/or societies, they often operate virtually undetected.

The psychological literature explains how individuals form stereotypes, and how they begin to act in conformity with those stereotypes, possibly leading to cognitive or unexamined bias where individuals might be unaware of their stereotyping.[143] It includes cognitive development theory that examines how children begin to label themselves as boys or girls, and social learning theory of how they develop sex appropriate and sex role behaviors consistent with those labels.[144] A young girl who acts boyishly may be accepted as a "tomboy," but it is derisory for an effeminate boy to be a "sissy." By the time children are five years old, they have developed sex role stereotypical activities and behaviors.[145] Cognitive processes and social pressures to conform are often cited as barriers to change gender stereotypes.[146] Once individuals accept a label from others, this secondary labeling results in them conforming their self-image and behavior to that label.

Research in social psychology has identified *situational* factors, that go beyond what happens in the minds of individuals to consider "how the individual is affected by and adapts to social contexts, ranging from proximal influences (e.g., the norms of one's immediate work group) to more distal influences (e.g., the division of male and female roles in society)."[147] Proximal influences might be thought about in terms of antecedent or predisposing conditions, which operate in different sectors to increase the likelihood of hostile gender stereotyping. This research has typically focused on situational factors in the employment sector,[148] but it may also have application to other sectors. Stereotyping is most likely to intrude when:

- The target or the subject of the stereotype is isolated; that is, when there are few of a kind in an otherwise homogeneous environment. Where there are many more men than women, there is more likelihood that women will be stereotyped in negative ways.[149]
- Members of a previously absent or omitted group move into an occupation or employment that is nontraditional for their group. That is, hostile gender stereotyping is more likely when members of a historically excluded group are introduced among traditional members of the group.[150]
- There is a gender mismatch.[151] That is, a preconceived lack of fit between the person's attributes and occupation. For example, the attributes often considered desirable in a manager—aggressive, competitive, directive, and tough—are not attributes usually expected of women. Women who behave in such managerial ways are often disliked, and often create dissatisfaction among their subordinates of both sexes.[152]

In addition to individual and situational factors, there are *broader factors*, including historical, cultural, religious, economic, and legal considerations, which might facilitate the perpetuation or elimination of a particular gender stereotype. The broader factors require understanding of how individual preconceptions and stereotypes are adopted by groups, and eventually integrated into *social structures* (institutions and practices) and *social meanings* (stories and reasons).[153] The perpetuation of stereotypes depends in part on the degree to which a group, community, or culture integrates the stereotypes into its social structures and meanings.

Explaining how a gender stereotype, and the ideology on which it is based, persists in different structures, meanings, and traditions, is "key to identifying and reshaping the base of shared understandings on which desirable change, or progress, can build."[154] This might require moving beyond the dichotomous approach of either repudiating the allegedly static traditions of the past, or promoting women's rights for the future. As has been explained, "This dichotomous view ignores the fact that the seemingly intractable views about gender which feminists seek to change are tied to individual and group identities, formed through ongoing accretions and synthesis of old and new understandings of self and other. Feminist revelations can have little impact on identities they completely reject. They must make sense *in terms of* these identities. This requires not the triumph of new over old, but an integration between them that can generate transformed and transforming views about gender."[155]

Gender stereotypes can be understood as arising out of a history of subordinate legal status of women.[156] Each country has its history of the legal subordination of women,[157] including in its customary laws and more formalized legislation and judgments. Historical inquiries on the "persons" cases, determining whether women are included among the "persons" to whom the law accords entitlements, have chronicled the challenges women have faced over the centuries in securing legal personality and capacity.[158] Women have advocated and continue to advocate for their right to vote,[159] run for election,[160] own and manage property independently of their husbands,[161] enter medical schools,[162] and enter other professions.[163] Some of these legal incapacities are rooted in gender stereotypes found in cultural traditions,[164] religious traditions,[165] or both.[166]

Gender stereotypes can be understood as arising out of different cultures. The broader contexts of gender stereotypes require an understanding of the different meanings of culture,[167] in part to avoid "widespread unreflective assumptions" about culture.[168] The term "culture" is used in multiple ways in international human rights law. Sometimes the term is used to include religion, as is the case under the Women's Convention,[169] and sometimes it is used to differentiate cultural practices from religious practices. The term may refer to customary laws, meaning laws that are not written into legislated statute books, and sometimes includes customary practices that are built on commonly accepted usages and traditions.

Another understanding of culture has emerged where women are increasingly challenging customary and religious laws, and are applying their rights to construct their own cultural and religious identities. Sandra Lovelace, a Canadian Maliseet Indian, challenged her loss of status and rights as an Indian when she married a non-Indian.[170] Canada's Indian Act, negotiated in the nineteenth century between sovereign agencies of both Britain and aboriginal communities represented by men, provided that Indian men gave Indian status to non-Indian women on marriage to them, but that Indian women lost their Indian status and entitlements on marriage to non-Indian men. The Human Rights Committee concluded that the government's refusal under the Indian Act, upheld by the Supreme Court of Canada,[171] to recognize her as a member of her Indian tribe, entitled to the rights and privileges available to men, was an unjustifiable denial of her right to enjoy her own culture as protected by the International Covenant on Civil and Political Rights.[172] The Human Rights Committee required a change in the law affecting all Indian women who marry non-Indians, which was undertaken.

Like Sandra Lovelace, subgroups of women are treating culture as a feature of group identity, and are insisting as a matter of right that they be able to enjoy, participate in, and formulate the culture of their communities equally with men. This view of culture celebrates cultural differences in ways that reinforce group identity.[173] It aims to understand how claims for women's equality might more effectively reinterpret cultural traditions of inequality to empower women's individual and collective identities.[174] Women might well find it easier to eliminate oppressive stereotypes within a culture that allows individuals to celebrate cultural difference and individual identities.

Prescriptive stereotypes can often be understood through the context of sex role ideologies, which tend to have their roots in cultures, religions, and, for example, colonial histories.[175] Cultures and religions have modesty, obedience, and chastity codes that dictate a woman's behavior, including her sexual behavior, dress, and role in society. As one commentator has explained in relation to modesty codes, they "often require segregation of the sexes in education, health, and employment. They may prohibit women from moving outside their home or country; prohibit women from meeting with others in public places; prohibit women from raising their voices; and mandate particular covering dress for women in public, including prohibiting women from showing their faces."[176]

Some chastity codes still require that brides, but not grooms, be virgin on marriage. The prescriptive stereotype that women must be virgin before marriage attributes virginity to virtuous women, which requires family control of unmarried women's sexuality, including the practice of virginity testing of young women before betrothal. Virginity testing has historical origins, because brides' virginity upon marriage ensures husbands' paternity of their children. Male lineage is especially important in some religions, such as Islam, suggesting religious roots to virginity testing. Male lineage is preserved in Islamic culture by the prohibition of adoption, and of sperm and embryo donation in medically assisted reproduction.[177]

The cultural context of virginity testing requires assurance of female virtue, to ensure the honor of families. Women are thought to embody the honor of men,[178] thus enabling the subordination of women through the control of behaviors not approved by family members.[179] Sex before marriage is thought to damage girls, and therefore makes them unfit for marriage. Sex before or outside of marriage has been used to justify or at least excuse, crimes of "honor"—including killing, assaulting, confining or imprisoning women—to save the honor of the family.[180] As has been explained, "the publicly articulated 'justification' is attributed to a social order claimed to require the preservation of a concept of 'honour' vested in male (family and/or conjugal) control over women and specifically women's sexual conduct: actual, suspected or potential."[181]

Historical factors that contribute to a particular gender stereotype are often found in patriarchal religious laws, some of which still govern women's personal status.[182] Religions have historical and sacred texts "with authoritative interpretations and applications, a class of officials to preserve and propagate the faith, a defined legal structure, and ethical norms for the regulation of the daily lives of individuals and communities,"[183] which often predate the principle of gender equality. As a result of these internally focused institutional characteristics, religions tend to be less amenable to outside pressures for change than many cultures. Therefore, one approach is that "change must be wrought within the religious hierarchy of the community and must be shown to conform to the religious dogmas of the written sources."[184] This is a particular challenge for women who live by their religious faith, but are seeking equal religious personality and status.[185] While many religions are evolving and internally contested,[186] their stereotypical views of women persist, and can disadvantage women in achieving spiritual and wider accomplishments and fulfillment.[187]

THEIR PERPETUATION AND ELIMINATION

Understanding the individual, situational, and broader sociocultural factors of the context of a gender stereotype is important in determining how and why a stereotype is *perpetuated* and how and why it is or can be *eliminated*. Although there are many different means of perpetuating gender stereotypes, this book is concerned primarily with the perpetuation of gender stereotypes through the laws, policies, and practices of States Parties to the Women's Convention. When a state applies, enforces, or perpetuates a gender stereotype in its laws, policies, and practices, it institutionalizes that stereotype,[188] giving it the force and authority of the law and of custom. The law, as a state institution, condones their application, enforcement, and perpetuation, and creates an environment of legitimacy and normalcy. When a state fails to adopt legal measures to eliminate and remedy the perpetuation of a gender stereotype through other means, such as through the media,[189] schools, and their curricula, a gender stereotype is also institutionalized and given the force and authority of the law. When a state legitimizes a gender stereotype in this way, it provides a legal framework to enable the perpetuation of discrimination over time and across different sectors of social life and experience.

Like understanding how a gender stereotype is perpetuated, understanding how a gender stereotype is or can be *eliminated* is also a complex task. The elimination of a gender stereotype presupposes that an individual, a community, or state is conscious of that stereotype, and how it operates to the detriment of a woman or a subgroup of women. Where a stereotype operates undetected, and is reinforced by the status quo, the prevailing gender hierarchy, or hierarchies of social and economic power more generally, a necessary measure toward its elimination is to become conscious of it and identify how it harms women. That is, diagnosing stereotypes as a social harm is a precondition to determining its treatment. Legal and human rights analysis can be instrumental in diagnosing a stereotype, which is a necessary prerequisite to its elimination.

Diagnosing and treating a gender stereotype is assisted by knowledge of how the individual, situational, and broader factors contribute to its perpetuation and elimination. Individuals may no longer apply a sex stereotype because they come to understand its harmful consequences, or realize that it is no longer apt, or an accurate generalization. A change in a situational factor, such as increasing the percentage of women in a sector, might lead to the dismantling of a hostile sexual stereotype in that sector. An evolution in broader factors of social structures and meanings, such as debunking the ideology of female domesticity, might help to deconstruct a stereotype of women as homemakers.

In order to determine how best to apply the Women's Convention to eliminate wrongful gender stereotyping, it is helpful to have a hypothesis or hypotheses about why such stereotypes are perpetuated in a particular sector, community, or culture. Hypotheses might emerge from considering some of the following questions concerning why individuals continue to stereotype, how a particular stereotype is institutionalized and causes harm in a certain sector, how it is reinforced by a gender ideology, and how it might best be eliminated.

i. Why do individuals continue to apply, enforce, or perpetuate a particular form of a gender stereotype?

- Do individuals perpetuate a gender stereotype because it is so socially ingrained, so embedded in the unconscious mind that it operates virtually undetected? What is the process that embeds a gender stereotype into the unconscious that makes it seem natural, intuitive, and self-evident? How can we gain insight into the processes of ingraining, and how might these insights reveal opportunities for eliminating a stereotype?[190]

- Do individuals perpetuate a gender stereotype because of the human need to maximize simplicity and predictability in human interactions, to assign differences to women or subgroups of women, or to prescribe or script women's identities?
- Do individuals, of either sex, perpetuate a gender stereotype because they are threatened by insecurity or uncertainty when women shed their service care giving roles? In response, a pattern or practice of hostile gender stereotyping may emerge to downplay women's competence, to try to keep women "in their place."

ii. How is a particular form of gender stereotype institutionalized into certain sectors, such as employment, education and health, or certain communities, or societal traditions and structures?

- Do communities and institutions perpetuate a gender stereotype because of antecedent or predisposing conditions, including situational factors like the proportion of women to men in certain sectors of social life?
- Do communities and institutions enforce a particular gender stereotype because of women's restricted participation in public life, due to historical, cultural, or religious factors?

iii. What are the individual, situational, or broader social factors that enable the dismantling and elimination of a particular form of a gender stereotype?

Answers to these, and other such questions, will help in formulating a hypothesis or hypotheses about how best to apply the Women's Convention to decode and deinstitutionalize harmful gender stereotypes in a particular community.

Chapter 2
Naming Gender Stereotyping

What Is the Significance of Naming Gender Stereotyping?

The ability to eliminate a wrong is contingent on it first being "named," by which is meant that a particular experience has been identified and publicly acknowledged as a wrong in need of legal and other forms of redress and subsequent prevention.[1] Naming is an important tool for revealing an otherwise hidden harm, explaining its implications, and labeling it as a human rights concern, grievance, or possible human rights violation. Once a wrong has been named, it is then possible to identify whether it is a form of discrimination and set about the task of securing its elimination through the adoption of legal and other measures. The significance of the naming process has been described by one commentator as follows: "Unless something is named as an injury, it cannot lead to a dispute. Unless the injured person knows that her experience is recognized as an injury, she cannot proceed with 'blaming' and 'claiming.' The first stage in the process, naming, requires information, which is essential to mobilize the process of demanding rectification and amelioration."[2]

Law has an important role to play in the naming process; indeed, it has been characterized as "the quintessential form of the symbolic power of naming."[3] One commentator has explained, for instance, that the judgment of a court "represents the quintessential form of authorized, public, official speech which is spoken in the name of and to everyone. These performative utterances . . . are magical acts which succeed because they have the power to make themselves universally recognized. They thus succeed in creating a situation in which no one can refuse or ignore the point of view, the vision, which they impose."[4] Law is an effective tool for naming precisely because it can publicly and authoritatively proclaim and transform an unacknowledged harmful experience into an experience, or wrong, that is recognized at law as one that is harmful and that requires legal redress.

The significance of naming is exemplified in the global campaign to eradicate gender-based violence against women, that is, "violence that is directed against a woman because she is a woman or that affects women disproportionately."[5] For too long, gender-based violence against women went unrecognized as a human rights violation. Indeed, even when the Convention on the Elimination of All Forms of Discrimination against Women ("Women's Convention" or "Convention"; see Appendix A)[6] was adopted in 1979, gender-based violence against women was not recognized as a harm against which women required legal protection, although the Women's Committee later interpreted the definition of "discrimination against women" in article 1 to include this harm.[7]

Today, gender-based violence against women is widely recognized as a critical concern for women in all parts of the world.[8] It is prohibited in a wide variety of legal instruments,[9] and is frequently named and condemned by international[10] and regional[11] human rights treaties bodies and domestic[12] courts. The adoption of legal and other measures to secure the eradication of gender-based violence was made possible precisely because grass-roots women's organizations and movements around the world identified it as a wrong, elaborated its many forms and manifestations, and characterized it as a form of discrimination and a serious violation of women's rights. According to one authoritative report,

As women sought to gain equality and recognition of their rights in many areas, they drew attention to the fact that violence against women was not the result of random, individual acts of misconduct, but was deeply rooted in structural relationships of inequality between women and men. . . . In calling for action and redress for these violations . . . *women exposed the role of violence against women as a form of discrimination and a mechanism to perpetuate it. This process led to the identification of many different forms and manifestations of violence against women . . . drawing them out of the private domain to public attention and the arena of State accountability.*[13]

The global campaign to eradicate violence against women can thus be said to have its foundations in the naming of that wrong.

Naming wrongful gender stereotyping, as with gender-based violence against women, is central to the effectiveness of efforts to eliminate this practice. Unless wrongful gender stereotyping is diagnosed as a social harm, it will not be possible to determine its treatment and bring about its elimination. Thus, the ability to eliminate wrongful gender stereotyping is contingent on the nature, forms, causes, and effects of stereotypes being examined. Moreover, arguments or claims alleging harm or discrimination on grounds of wrongful gender stereotyping are more likely to be accepted in circumstances where the nature of the operative gender stereotypes, the extent to which they operate, and the harm that those stereotypes inflict are fully understood.[14] As has been explained, exposing operative gender stereotypes "makes it more likely that the classifications will be acknowledged as a form of . . . sex discrimination by demonstrating a real 'harm' caused by the sex based classifications."[15]

For instance, naming allows a work experience in which a qualified woman is denied access to a leadership or decision-making position to be understood not as an illustration of her personal inadequacies as an employee, but as an example of sex role stereotyping of men (rather than women) as leaders or decision-makers. Naming this situation as a wrong involving sex role stereotyping allows the woman to understand her experiences of stereotyping in relation to those of other women and, perhaps more important, it enables the employer's workplace practices to be challenged on legal grounds of sex or gender discrimination. In contrast, characterizing the situation as one of personal inadequacy shifts blame for the treatment of the employee to her own shoulders; it becomes her fault that she has not been chosen to assume a leadership or decision-making position, and the employer is divested of legal responsibility for any wrongdoing.

On a global scale, the naming process promotes understanding of women's collective experiences of gender stereotyping. It helps to raise consciousness[16] of the socially pervasive and persistent forms of gender stereotyping that operate within and across different cultures by creating knowledge of "common experiences and patterns that emerge from shared telling of life events."[17] In so doing, it helps us to understand how individual preconceptions and stereotypes are adopted by groups, and eventually integrated into social structures and social meanings.[18] The naming process also helps to foster understanding of the common ways in which stereotyping harms women throughout all regions of the world; that is to say, naming enables the individual harms of stereotyping to be revealed as a collective experience of oppression.[19] This knowledge can, in turn, help to promote awareness of the significance and urgency of adopting legal and other measures that are aimed at eliminating gender stereotyping.

A particular challenge in naming gender stereotyping concerns the identification as problematic of gender stereotypes that are often deeply ingrained in our subconscious minds and frequently accepted as a culturally "normal" aspect of our sexed and gendered lives.[20] Consider the example of gender-based violence against women. Because such violence has long been constructed as a "normal" part of gender relations, we have difficulty in identifying how gender stereotypes contribute to its practice. It has been explained that "A big difficulty for the attention and prevention of violence against women is that it appears as culturally naturalized, as an intrinsic characteristic of the social relations and accepted gender model. In the collective imagination, the acceptation of scorn, inequality, unworthiness and violence is linked to the roles that give a 'natural' form to what must be accomplished in order to be a woman."[21] As a feminist legal scholar reasoned, "I think we are in danger of being politically immobilized by a system for the production of what sex means that makes particular sex differences seem 'natural.'"[22] Even where the stereotypes that underpin gender-based violence against women have been identified,[23] history has demonstrated a societal reluctance to abandon pervasive and persistent gender stereotypes, particularly those that reflect actual modes of social organization and behavior. For instance, even though some of the gender stereotypes that facilitate gender-based violence against women have been identified and exposed, such stereotypes continue to regularly play a role in the violent treatment of women.[24]

Notwithstanding the challenges of naming the conscious and subconscious forms of gender stereotyping, a rethinking of how best to name everyday, often invisible encounters with gender stereotypes is already underway. An analysis of domestic, regional, and international jurisprudence suggests that courts and human rights treaty bodies are increasingly naming gender stereotypes in their majority,[25] concurring,[26] and dissenting[27] opinions, and also in their decisions that address gender stereotyping more generally.[28] A comparative analysis of legal scholarship suggests a similar trend.[29]

This chapter attempts to develop a legal methodology to advance the effective naming of gender stereotypes. There are many different ways one might seek to name gender stereotypes; this chapter explores but one example. It is hoped that the approach explored here will provoke discussion about other approaches that might be used to name gender stereotypes, which approaches might prove most useful in different contexts, and the reasons why those approaches might be helpful for naming gender stereotypes in one context but not another.

The methodology of naming gender stereotyping presented in this chapter consists of two key questions:

- How does a law, policy, or practice stereotype men or women?
- How does the application, enforcement, or perpetuation of a gender stereotype in a law, policy, or practice harm women?

In order to demonstrate how naming gender stereotypes can strengthen efforts to secure their elimination, this chapter will apply these questions to three substantively and geographically distinct cases. While the methodology has been intentionally applied to these three cases and the gender stereotypes that operate therein, it is intended to be applicable to all forms of gender stereotyping.

The first case, *Morales de Sierra v. Guatemala*[30] ("the *Morales de Sierra* case"), concerned a married woman's challenge to several provisions of the 1963 Civil Code of the Republic of Guatemala, which defined spousal roles and responsibilities within marriage. The impugned provisions conferred upon husbands the power and responsibility to financially sustain the marital home, publicly represent the marital union, and administer marital property. In contrast, the impugned provisions conferred upon wives the right and obligation to care for children and the marital home. In addition, they made the right of married women to take paid work conditional on discharging their roles as mothers and homemakers, as well as on the consent of their husbands.

In its decision, the Inter-American Commission on Human Rights identified and exposed in the impugned provisions "stereotyped notions of the roles of women and men."[31] The Inter-American Commission concluded that, in enforcing these sex role stereotypes, the impugned provisions of Guatemala's Civil Code had discriminated against Ms. Morales de Sierra, as a married woman.[32] They had also subordinated wives' ability to act in a variety of situations to the will of their husbands, divested wives of their autonomy, and deprived them of their legal capacities.[33] Moreover, the impugned provisions had established a situation of dependency on husbands, created "an insurmountable disequilibrium in the spousal authority within the marriage," and had also institutionalized imbalances in family life.[34] On the basis of this reasoning, the Inter-American Commission invalidated the provisions[35] and, in so doing, decided that it is impermissible to rely on gender stereotypes to define spousal roles and responsibilities within marriage.

The second case, *R. v. Ewanchuk*[36] ("the *Ewanchuk* case"), concerned the role of sexual stereotypes in the adjudication of a case related to the sexual assault of a seventeen-year-old female complainant. The complainant alleged that Mr. Steve Brian Ewanchuk, the respondent, had sexually assaulted her. Specifically, she claimed that following a job interview in Ewanchuk's van, she accepted an invitation to see some of his work in the attached trailer. Upon entering the trailer, the complainant deliberately left the door open, but Ewanchuk reportedly closed and appeared to lock it when he followed her inside. Ewanchuk then allegedly initiated several incidents involving touching, each more intimate than the last. On each occasion, the complainant said "no," but Ewanchuk reportedly continued to assault her. The complainant claimed she was frightened throughout the ordeal, but that she had attempted to disguise her fear so as not to provoke Ewanchuk to aggravated sexual assault. She also claimed that Ewanchuk was aware that she had not consented to his sexual advances.

In the trial decision, the complainant was found to be a credible and intelligent witness who had given reliable testimony regarding her non-consensual encounter with Ewanchuk. Notwithstanding, Ewanchuk was acquitted based on the defense of "implied consent," a decision later upheld by the Alberta Court of Appeal. On further appeal, a unanimous Supreme Court of Canada overturned Ewanchuk's acquittal, holding that implied consent is not a defense to sexual assault under Canadian law.[37] On the basis of that finding, the Supreme Court convicted Ewanchuk of sexual assault and remanded the matter for sentencing. In her concurring opinion, Justice L'Heureux-Dubé named the impermissible sexual stereotypes enforced by the lower courts, and described how they had harmed the complainant and enabled Ewanchuk's earlier acquittal.

The final case to be considered, *President of the Republic of South Africa v. Hugo*[38] ("the *Hugo* case"), concerned a constitutional challenge to a pardon issued by President Nelson Mandela remitting the sentences of certain categories of prisoners, including mothers convicted of nonviolent offenses who had children younger than twelve years of age. The respondent, Mr. John Hugo, sole caregiver of his son, would, had he been a mother, have qualified for remission of sentence. He sought an order declaring the pardon unconstitutional and requiring its correction to apply equally to fathers, including himself. He submitted that in remitting the sentences of mothers, and not fathers, the President had discriminated against him on the ground of sex, in violation of the equality provision of the South Africa (Interim) Constitution of 1993.

In an affidavit submitted to the Constitutional Court of South Africa, President Mandela claimed that he had based his decision to remit the sentences only of mothers on the best interests of children. In so doing, he relied, among other factors, on the sex role stereotype that women are or should be primary caregivers,[39] which provides that women do or should play a "special role" in the care and nurturing of young children. Ms Helen Starke, national director of the South African National Council for Child and Family Welfare, submitted an affidavit in support of President Mandela's claim regarding women's "special role" in child-rearing in South African society.[40]

Justice Goldstone, writing for a majority of the Constitutional Court, held that although the pardon treated mothers and fathers differently based on sex role stereotypes, that treatment did not violate the South Africa (Interim) Constitution on grounds of discrimination.[41] Justice O'Regan concurred.[42] Taking a different legal route in her concurring opinion, however, Justice Mokgoro found that the pardon did discriminate against fathers, but that such discrimination was justified; that is, it served a legitimate purpose, namely, to ensure the adequate care of young children, and the means chosen to attain that purpose were both reasonable and proportionate.[43] Justice Kriegler found, in dissent, that the act of denying fathers the opportunity for remission of sentence violated the South Africa (Interim) Constitution on grounds of sex discrimination.[44]

How Does a Law, Policy or Practice Stereotype Men or Women?

A helpful first step in naming gender stereotyping is to ask: how, if at all, does a law, policy or practice stereotype men or women? One approach to this question is to inquire:

- Is there evidence of gender stereotyping?
- What are the operative gender stereotypes and their forms?
- What are their contexts, means of perpetuation, and means of elimination?

IDENTIFYING GENDER STEREOTYPING

The term "gender stereotype" has been employed in this book as an overarching concept that encompasses sex, sexual, sex role, and compounded stereotypes (see Chapter 1). It will be recalled that a "sex stereotype" refers to a generalized view or preconception concerning the physical, including biological, attributes or characteristics possessed by men or women. A "sexual stereotype" is a generalized view or preconception concerning sexual characteristics or qualities possessed by men or women. A "sex role stereotype" describes a normative view or preconception regarding appropriate roles or behavior for men and women. It will be recalled, also, that the term "compounded stereotype" refers to a gender stereotype that coincides with another type of stereotype, for example, one that relates to race, age, and/or disability.

A finding that a law, policy, or practice stereotypes men or women thus hinges on the existence of a generalized view or preconception concerning the attributes or characteristics that are or should be possessed by, or the roles that are or should be performed by, men and women, respectively. For example, it might be determined that a woman was stereotyped by a restrictive health law that enforces a generalized view that women should be mothers.[45] A finding that a law, policy, or practice involves compounded stereotyping requires a generalized view or preconception concerning the attributes or characteristics possessed by, or the roles that are or should be performed by, men or women, based on their membership in the social group of men or women plus another group, such as a particular racial or ethnic group. For example, it might be found that an Asian woman was stereotyped by an administrative policy that applied a racialized sex role stereotype of Asian women.[46]

There is no single correct way to determine whether a law, policy, or practice applies, enforces, or perpetuates a gender stereotype; a variety of approaches might usefully be employed to identify and expose gender stereotyping. Which approach will prove most effective in any given situation might vary widely, depending on such factors as whether gender stereotyping is explicit or implicit, and the context within which it arises. For example, the process of determining whether gender stereotyping is present may differ, depending on whether a specific situation concerns the allocation of spousal roles and responsibilities in a civil code,[47] a judge's decision to acquit an alleged perpetrator of sexual assault,[48] or a presidential pardon remitting the sentences of certain categories of prisoners.[49]

A careful analysis of the facts will help to determine what the law, policy, or practice provides, either explicitly or implicitly, about men or women and the nature and hierarchy of gender relations. The decision of which approach will prove most effective in exposing gender stereotyping is therefore best left to those who undertake the task of examining a law, policy, or practice, having regard to the context at hand. For instance, a judge presiding over a particular case is best placed to determine which will be an effective method to identify gender stereotyping in that case.

At times, it might be obvious that a law, policy, or practice applies, enforces, or perpetuates a gender stereotype. In cases where gender stereotyping is obvious, it may be possible to expose this fact without having to engage in a careful analysis of the facts. Nevertheless, it is still important to publicly identify gender stereotyping as a problem, and to explain the reasons why such cases involve gender stereotyping. This is because the process of using law to authoritatively and publicly identify this problem can serve as a powerful tool for proclaiming and transforming an unacknowledged harmful experience of gender stereotyping into a recognized wrong,[50] and determining its treatment. The process of identifying and exposing even obvious forms of gender stereotyping can help us to understand how stereotypes are integrated into social structures and social meanings. It also helps to raise global awareness of this wrong and its harmful effects, further pressuring governments to modify the social and cultural patterns of conduct of men and women in their jurisdictions.

Psychologists often look for symptoms or indicators of the cognitive processes that give rise to stereotyping as a way to identify and expose

the wrong. Such an inquiry might prove useful where gender stereotyping may not be immediately obvious. It might also prove useful in
circumstances where gender stereotyping operates unnoticed because
a particular stereotype is deeply embedded in our subconscious minds.
Symptoms or indicators of stereotyping include

- category-based judgment, for example evaluating a woman's leadership potential based on her membership in the social group of
  women, rather than on her demonstrated abilities as a leader;
- evaluation of qualifications or credentials based on information
  that is only tangentially relevant, for example, evaluating a woman
  in terms of her social skills, rather than her business-generating
  abilities;
- selective perception and interpretation, for example, interpreting
  a woman's aggressiveness as meaning that she must be difficult to
  deal with; and
- extreme evaluation or judgment based on limited evidence, for example, assuming a woman was late to a meeting because she was
  caring for her children when, in fact, she was delayed because of a
  medical appointment.[51]

When seeking to identify gender stereotyping, some feminists have
relied on an approach known as asking the "woman question." This
method aims to expose the sexed and gendered nature of a law, policy,
or practice, and how it operates to the detriment of women.[52] Building on the woman question, it is helpful to ask: does a law, policy, or
practice make an assumption about women, specifically, an attribute or
characteristic that women have or should have, or a role that women do
or should perform in society? Asking this question directs attention to
what a law, policy, or practice implies about women. For this reason, the
woman question is a helpful tool for uncovering gender stereotyping.
Asking the woman question in the context of a law that prefers male es-
tate administrators to females, for example, might uncover stereotyping
around the business aptitudes of men and women.[53]

In the *Morales de Sierra* case, the Inter-American Commission on
Human Rights was explicit in naming gender stereotyping. It stated
empathically that the impugned provisions of Guatemala's Civil Code
rested on "stereotyped notions of the roles of women and men which
perpetuate de facto discrimination against women in the family sphere,
and which have the further effect of impeding the ability of men to
fully develop their roles within the marriage and family."[54] The Inter-
American Commission reached this conclusion by carefully analyzing
the text of the impugned provisions of the Civil Code for implicit as-

sumptions about men and women, in particular, the roles that they do or should perform in Guatemalan society. In so doing, it considered how the impugned provisions compelled men and women to fulfill traditional sex roles while at the same time denying them the opportunity to pursue roles deemed to be untraditional. Exposing sex role stereotyping enabled the Inter-American Commission to frame the question, as a central issue for determination, of whether Guatemala's Civil Code violated Morales de Sierra's rights to equality and nondiscrimination, because it stereotyped her into specific sex roles by virtue of being a married woman.

Justice L'Heureux-Dubé's concurring opinion in the *Ewanchuk* case is further illustrative in its explicit recognition of sexual stereotyping. The *Ewanchuk* case, as she described it, was "not about consent, since none was given. It [was] about myths and stereotypes"[55] concerning the sexuality of men and women. More specifically, it was about how sexual stereotypes of men and women enabled and justified the sexual assault of the complainant. Justice L'Heureux-Dubé was able to characterize the *Ewanchuk* case as one involving sexual stereotyping by first invalidating the finding that it was about "implied consent." She did this by engaging in a detailed factual analysis of the case. For example, in recalling that the complainant had not consented to sexual relations and that Ewanchuk was aware that she had not consented, Justice L'Heureux-Dubé explained: "The complainant clearly articulated her absence of consent: she said no. Not only did the accused not stop, but after a brief pause . . . he went on to an 'increased level of sexual activity' to which twice the complainant said no. What could be clearer?"[56]

Justice L'Heureux-Dubé also recalled that the trial judge had believed the complainant to be a truthful witness, and had accepted her testimony that she had not consented and had been afraid of Ewanchuk. Yet, as Justice L'Heureux-Dubé explained, the trial judge gave no legal effect to the finding that the complainant had submitted to sexual activity out of fear of aggravated assault.[57] Considering these facts, Justice L'Heureux-Dubé observed, "it is difficult to understand how the question of implied consent even arose. Although the trial judge found the complainant credible, and accepted her evidence that she said 'no' on three occasions and was afraid, the trial judge nevertheless did not take 'no' to mean that the complainant did not consent. Rather, he concluded that she implicitly consented and that the Crown (prosecutor) had failed to prove lack of consent. This was a fundamental error."[58]

Having invalidated the finding of implied consent, Justice L'Heureux-Dubé then carefully analyzed the reasoning of the lower courts for implicit assumptions about men and women, including their sexuality. That is to say, Justice L'Heureux-Dubé considered whether the lower courts had ascribed to the complainant or Ewanchuk specific sexual attributes or characteristics. It was this detailed analysis of the lower courts' reasoning that led Justice L'Heureux-Dubé to conclude that the "fundamental error" in their reasoning derived not from the findings of fact, but from prescriptive sexual stereotypes of men and women.[59] For instance, she explained that the error derived "from mythical assumptions that when a woman says 'no' she is really saying 'yes,' 'try again,' or 'persuade me'."[60]

Like Justice L'Heureux-Dubé's concurring opinion, the decision of the Constitutional Court of South Africa in the *Hugo* case is instructive for its recognition of stereotyping. For all but one judge, sex role stereotyping formed the cornerstone of the case. The Constitutional Court reached this conclusion by carefully examining the reasoning behind President Mandela's decision to remit the sentences of nonviolent mothers with children younger than twelve years of age, but not similarly situated fathers, for implicit assumptions about men and women, specifically the roles that they do or should perform in South African society. Particular emphasis was placed on the affidavit that President Mandela submitted to the Constitutional Court, in support of his decision to remit the sentences of, among other categories of prisoners, nonviolent mothers with children younger than twelve. Attention was also paid to the supporting affidavit of Helen Starke.

In his affidavit, President Mandela explained that he "was motivated predominantly by a concern for children who had been deprived of the nurturing and care which their mothers would ordinarily have provided,"[61] and that "Account was taken of the special role I believe that mothers play in the care and nurturing of younger children."[62] In Starke's supporting affidavit, it was explained that

the identification of this special category for remission of sentence is rationally and reasonably explicable as being in the best interests of the children concerned. It is generally accepted that children bond with their mothers at a very early age and that mothers are the primary nurturers and care givers of young children. . . . The reasons for this are partly historical and the role of the socialisation of women who are socialised to fulfil the role of primary nurturers and care givers of children, especially pre-adolescent children and are perceived by society as such (sic).[63]

It was further explained that "there are only a minority of fathers who are actively involved in nurturing and caring for their children, particularly their pre-adolescent children. There are, of course, exceptions to this generalisation, but the *de facto* situation in South Africa today is that mothers are the major custodians and the primary nurturers and care givers of our nation's children."[64]

In delivering the majority opinion, Justice Goldstone explained that the reasons given by President Mandela for his decision to remit the sentences of mothers were based on generalizations, or preconceptions, about men and women and their roles within South African society. That is to say, in deciding which categories of prisoners should have their sentences remitted, President Mandela engaged in sex role stereotyping. He ascribed to individual men and women particular sex roles by reason only of their respective membership in the social group of men and women. Justice Goldstone noted that neither President Mandela nor Starke had offered statistical or survey evidence to support their assertion regarding the sex roles assumed by men and women in South Africa. Nevertheless, Justice Goldstone determined that there was "no reason to doubt the assertion that mothers, as a matter of fact, bear more responsibilities for child-rearing in our society than do fathers. This statement, of course, is a generalisation. There will, doubtless, be particular instances where fathers bear more responsibilities than mothers for the care of children. In addition, there will also be many cases where a natural mother is not the primary care giver."[65] Identifying and exposing stereotyping allowed the Constitutional Court to frame the central issue for determination in terms of whether President Mandela had violated Hugo's rights to equality and nondiscrimination, on the ground of sex role stereotyping.

EXPOSING OPERATIVE GENDER STEREOTYPES AND THEIR FORMS

For analyzing gender stereotyping, it is important, but not sufficient, to have identified gender stereotyping as a legal wrong in need of redress. In order to determine the appropriate treatment for this wrong, specific reference should also be made to the operative gender stereotype concerning the attributes or characteristics that are or should be possessed by, or the roles that are or that should be performed by, men and women. This requires that operative gender stereotypes (e.g., women are passive) be uncovered and publicly named, and that their forms (e.g., sex, sexual, sex role, or compounded) be identified.

As our understanding of gender stereotyping has evolved, it has become apparent that gender stereotypes of both men and women can operate to the detriment of women. Take as an example the gender stereotype that men are primary breadwinners. While outwardly concerned with men's socially and culturally constructed roles within society, this stereotype may operate to exclude women from the role as breadwinners and entrench their role as homemakers and caregivers. It might also operate to deny women equal pay for work that is equal to men's, and to deny or restrict women's access to social security or other benefits.[66] It is thus important that efforts to identify operative gender stereotypes extend to stereotypes of both men and women.

Just as there is no single correct way to identify gender stereotyping, there is no single right way to recognize and expose operative gender stereotypes and their forms. It is important that close attention be paid to the facts, to discover what generalized views or preconceptions they reveal about the attributes or characteristics possessed by, or the roles that are or should be performed by, men and women. One way to bring underlying gender stereotypes and their forms to the fore is to ask: what does a law, policy, or practice imply about men or women? More specifically, what attributes, characteristics, or roles does it ascribe to them? For example, does a law, policy, or practice ascribe to men or women a physical or sexual characteristic or attribute? If so, what is that characteristic or attribute? Does it prescribe or enforce sex roles or gender-specific behaviors for men or women? What are those roles or behaviors?

Once identified and exposed, the significance of gender stereotypes can be elaborated. Put simply, one might ask: what does it mean to ascribe to women certain attributes, characteristics, or roles? Were the sex role stereotype of women as primarily mothers to be identified and exposed in a law, policy, or practice, it might be helpful to explain what the ascription of motherhood signifies for women. Does it signify, for example, that women should be concerned with matters only related to the bearing and rearing of children? Does it mean that women's childbearing and childrearing responsibilities should be prioritized over other roles they might perform or choose? It might also be helpful to explain the implications of the stereotype for different subgroups of women. For example, does the stereotype of women as primarily mothers apply to all women insofar as they are actual or potential mothers, or does it apply only to married women, or women of childbearing age?

In the *Morales de Sierra* case, the Inter-American Commission on Human Rights named several sex role stereotypes operating in Guatemala's Civil Code. It did this by identifying and exposing the specific roles that the impugned provisions attributed to individual men and women by virtue of their membership in the social groups of men and women, respectively, and by explaining the consequences of ascribing such roles to them. The Inter-American Commission explained that the Civil Code applied stereotyped notions that

- *women should be mothers* and, therefore, they and not men ought to be concerned with matters related to the bearing and rearing of children;[67]

- *women should be homemakers* and, therefore, they and not men ought to be the center of the home and family life, tending, among other things, to domestic responsibilities;[68] and,
- *women should be caregivers* and, therefore, they and not men ought to assume responsibility for the primary care and nurturing of dependent children.[69]

The Inter-American Commission referred to a decision of the Court of Constitutionality of Guatemala, in which the impugned provisions of the Civil Code were upheld on grounds that they provided certainty and juridical security concerning the allocation of spousal roles within marriage. In discussing this decision, the Inter-American Commission named the additional sex stereotype that *women are vulnerable* and, therefore, are in need of men's protection.[70] Because of her membership in the social group of women, the Inter-American Commission explained that Morales de Sierra was stereotyped as a mother, a homemaker, and a caregiver. It was also assumed that she was vulnerable and in need of her husband's protection.

Regarding men's roles, the Inter-American Commission named the sex role stereotype that *men should be their family's primary breadwinner,* meaning that they, and not women, ought to assume the burden of sustaining and protecting their families and meeting their financial needs and responsibilities.[71] Since Morales de Sierra's husband belonged to the social group of men, he was stereotyped as his family's primary breadwinner; as a woman, Morales de Sierra was not stereotyped as such. Also implicit in the Civil Code were the sex role stereotypes that *men should be decision-makers* and *men should be heads of households,* and therefore they, and not women, ought to bear the burden of representing the marital union and, for example, administering marital property.

In the *Ewanchuk* case, Justice L'Heureux-Dubé successfully uncovered and named numerous sexual stereotypes in the reasoning of the lower courts, as well as in society more generally. Adopting a similar approach to the Inter-American Commission in the *Morales de Sierra* case, Justice L'Heureux-Dubé identified and exposed the specific sexual characteristics and attributes attributed to the complainant and Ewanchuk through the reasoning of the lower courts, and by explaining the consequences of ascribing such characteristics and attributes to each of them. The following sexual stereotypes about women are among those identified in Justice L'Heureux-Dubé's concurring opinion:

- *women are sexually passive* and, therefore, they are disposed submissively to surrender to men's sexual advances;[72]

- *women should physically resist sexual assault* and, therefore, failure to resist on the part of a female complainant signals consent to sexual activities;[73]
- *women should dress modestly* and, therefore, an immodestly dressed woman is responsible for her own sexual assault;[74] and
- *women are in a state of perpetual consent to sexual activity* and, therefore, when a woman says "no" to sexual activities she does not really mean it.[75]

As a woman, the complainant was stereotyped by the lower courts as sexually passive and as being in a state of perpetual consent to sexual activity. Sex role stereotypes were also applied to her that required her to dress modestly, and to physically resist the sexual assault perpetrated by Ewanchuk. Stereotypes about men included the belief that *men are unable to control their hormonal urges*, and that therefore they, including Ewanchuk, are not responsible for their own sexual misconduct.[76]

In the *Hugo* case, a number of different sex role stereotypes were identified in the reasoning underpinning President Mandela's decision to remit the sentences of mothers only. The Constitutional Court of South Africa was able to identify and expose these sex role stereotypes by recognizing the way in which President Mandela constructed the caregiving responsibilities of individual men and women by reason only of their respective membership in the social groups of men and women. The sex role stereotypes identified by the various members of the Constitutional Court included

- *women are/should be primary caregivers* and, therefore, women, as opposed to men, play or should play a special role in the care and nurturing of young children;[77]
- *men are/should be primary breadwinners* and, therefore, because they lack the nurturing and caring attributes that women possess, men are less capable caregivers than women;[78] and
- *women are/should be homemakers* and, therefore, women are or should be the center of the home and family life, tending, among other things, to domestic responsibilities.[79]

Although not discussed in the case, there appear to be at least two further stereotypes implicit in President Mandela's pardon. First, *mothers should subjugate their own needs and interests to those of their children*, and therefore, if released, mothers, and not fathers, ought to resume primary childcare responsibility. Second, *mothers* (as opposed to fathers) *are less likely to be repeat offenders* ("recidivists") *because they are caring and nurturing*: therefore, remitting their sentences was unlikely to endanger the public or cause public outcry.

The application of these sex role stereotypes to Hugo meant that he was stereotyped as a breadwinner, and was therefore treated as less capable of caring for his child than a woman might have been. Despite his status as the sole parent of his child, Hugo was not stereotyped as the caregiver of his child or as the family homemaker.

EXAMINING THEIR CONTEXTS, MEANS OF PERPETUATION, AND MEANS OF ELIMINATION

In order to accurately diagnose wrongful gender stereotyping, once an operative gender stereotype has been identified and exposed, it is necessary to consider the contexts within which the stereotype operates, how it has been perpetuated, and the process by which it might be eliminated. Understanding the individual, situational, and broader contextual factors of a gender stereotype can help to explain how a stereotype contributes to the conditions for the social stratification or subordination of women.[80] Understanding how and to what extent individual stereotypes are integrated into social structures and social meanings is key to determining how they are perpetuated and how they might be treated, or eliminated.

In examining the contextual factors of a gender stereotype, it might be helpful to ask: what are the individual, situational, and broader factors that are relevant to the application, enforcement, or perpetuation of different gender stereotypes? For example, do the facts reveal *individual factors*, such as stereotypes of women's intellectual or cognitive abilities, a psychosocial profile or biological differences, which render unnecessary any consideration of the attributes or characteristics of particular individuals in these three regards? Do the facts reveal *situational factors* specific to a particular sector? For example, do the facts reveal a situational factor specific to the family, such as tolerance of gender-based violence against women as a natural element of family relations, perhaps as a way a husband shows his possessiveness, and therefore that he values his wife? And, do the facts reveal *broader factors*, such as rapid industrial growth or economic expansion, which has altered existing gender relations, and created an environment of hostile stereotyping of women?

The significance of examining the contextual factors of a gender stereotype is evident from an analysis of Executive Order No. 003: Declaring Total Commitment and Support to the Responsible Parenthood Movement in the City of Manila and Enunciating Policy Declarations in Pursuit Thereof (2000).[81] The Executive Order provides that Manila

City "promotes responsible parenthood and upholds natural family planning not just as a method but as a way of self-awareness in promoting the culture of life while discouraging the use of artificial methods of contraception like condoms, pills, intrauterine devices, surgical sterilization, and other." Although, in practice, the Executive Order does not prohibit use of "artificial" contraception, it has severely impeded women's access to affordable contraceptives and related health care services in Manila City, by prohibiting their distribution in public health care facilities.

In issuing the Executive Order, Manila City Mayor Atienza enforced prescriptive sex role stereotypes of women as primarily child bearers and caregivers. These stereotypes imply that women's "natural" role and destiny in Filipino society is as mothers; that is to say, Filipino women should prioritize childbearing and caregiving over all other roles they might perform or desire to choose. The stereotypes also imply that all Filipino women should be treated first and foremost as mothers or potential mothers, and not according to their individual needs not to become mothers at certain points in their lives. According to this stereotypical thinking, women do not need access to affordable methods of contraception, as this would prevent them from fulfilling their "natural" roles.

The enforcement of these stereotypes has occurred in a broader context "of the growing Catholicization of public health policies."[82] For example, a number of state agents and officials, including Filipino President Arroyo, have justified the Executive Order on the ground that it is congruent with the Catholic Church's teachings on family planning.[83] It has also occurred in a broader context of a legal culture that perpetuates stereotypes within the family, and promotes a climate of impunity around women's subordinate status. Take as examples articles 96 and 211 of the Family Code of the Philippines.[84] These provisions respectively provide that, in the case of disagreements regarding marital property or the exercise of parental authority over children, the husband's/father's decision shall prevail. In so providing, these provisions perpetuate the sex role stereotype that men should be decision-makers, with the implication that it is men who bear ultimate power and authority within the family, especially "in issues of sexual relations, childbearing and child-rearing."[85]

Situational factors, such as the widespread state practice of rewarding women, through compensation and other gifts, for stereotype-conforming behavior, has further enforced the operative stereotypes.[86] For example, it has been explained that "The mayor gives prizes for having the most number of children, and the current champion has 21 kids."[87] The state practice of rewarding such behavior restricts women to culturally acceptable roles and behavior, even where doing so poses serious risks to their health and lives. The operative stereotypes have been further institutionalized by the state practice of harassing and intimidating individuals and organizations that provide artificial methods of contraception, resulting in the closure of many of these facilities and further impeding women's ability to access essential health care and decide freely and responsibly on the number and spacing of children.[88]

In the *Hugo* case, Justice Kriegler located the operative sex role stereotypes within the broader social context of patriarchy. According to him, the sex role stereotype of women as primary caregivers "is both a result and a cause of prejudice; a societal attitude which relegates women to a subservient, occupationally inferior yet unceasingly onerous role. *It is a relic and a feature of the patriarchy* which the Constitution so vehemently condemns."[89] The South Africa (Interim) Constitution, he explained, was intended to undermine the state's institutionalization of this ideology in South Africa's laws, policies, and practices.[90] For Justice Kriegler, then, the South Africa (Interim) Constitution was a tool that should be used to deinstitutionalize the sex role stereotype that women are or should be mothers; it should not be used to perpetuate this prescriptive stereotype and the ideology of patriarchy upon which it rests.

In the *Ewanchuk* case, Justice L'Heureux-Dubé engaged in a careful analysis of situational factors as a way to shed light on the power imbalance between Ewanchuk and the complainant. As Justice L'Heureux-Dubé characterized the circumstances of the complainant, the *Ewanchuk* case was not simply a case about sexual assault, but a case concerning the sexual assault of a seventeen-year-old girl by a man almost twice her size, which immediately followed a job interview.[91] In her opinion, this power imbalance—or, situational factor—contributed directly to the complainant's fear of aggravated sexual assault and her decision not to physically resist Ewanchuk's sexual advances, as the lower courts' stereotypical reasoning required her to do.[92] Taking into account this situational factor, Justice L'Heureux-Dubé concluded that not only did the complainant repeatedly communicate her desire not to engage in sexual relations with Ewanchuk, but also her failure to physically resist could not be taken to signal consent to his sexual behavior. In basing their decision on prescriptive sexual stereotypes instead of making a genuine evaluation of the facts, the lower courts had privileged Ewanchuk's (i.e., male) sexuality, while subordinating the importance of voluntary consent to sex to the complainant.

In determining how a state has enabled the perpetuation of a gender stereotype, it is helpful to ask: has a state, through its laws, policies, or practices, perpetuated a gender stereotype, which, in turn, has created an environment of legitimacy and normalcy of its usage? For example, has a state's failure to adequately respond to gender-based violence against women perpetuated the view that such violence is not a serious crime because, according to the sex stereotype, women are inferior and less valuable than men, and therefore crimes against them are lesser crimes that do not warrant the concern or resources of the state? Has a state enabled the perpetuation of a gender stereotype through means other than the law, because it failed to adopt legal measures to prevent the stereotype's perpetuation through those means? For example, has a state enabled the perpetuation of wrongful sexual stereotypes through the media, because it failed to issue guidelines specifying that such perpetuation violates the rights to equality and nondiscrimination?

In the *Morales de Sierra* case, the Inter-American Commission on Human Rights situated Guatemala's perpetuation of operative sex role stereotypes in the impugned provisions of its Civil Code. It explained that, by enacting the Civil Code, the Guatemalan legislature had institutionalized sex role stereotypes and given them the force of law. In so doing, it created a legal framework that enabled their perpetuation. While the Inter-American Commission acknowledged the government's commitment to reforming the Civil Code, it emphasized that the decision of the country's Court of Constitutionality, which upheld these provisions, remained "the authoritative application and interpretation of national law."[93] In upholding these provisions, the Court of Constitutionality had further institutionalized the operative sex role stereotypes and, in turn, strengthened the legal framework that enabled their perpetuation.

Like the Inter-American Commission in the *Morales de Sierra* case, the Supreme Court of Canada in the *Ewanchuk* case addressed the way in which law had become a site for perpetuating sexual stereotypes of men and women. In contrast to the Inter-American Commission placing its primary focus on the legislature's role in enforcing and perpetuating sexual stereotypes, the Supreme Court in the *Ewanchuk* case centered its attention on the role of the judiciary. According to Justice L'Heureux-Dubé, judges' use of discretion has played a significant role in the institutionalization and perpetuation of sexual stereotypes. She explained that "History demonstrates that it was discretion in trial judges that saturated the law in this area with stereotype. My earlier discussion shows that we are not, all of a sudden, a society rid of such beliefs."[94] The lower courts' exercise of discretion had in this case, she said, further perpetuated the operative sexual stereotypes, imbuing them with the force and authority of law.

The Constitutional Court of South Africa's decision in the *Hugo* case focused on the role of the executive—specifically, the role of President Mandela—in institutionalizing and perpetuating sex role stereotypes of men and women. While a majority of the Constitutional Court accepted that President Mandela's justification for remitting the sentences of mothers, but not fathers, rested on a sex role stereotype that mothers are or should be primary caregivers,[95] the majority did not suggest that his reliance on this stereotype in any way contributed to its perpetuation. In dissent, Justice Kriegler asserted that President Mandela's reliance on this stereotype "put the stamp of approval of the head of state on a perception of parental roles that has been [prescribed]."[96] For Justice Kriegler, then, the fact that President Mandela based his decision on sex role stereotypes not only contributed to their perpetuation, it also imbued them with added legitimacy by virtue of the fact that the head of state prescribed those roles.

The process of identifying the contextual factors of a gender stereotype and its means of perpetuation provides important insights into the measures that could be adopted to dismantle or eliminate that stereotype. For example, where, as in the *Ewanchuk* case, it has been determined that stereotypes have been perpetuated through the discretionary decision-making of the judiciary, steps can be taken to rid the legal system of those stereotypes. In *Ewanchuk*, Justice L'Heureux-Dubé asserted that "Complainants should be able to rely on a [legal] system free from myths and stereotypes, and on a judiciary whose impartiality is not compromised by these biased assumptions."[97] Considering that the Criminal Code of Canada had been twice amended to eliminate wrongful gender stereotyping, Justice L'Heureux-Dubé was emphatic that sexual stereotypes should not be permitted to resurface through the reasoning of the lower courts in that case. Instead, she concluded, the Supreme Court had an obligation to denounce such reasoning, precisely because it perpetuates sexual stereotypes and ignores the law.[98] By denouncing such reasoning in her concurring opinion, Justice L'Heureux-Dubé was able to take concrete steps to bring about the demise of those stereotypes.

In an effort to eliminate some of the same sexual stereotypes that have permeated the courts in Australia, the state parliament of Victoria enacted legislative requirements regarding matters on which a judge must direct a jury in cases of alleged rape or sexual assault. The Crimes Act 1958 (Vic) provides that in matters relating to consent to sexual activities, a judge must, among other things, direct the jury that it "is not to regard a person as having freely agreed to a sexual act just because she or he did not protest or physically resist."[99]

How Does the Application, Enforcement, or Perpetuation of a Gender Stereotype in a Law, Policy, or Practice Harm Women?

Once gender stereotyping has been identified, the operative gender stereotype has been named and described, and its contexts, means of perpetuation and means of elimination have been explored, it is possible to analyze the different ways in which its application, enforcement, or perpetuation in a law, policy, or practice has harmed women. Making the harms of gender stereotyping explicit is important, since this exposes their malignant nature. It enables us to more fully understand the disease, or wrong, and the type of legal and other means of redress that might be required to treat or eliminate it. Moreover, when the harms of gender stereotyping are revealed and acknowledged, it becomes clear precisely why combating such stereotyping is essential to the goals of eliminating all forms of discrimination against women and of achieving substantive equality for women.

An analysis of jurisprudence and scholarship on gender stereotyping suggests that the application, enforcement, or perpetuation of gender stereotypes can harm women, or subgroups of women, in complex and profound ways. It has been explained, for instance, that stereotypes can affect "self-image, views of what is good or bad in others, whom we marry, the careers we pursue, our leisure-time interests, how we raise our children, and so on."[100] Stereotypes can also create adaptive problems for women across a range of social sectors[101] and, in the case of hostile stereotyping, they can, for example, have consequences that range from poor self-image of individual women to weak social integration of different subgroups of women. For instance, denying a woman the right to serve on a jury on the basis of a gender stereotype will, in addition to excluding that woman from the civic responsibility of participation in the justice system,[102] diminish personal expectations of women's life options, specifically of women having a role and equal status with men in the ordering of civil society.

Stereotyping results in different kinds of harms. Harms can be understood in terms of their denial of recognition of individual dignity and worth ("recognition effects"),[103] and in terms of their denial of the fair allocation of public goods ("distribution effects").[104] Often, consequential harms of stereotyping can have both recognition and distribution effects. In the example of women requiring the authorization of their husbands to obtain health care services, women are stereotyped as incapable of making medical and moral decisions, thus denying them recognition of their intellectual capacities and their moral agency.[105] This nonrecognition can also lead to women being denied the distribution of necessary health services, resulting in a distributional harm.

It is important to understand that the harms that result from gender stereotyping might vary according to community, country, or region, and according to the nature of the group stereotyped. A stereotype that positions women as a form of property may impact women's lives differently in different parts of the world. For instance, the gender stereotype of women as men's possessions may enable the marriage of girl children before the legal age of marriage in one community,[106] contribute to some of the preconditions for forced marriage in another,[107] or, elsewhere, the rape of a sister to punish her brother.[108] For that reason, in determining the harms of gender stereotyping, it is important to consider how certain individual women or subgroups of women are differently affected by the application, enforcement, or perpetuation of gender stereotypes in different parts of the world.

It is not the purpose of this section to identify all the ways in which gender stereotypes can harm women. Rather, this section is intended to illuminate the types of questions that might prove helpful in exposing and acknowledging the harms of gender stereotyping for women in different contexts. Moreover, it must be emphasized that, as awareness of gender stereotyping evolves, new understandings of the complex and profound harms of this phenomenon are likely to emerge. It is therefore important to demonstrate the different ways in which gender stereotyping harms women, so that we might more fully comprehend and expose its oppressive and unjust nature.

One way to identify the serious, sometimes tragic harms of gender stereotyping is to ask the following series of questions:

- Does a gender stereotype deny women a benefit?
- Does a gender stereotype impose a burden on women?
- Does a gender stereotype degrade women, diminish their dignity, or otherwise marginalize them?

In general terms, the first and second questions seek to identify whether the application, enforcement, or perpetuation of a gender stereotype in a law, policy, or practice has resulted in the denial of a fair allocation of public goods ("distribution effects"). The last question seeks to ascertain whether gender stereotyping has resulted in the denial of recognition of women's dignity and worth ("recognition effects"). However, as the cases discussed below demonstrate, it is important to acknowledge that there is potential for overlap in circumstances where the consequential harms of stereotyping have both recognition and distribution effects.

DENYING WOMEN A BENEFIT

A woman can be harmed when she is denied a benefit because of the application, enforcement, or perpetuation of a gender stereotype in a law, policy, or practice that does not correspond to her actual needs, abilities, and circumstances. In such a case, she has been treated according to an impersonal generalized belief or preconception that does not describe her accurately.[109]

The example of Mary, the female firefighter, is illustrative of a woman who has been harmed because of the application of a sex stereotype that failed to take account of her actual situation. In that case, it will be recalled, the employer denied Mary the benefit of employment as a firefighter based on his stereotypical belief that women are physically weak and, therefore, lack the strength needed to be a firefighter. The employer's decision to deny Mary employment on the basis of this belief failed to take into account that she was in fact physically capable of performing all the functions of that role. The employer's decision harmed Mary because it denied her the benefit of employment of her choice on the basis of a sex stereotype that did not accurately describe her abilities.[110]

Similarly, in the *Hugo* case, Hugo was denied a benefit on the basis of President Mandela's enforcement of sex role stereotypes, which failed to take account of his actual situation. President Mandela based his decision to remit the sentences of mothers on the sex role stereotype that it is mothers, and not fathers, who assume or should assume primary responsibility for caregiving and who, therefore, would be best placed to ensure the adequate care of young children. However, Hugo was his child's only parent and caregiver; there was no mother to perform the traditionally gender-identified role of caregiving. Thus, Hugo was harmed as he was deprived of the benefit of early release from prison under the President's prerogative discretion, on the basis of a sex role stereotype that did not address his status as sole caregiver of his child. However, he was, as Justice Goldstone pointed out, able to apply to President Mandela on an individual basis for remission of sentence.[111]

In the *Morales de Sierra* case, the codification and institutionalization in Guatemala's Civil Code of the operative sex role stereotypes segregated married men and women into rigid and unequal spousal roles, resulting in the denial of numerous benefits and capacities to Morales de Sierra. The impugned provisions of the Civil Code constructed Morales de Sierra as a mother, a homemaker, and a caregiver, confining her to the private sphere where she was expected to attend to domestic and caring responsibilities. Her husband, on the other hand, was constructed as a breadwinner and granted the authority and responsibility, among other things, to financially sustain the marital home and represent the marital union. Significantly, the impugned provisions failed to take into account that Morales de Sierra did not wish to be confined to these traditional sex roles; she wanted to be able to legally exercise and enjoy the same rights granted to her husband. She was thus denied access to a number of benefits, such as the right to represent the marital union, on the basis of sex role stereotypes, which failed to take into account her actual situation.

A law, policy, or practice that aims to eliminate discrimination against women and ensure substantive equality should seek to treat women according to their actual needs, abilities, and circumstances. It is therefore important that states not treat women according to generalized attributes, characteristics, or roles that might have been falsely ascribed to them by virtue of them being women, or that do not take into account their actual needs, abilities, and circumstances.

IMPOSING A BURDEN ON WOMEN

Women can be harmed when the application, enforcement, or perpetuation of a gender stereotype in a law, policy, or practice burdens them.[112] Gender stereotypes can impose a burden on women, and therefore harm them, in a number of different ways:

A gender stereotype might burden women when it *forces them to bear an unequal share of domestic or caregiving responsibilities*[113] or, for example, when it *enables or justifies gender-based violence against them*.[114] In the *Ewanchuk* case, the stereotypical reasoning of the lower courts burdened women by making them more vulnerable to sexual assault and by reducing the likelihood that sexual assault perpetrators would be held legally accountable, and so deterred. It will be recalled, for instance, that, in her concurring opinion, Justice L'Heureux-Dubé was critical of the trial judge's decision to acquit Ewanchuk, in spite of his finding that the complainant did not consent to Ewanchuk's sexual advances.[115] In enforcing the sexual stereotype that women are in a state of perpetual consent to sexual activity, or find any man's advances irresistible, Justice L'Heureux-Dubé explained that the trial judge sexualized the complainant and her body, suggesting that she was willing to engage in sexual relations, even when she refused.[116] Significantly, the trial judge effectively afforded men permission to engage in sexual relations with women, even when women express clear refusal. Moreover, he decreased the likelihood that sexual assault perpetrators would attract legal liability for their actions.

The stereotypical reasoning of the lower courts in the *Ewanchuk* case also burdened women by shifting responsibility for sexual assault to them. In this connection, Justice L'Heureux-Dubé singled out the comment of Justice McClung of the Alberta Court of Appeal regarding how "In a less litigious age going too far in the boyfriend's car was better dealt with on site—a well chosen expletive, a slap in the face or, if necessary, a well-directed knee."[117] She explained that this comment rested on the sexual stereotype that women should physically resist sexual assault, and that, according to this stereotype, "it is not the perpetrator's responsibility to ascertain consent . . . but the women's not only to express an unequivocal 'no,' but also to fight her way out of such a situation."[118] Since the complainant had not physically resisted Ewanchuk's sexual advances, Justice McClung found a reasonable belief that she may have implicitly consented to sexual relations. In making this finding, Justice McClung denied female sexual agency and privileged male sexuality. Moreover, he harmed the complainant by holding that she may have been responsible for the assault. Yet, as Justice L'Heureux-Dubé insightfully pointed out, the enforcement of this sexual stereotype obscured the real reason that the complainant did not physically resist Ewanchuk's sexual advances: her fear of aggravated sexual assault.[119]

A law, policy, or practice that applies, enforces or perpetuates a gender stereotype might burden women when it *restricts them to culturally acceptable roles or behavior*, such as motherhood, or, for example, when it *stigmatizes or punishes women for their failure to conform to such roles or behavior*.[120] For instance, a qualified woman denied a promotion due to her failure to conform to prescriptive sex role stereotypes of how women should behave in the workplace was found to be harmed.[121] She was burdened by her employer's rigid beliefs about what it means to be a woman or a man. In that employer's view, she was insufficiently feminine (e.g., she did not wear make-up) or, put differently, was too masculine (e.g., she was "macho" and regularly used profanity); she was, according to the employer, therefore unworthy or unqualified to fulfill the requirements of the more prestigious position.

The rights to equality and nondiscrimination require that states, through their laws, policies, and practices, value and respect the needs, abilities, and circumstances of women. A state that imposes a burden on women through the application, enforcement, or perpetuation of a gender stereotype in a law, policy, or practice that does not accurately describe their needs, abilities, or circumstances, harms them.[122]

DEGRADING WOMEN, DIMINISHING THEIR DIGNITY, OR OTHERWISE MARGINALIZING THEM

Women can be further harmed when the application, enforcement, or perpetuation of a gender stereotype in a law, policy, or practice degrades them, diminishes their dignity, or otherwise marginalizes them in their relationships and in society more generally.

Gender stereotypes can *degrade women* in a number of different ways. One example involves the lowering of women's status, position, or rank in their marriages, families, and communities. We see evidence of such harm in laws, policies, or practices that deny women legal capacity in matters related to the representation of their children, and to the management of marital property,[123] or that downplay or undermine women's competence, such as in cases where stereotypes posit that women are incapable of rigorous, abstract thought.[124] One commentator has explained that "if females are expected to be less rational than males, some may view themselves that way and not participate in problem-solving activities or take advanced math courses, since such behaviors are not gender-appropriate. As a result, some females may indeed develop fewer problem-solving abilities than males who have had those experiences, thereby fulfilling the stereotype. Such beliefs can powerfully influence behavior in either a negative way, if the expectations are negative, or a positive way, if the expectations are positive."[125]

A further example of the degrading effect of gender stereotypes concerns laws, policies, or practices that lower a woman's personal or professional reputation through a gender stereotype, such as the historical practices that precluded women from entry into learned professions and universities. It also includes laws that criminalize the conduct of sex workers (who are overwhelming women), but not their patrons (who are typically men), and that devalue sex workers through the insinuation that they undertake sex work because they are "loose" or "fallen," when in fact their motives might be to financially support themselves or their families.[126]

Sometimes, a woman might have been subject to degrading treatment simply by being treated differently than a man on account of a gender stereotype.[127] For instance, when doctors exploit their professional authority to treat female, but not male, patients according to their own beliefs and gender stereotypes, rather than according to the actual needs, priorities, and aspirations of such patients, there is a form of degrading treatment.[128] There is also a form of degrading treatment when a doctor sterilizes a woman without her free and informed consent, because he or she stereotyped the patient as an irresponsible and excessive child bearer by virtue of her status as a Roma woman.[129]

When a gender stereotype fails to respect the basic choices women have made (or would like to make) about their own lives, when it interferes with their ability to shape, or carve out, their own identities, when it lowers expectations of them, or, for example, negatively impacts their sense of self, goals, and/or life plans, it degrades them. The gender stereotype constricts women's identities, meaning that it prevents women from defining and presenting themselves as they would like. Instead, women have been publicly defined or presented in the manner of another's choosing, and their ability to shape their own identities and direct their lives according to their own values, priorities, and aspirations has been denied.[130]

In the *Hugo* case, the Constitutional Court of South Africa considered the restriction of men's and women's identities as a result of President Mandela's enforcement of the operative sex role stereotypes. Justice Kriegler explained that "Reliance on the generalisation that women are the primary care givers is harmful in its tendency to cramp and stunt the efforts of both men and women to form their identities freely."[131] In addition, Justice Mokgoro explained that this stereotype had prevented women from "forging identities for themselves independent of their roles as wives and mothers," and that it had also "denied fathers the opportunity to participate in child rearing."[132]

In the *Morales de Sierra* case, the Inter-American Commission on Human Rights concluded that the enforcement of the operative sex role stereotypes in the impugned provisions of Guatemala's Civil Code severely limited Ms. Morales de Sierra's ability to define and present herself in a manner of her own choosing; that is to say, it restricted her ability to shape her own identity and, in the process, it degraded her. The Civil Code, the Inter-American Commission explained, unjustly determined her role and identity within Guatemalan society. She was a wife and a mother, with the special right and obligation to be a homemaker and caregiver. She was only allowed to step outside these rigidly defined roles if her husband granted her permission. While Morales de Sierra's husband had in fact granted her permission to engage in professional work, he could by law have revoked that permission at any time. Moreover, Guatemala's Civil Code denied Morales de Sierra's legal capacities in civil matters such as administering property and representing the marital union in a manner of her own choosing. The Civil Code treated her as a dependent of her husband; she was not defined and presented as an autonomous individual capable of making decisions about her own life.[133]

A gender stereotype can harm women when it *diminishes their dignity as human beings*.[134] A gender stereotype infringes women's dignity when it fails to recognize their intrinsic and equal worth as human beings or when, for example, it treats them in ways that do not take into account their actual situations. The application, enforcement, or perpetuation of benign gender stereotypes can, for example, harm women when it precludes consideration of their actual situations because of others' paternalistic attitudes or instincts that mothers, and not fathers, should be at home looking after dependent children rather than staying late at work.[135] A gender stereotype can also have a dignity-diminishing effect when it treats women as second-class citizens or as less capable or competent than men, by virtue of the fact that they are women.

In her concurring opinion in the *Hugo* case, Justice Mokgoro found that the differential treatment of mothers and fathers, which was based on sex role stereotypes, impaired the dignity of fathers and of Hugo, specifically. She explained that "denying men the opportunity to be released early from prison in order to resume rearing their children, entirely on the basis of stereotypical assumptions concerning men's aptitude at child rearing is an infringement upon their equality and dignity."[136] In her view, the pardon failed to recognize the equal worth of fathers involved in caregiving, and treated men "as less capable parents on the mere basis that they are fathers and not mothers."[137] Even so, she considered the discrimination justified in this case. In contrast, Justice Goldstone, delivering the majority opinion, concluded that Hugo's dignity had not been fundamentally impaired, since the curtailment of his freedom derived not from the differential treatment but from his conviction alone. Moreover, Hugo could apply, on an individual basis, for remission of sentence.[138]

In the *Morales de Sierra* case, the Inter-American Commission on Human Rights explained that the right to honor and dignity, as guaranteed in the American Convention on Human Rights, embodies a number of elements related to the dignity of the individual, "including, for example, the ability to pursue the development of one's personality and aspirations, determine one's identity, and define one's personal relationships."[139] The Inter-American Commission acknowledged that the enforcement of sex role stereotypes in the impugned provisions of Guatemala's Civil Code had prevented Morales de Sierra from developing her personality, pursuing her aspirations, shaping her own identity, and defining her own personal relationships. In the view of the Inter-American Commission, the Civil Code did not accord Morales de Sierra, as a married woman, the same rights or recognition as married men (or single men and women), nor did it allow her the same freedoms they enjoyed in pursuing their aspirations.[140] This, in turn, negatively affected Morales de Sierra's position within Guatemalan society, as well as her status within her own family and community, thereby demeaning her dignity.[141]

In the *Ewanchuk* case, Justice L'Heureux-Dubé was critical of Justice McClung, who observed that "the complainant did not present herself to Ewanchuk or enter his trailer in a bonnet and crinolines."[142] Comments like this, she explained, derive from the sexual stereotype that women should dress modestly.[143] The enforcement of this sexual stereotype suggested that the complainant invited the sexual assault, because she was not modestly dressed as a "good" woman should be. It harmed the dignity of the "immodestly" dressed complainant, by implying that she was not as worthy of protection against sexual assault as other more modestly dressed women, and by suggesting that she was in some way less worthy of respect and physical integrity as a human being because of the way she dressed.

Gender stereotypes can further harm women by otherwise *marginalizing them in their relationships and in society more generally*. In the *Morales de Sierra* case, for example, the Inter-American Commission on Human Rights considered the different ways in which Guatemala's Civil Code marginalized married women through enforcement of sex role stereotypes. The Inter-American Commission explained that the sex role stereotypes in Guatemala's Civil Code segregated married men and women into rigid and unequal spousal roles within the family and marriage. These stereotypical distinctions institutionalized imbalances in spousal rights and duties, by subordinating wives to their husbands, denying wives their autonomy and legal capacities, and creating wives' dependency.[144] The Inter-American Commission understood that, in its application of stereotyped notions of the roles of men and women, Guatemala's Civil Code had infantilized women; it effectively denied wives' status as independent, adult legal persons and, in the process, restricted wives' access to resources and administrative or judicial recourse, and their ability to execute contracts and administer property.[145] It had also reinforced women's systemic disadvantage.[146]

The Constitutional Court of South Africa's decision in the *Hugo* case provides a further illustration of how gender stereotypes can marginalize women in their relationships and in society more generally. In writing for the majority, Justice Goldstone observed that the sex role stereotype of women as primary caregivers has been a root cause of women's inequality and a primary source of women's disadvantage in South African society.[147] As well, Justice Mokgoro noted that this stereotype has "for too long deprived women of a fair opportunity to participate in public life, and deprived society of the valuable contributions women can make. Women have been prevented from gaining economic self-sufficiency, or from forging identities for themselves independent of their role as wives and mothers."[148] Moreover, it has "denied fathers the opportunity to participate in child rearing, which is detrimental both to fathers and their children,"[149] as well as to women. The Constitutional Court concluded, however, that women's disadvantage in this case derived not from the President's stereotype-informed pardon, but from the "social fact of the role played by mothers in child rearing and, more particularly, in the inequality which results from it."[150] While it conceded that the President had relied on the stereotype of women as primary caregivers, it concluded that he had done so in a way that afforded mothers of young children—a particularly vulnerable group, subject to past discrimination—an advantage (early release from prison).[151]

A law, policy, or practice that aims to promote substantive equality and nondiscrimination must recognize and respect the equal and intrinsic worth of all human beings, both men and women. It must also honor the basic choices women make (or would like to make) about their own lives, and enable them to shape, or carve out, their own identities.[152] To achieve this goal, laws, policies, and practices must be free of gender stereotyping in all its forms and manifestations, especially those that degrade or devalue women, restrict their capacity to define their own identities, lower expectations of them, or subordinate them to men. Such provisions must also be sensitive to women's needs, interests, and circumstances, and ensure that women are treated as human beings equally deserving of concern, respect, and consideration.

* * *

As our understanding of gender stereotyping has grown, it has become apparent that gender stereotypes of men can, in addition to harming men, also harm women. In considering the harms of gender stereotyping, it is therefore important that gender stereotypes of both men and women be taken into account. The preamble to the Women's Convention underscores the importance of addressing gender stereotypes of men and women insofar as it requires "a change in the traditional role of men as well as the role of women in society and in the family"[153] to achieve full equality between men and women. The importance of addressing stereotypes of men and women is further underscored in article 5(a) of the Convention in that it requires the modification of "the social and cultural patterns of conduct of men and women" with a view to eliminating "prejudices and . . . practices which are based on the idea of the inferiority or the superiority of either of the sexes or on stereotyped roles for men and women." Social and cultural patterns of conduct include gender conventions that organize social practices that stereotype men and women into distinct yet mutually reinforcing roles. Focusing exclusively on stereotypes of women, to the exclusion of stereotypes of men, and how they both impact gender dynamics, ignores the complexity of "the social and cultural patterns of conduct of men and women."

Justice O'Connor, delivering the opinion of the majority of the U.S. Supreme Court in *Mississippi University for Women v. Hogan*, addressed the mutually reinforcing nature of sex role stereotypes of men and women.[154] The Supreme Court determined that the university's decision to deny admission to its all-female nursing program to an other-wise qualified male applicant because of his sex violated the Fourteenth Amendment to the U.S. Constitution.[155] In reaching this conclusion, Justice O'Connor emphasized the importance of avoiding gender ste-reotypes,[156] and explained that the exclusion of men from the nursing program perpetuated the stereotypical view of nursing as "women's work." She elaborated: "By assuring that Mississippi allots more open-ings in its state-supported nursing schools to women than it does to men, MUW's admissions policy lends credibility to the old view that women, not men, should become nurses, and makes the assumption that nurs-ing is a field for women a self-fulfilling prophecy."[157] Because of the his-tory of devaluing "women's work," this conceptualization had harmed women in the form of lower wages.

In contrast to Justice O'Connor's recognition of the harm of mutu-ally reinforcing gender stereotypes, a majority of the European Court of Human Rights overlooked this harm in *Petrovic v. Austria*,[158] when it upheld the denial of parental leave to a father, Mr. Petrovic, under the Austrian Unemployment Benefit Act of 1977. The Act, which rested on implicit sex role stereotypes of women as primarily caregivers and of fathers as primary breadwinners entitled mothers, and not fathers, to parental leave. The majority concluded that since there was no com-mon European standard on the provision of parental leave to fathers, Austria's refusal to grant leave to Petrovic fell within its margin of ap-preciation,[159] meaning the latitude all States Parties to the European Convention on Human Rights[160] have in compliance with this treaty. While the judicial majority recognized a gradual change in traditional childcare responsibilities, in deferring to the absence of a common stan-dard in this field, it effectively perpetuated the sex role stereotypes im-plicit in the Act.

Judges Bernhardt and Spielmann ruled in dissent, however, that Petrovic had been discriminated against on the basis of his sex.[161] While they conceded that Austria had no obligation to pay parental leave, they determined that in the event that it did so, sex role stereotypes could not justify the differential treatment of mothers and fathers. Judges Bern-hardt and Spielmann reasoned that reliance on the sex role stereotype of men as breadwinners not only harmed the petitioner in that he was unable to claim parental leave, but also his wife, because absence of pro-vision for paternal leave entrenched and perpetuated the stereotype that women, and not men, are suited to caregiving roles. As they explained, "The discrimination against fathers perpetuates this traditional distri-bution of roles and can also have negative consequences for the mother; if she continues her professional activity and agrees that the father stay at home, the family loses the parental leave allowance to which it would be entitled if she stayed at home."[162] Thus, for Judges Bernhardt and Spielmann, the absence of a common European standard was not conclusive, nor was it a sufficient justification to perpetuate harmful sex role stereotypes of men and women.[163]

Justice O'Connor and Judges Bernhardt and Spielmann understood that in order "to modify the social and cultural patterns of conduct of men and women," the consequences of stereotyping of men on women need to be addressed. In contrast to the judicial majority of the European Court of Human Rights in *Petrovic v. Austria,* who were silent on the detrimental impact of the stereotyping of Petrovic on his wife, Justice O'Connor and Judges Bernhardt and Spielmann did draw out the impact of gender stereotyping of men on women. Significantly, they did this even though the respective cases involved a male applicant claiming sex discrimination.

Chapter 3
State Obligations to Eliminate Gender Stereotyping

What Are the Obligations of States Parties to Eliminate Gender Stereotyping?

The Convention on the Elimination of All Forms of Discrimination against Women ("Women's Convention" or "Convention"; see Appendix A) requires that States Parties take all appropriate measures to eliminate wrongful gender stereotyping.[1] The content of the obligations of a State Party under the Convention is determined as a matter of treaty interpretation. One or more of the issue-specific articles (articles 6–16) need to be interpreted in conjunction with the articles outlining general obligations (articles 1–5 and 24), and in light of the Convention's overall object and purpose, taking account of the actual practice of how the treaty has been applied by the Women's Committee over time. The Committee has explained that "The Convention is a dynamic instrument. Since the adoption of the Convention in 1979, the Committee as well as other actors at the national and international levels have contributed through progressive thinking to the clarification and understanding of the substantive content of the Convention's articles and the specific nature of discrimination against women and the instruments for combating such discrimination."[2]

While the Committee has stressed that addressing wrongful gender stereotyping is central to the elimination of all forms of discrimination against women and the achievement of substantive equality,[3] it has yet to develop the general and specific nature of the obligations in the Women's Convention. As a result, this chapter will explore what might be the nature of such obligations, given that a "treaty shall be interpreted in good faith in accordance with the ordinary meaning to be given to the terms of the treaty in their context and in the light of its object and purpose."[4]

THE NATURE AND SCOPE OF OBLIGATIONS TO ELIMINATE
GENDER STEREOTYPING

States Parties are obligated by article 2(f) "to take all appropriate measures, including legislation, to modify or abolish existing laws, regulations, customs and practices which constitute discrimination against
women." Where "laws, regulations, customs and practices" are based on
discriminatory forms of gender stereotypes, States Parties are obligated
"to modify or abolish" them. In other words, where a law, policy, or practice makes a difference in treatment on the basis of a gender stereotype
in any sector that has the purpose or effect of impairing or nullifying
women's equal rights and fundamental freedoms, it is a form of discrimination that States Parties are obligated to eliminate.

Article 5(a) requires States Parties to "modify the social and cultural
patterns of conduct of men and women, with a view to achieving the
elimination of prejudices and customary and all other practices which
are based on the idea of the inferiority or the superiority of either of
the sexes or on stereotyped roles for men and women." The obligation
under article 5(a) is for all branches of government to take appropriate
measures to achieve the modification of social and cultural patterns of
conduct to eliminate such prejudices and practices in all sectors. Under
this article, it is not necessary to determine whether stereotypes that are
based on the inferiority, or the stereotyped roles, of women, are a form
of discrimination. It is sufficient that there is a finding that the stereotypes are "based on the idea of inferiority or superiority of either of the
sexes or on stereotyped roles for men and women."

Consequently, where "laws, regulations, customs and practices" that
are based on gender stereotypes do not constitute a form of discrimination for purposes of article 2(f), a State Party is nevertheless obligated
to pursue the objectives of article 5(a). Whether the action is under 2(f)
or 5(a), it can be brought in conjunction with an issue-specific article,
such as wrongful gender stereotyping in the employment sector (article 11), the health sector (article 12), or marriage and family relations
(article 16).

Articles 2(f) and 5(a) of the Convention have roots in article 3 of
the United Nations Declaration on the Elimination of Discrimination
against Women ("Women's Declaration").[5] Article 3 requires members
of the United Nations to take "All appropriate measures . . . to educate
public opinion and to direct national aspirations towards the eradication of prejudice and the abolition of customary and all other practices
which are based on the idea of the inferiority of women." Article 5(a)
of the Women's Convention goes beyond article 3 of the Women's Declaration, because it requires modification of "the social and cultural

patterns of conduct," not just education of public opinion. Article 2(f) further requires a showing that laws, regulations, customs, and practices that are rooted in gender-based judgments or stereotypes, constitute discrimination.

Sometimes a practice might not be considered discriminatory because in the particular circumstances the discrimination is justified. However a State Party might, nonetheless, have a transcending obligation under article 5(a) to take appropriate measures "to modify social and cultural patterns of conduct." That is, the obligation to change social and cultural patterns of conduct to ensure that the inherent dignity of women is respected, protected, and fulfilled, transcends the more particular obligations to eliminate all forms of discrimination against women. This transcending obligation also requires understanding how to eliminate gender hierarchies as well as gender differences per se.[6] The elimination of gender hierarchies means addressing how laws construct men as superior to women, and how laws construct certain subgroups of women as inferior to men, or vice versa, or other subgroups of women or men. The obligation to eliminate gender hierarchies is established in article 5(a) of the Women's Convention, which requires States Parties to take all appropriate measures to eliminate prejudices and practices "which are based on the idea of the inferiority or the superiority of either of the sexes."

The law can construct men or women as inferior or superior through its application of bias, prejudice, and stereotypes. It will be recalled that the *Hugo* case concerned the remission of sentences of mothers convicted of nonviolent crimes, with children under the age of twelve, but not fathers in similar circumstances.[7] Justice Mokgoro in a concurring opinion reasoned that there was discrimination, but that it was justified to ensure adequate care of young children.[8] Taking into account Justice Mokgoro's finding that gender stereotyping was justified in the *Hugo* case, she would not have found a violation of article 2(f) of the Women's Convention, but she could have found a violation of article 5(a).

Justice Kriegler dissented, finding that the pardon constituted a form of discrimination because it perpetuated a stereotype of women as caregivers and men as breadwinners.[9] Had Justice Kriegler applied the Women's Convention, he almost certainly would have found a violation of article 2(f), in conjunction with article 5(a) to take appropriate measures "to modify the social and cultural patterns of conduct of men and women" and article 16(d) requiring that States Parties should "take all appropriate measures to eliminate discrimination against women in all matters relating to . . . family relations and in particular shall ensure, on a basis of equality of men and women . . . [t]he same rights and responsibilities as parents."

The nature and scope of States Parties' obligations to eliminate wrongful forms of gender stereotyping are both general and particular. The general obligation is to dismantle, eliminate, and remedy wrongful gender stereotypes. States Parties need to decode the biases and prejudices that compromise the full application of the rights of men and women. States Parties also need to recognize women's individual worth, their talents, and capacities as individuals, and take measures that value those activities and roles traditionally associated with women.

The general obligation might require government to undertake an assessment to identify the stereotypes that operate to the detriment of women and men, and to determine which measures are appropriate to dismantle and eliminate them. An assessment might show that a government might have to adopt temporary special measures (affirmative action) to ensure that there is a critical mass of women sufficient to break a harmful gender stereotype in a particular sector. An assessment might suggest that an effective measure in a certain sector might be for a government to institute a training program to sensitize people and officials about how a gender stereotype operates in ways that prevent women from using all their capabilities in that sector. In certain situations, eliminating a sex role stereotype of women as homemakers might require recognizing that it was due to prescriptive expectations that society had of them early in their lives. Those prescriptive expectations might be due to the fact that a society had not created, valued, and sustained positive alternative role models for women, or had not debunked the ideology of domesticity underlying it in the larger society. An assessment might finally show the kinds of resources that are lost to a society, or a particular sector of a society, by denying women and men their ability to exercise fully their capabilities and talents, through the application of wrongful stereotypes.

The particular obligation is to understand, name, eliminate, and remedy wrongful gender stereotypes that fall under the Women's Convention's issue-specific articles 6–16, such as exploitation of women and women's exclusion from public office, the franchise, choice of nationality, education, employment and health services, and the other human rights and fundamental freedoms that are addressed through articles 1 and 3. Through article 3, States Parties agree "to ensure the full development and advancement of women, for the purpose of guaranteeing them the exercise and enjoyment of human rights and fundamental freedoms on a basis of equality with men." This would require States Parties to eliminate wrongful gender stereotyping of women to ensure that they exercise rights and freedoms not specifically mentioned in the Convention. For example, it might be necessary to apply domestic laws or other conventions to eliminate stereotyping of women in order for them to be free from inhuman and degrading treatment,[10] and to ensure their rights to privacy, to freedom of thought, conscience, and religion, and to freedom of opinion and expression. Article 23 encourages States Parties to apply "any provisions that are more conducive to the achievement of equality between men and women which may be contained" in state laws or other conventions or agreements in force for a particular state, which would include provisions regarding the elimination of wrongful gender stereotyping.

Articles 2(f) and 5(a) are overarching, cross-cutting obligations that need to be read in conjunction with other human rights and fundamental freedoms, because gender stereotyping does not exist in isolation.[11] The nature of the obligation to eliminate wrongful gender stereotypes will vary according to each human right and fundamental freedom. For example, the right to equality in education, protected by article 10, specifically obligates States Parties to eliminate "any stereotyped concept of the roles of men and women at all levels and in all forms of education by encouraging coeducation and other types of education which will help to achieve this aim and, in particular, by the revision of textbooks and school programmes and the adaptation of teaching methods."[12]

Where there is no specific textual support in the Convention, the Women's Committee has interpreted issue-specific articles to require the elimination of gender stereotypes on that issue in its General Recommendations and Concluding Observations (see Chapter 5). For example, the Committee, in its General Recommendation No. 19 on violence against women, has underscored how "Traditional attitudes by which women are regarded as subordinate to men or as having stereotyped roles perpetuate widespread practices involving violence or coercion, such as family violence and abuse."[13]

Where there is no specific textual support or a General Recommendation or Concluding Observation addressing the gender stereotyping dimensions of an issue-specific equality right, the State Party is still obligated to examine how wrongful gender stereotypes inhibit the exercise of that right. International human rights treaties are to be interpreted generously, rather than strictly, in order to promote maximum advantage for those their terms are designed to protect. This requires understanding the contexts of the particular gender stereotype, how it was created, and how it is perpetuated. The State Party will be required to take both positive and negative measures to transform prejudices and practices that are based on the stereotyped attributes, characteristics, and roles of men and women.[14] In some cases, this will require challenging wrongful forms of gender stereotypes that are perpetuated through the legislature, the judiciary, or the executive branch of government, including both civil and military services. It will require critically analyzing enacted and proposed laws, policies, and practices for hidden wrongful forms of gender stereotypes.

The nature and scope of States Parties' obligations will evolve over time as our understanding of the wrongful nature of gender stereotypes grows. One way to approach the content of the obligations of States Parties to eliminate wrongful gender stereotyping is to use the tripartite framework that has been widely applied by international and regional human rights bodies,[15] such as by the Committee on Economic, Social and Cultural Rights in its General Comment No. 16 on equality.[16] This framework incorporates

• the obligation to respect;
• the obligation to protect, and;
• the obligation to fulfill

human rights and fundamental freedoms.

(a) The obligation to respect
This obligation requires all organs of states to refrain from wrongful gender stereotyping that would directly or indirectly result in the denial of the equal human rights and fundamental freedoms of men and women. This obligation includes naming the gender stereotype, identifying its harm, and examining how it affects the equal application of a law, policy, or practice.[17] Where laws, policies, or practices that embody a gender stereotype are found to be wrongful, States Parties have to refrain from implementing them, and/or amend them appropriately.

The executive branch of government must refrain from gender stereotyping in all its ministries and departments functioning either domestically or internationally. It must ensure, when it designs and implements its administrative policies that, as an organ of the state, it does not engage in wrongful gender stereotyping. The executive might well need to review its laws, policies, and practices in all sectors to ensure that wrongful gender stereotypes are not perpetuated. The vice lies in using the power of the executive to support the perpetuation of wrongful gender stereotypes.[18] As was said by Justice Kriegler in the *Hugo* case, "the Constitution enjoins all organs of state—here the President—to be careful not to perpetuate the distinctions of the past based on gender type-casting. In effect the Act put the stamp of approval of the head of state on a perception of parental roles that has been [prescribed]."[19] For Justice Kriegler, President Mandela's reliance on sex role stereotypes not only contributed to their perpetuation, but also imbued them with added legitimacy by virtue of the fact that the head of state prescribed women's roles within South African society.

The obligation of the executive extends to its departments of immigration and foreign affairs. Immigration services have been known to deny visas to husbands of resident women, and not to wives of resident men.[20] This distinction is based on an improper gender classification rooted in sex role stereotypes of men as breadwinners and women as homemakers that immigration services need to eliminate. A ministry of foreign affairs, which usually is the ministry responsible for reservations to international treaties, has an obligation only to file reservations that are compatible with the object and purpose of the Women's Convention to eliminate wrongful forms of gender stereotyping. Where a ministry of foreign affairs files a reservation that is incompatible, it needs to withdraw it, or at least state when it will do so.

The legislative branch of government must refrain from applying and perpetuating wrongful forms of stereotyping in enacting new legislation. In addition, the legislative branch must take positive measures such as reviewing enacted or proposed legislation and customary laws, through law-reform initiatives to ensure that they do not contain wrongful gender stereotypes. A former Justice of the Supreme Court of Canada, L'Heureux Dubé, has explained that "Legislators have a very important role to play in the elimination of myths and stereotypes because legislation contributes, on a collective scale, to the development of social values and norms. As we have seen over the course of this [20th] century in particular, laws not only reflect societies' views, but they sometimes also go beyond current norms and seek to modify them in order to achieve a higher principle, such as equality, where there is a political will to do so."[21]

A favorable example of a parliament removing stereotypes from the law includes legislative reform in Botswana when, following the groundbreaking decision of the Court of Appeal in *Attorney General of Botswana v. Unity Dow*,[22] its Parliament changed its nationality law to allow female citizens to convey nationality to their children, like male citizens can.[23] While neither the Court of Appeal nor the Parliament directly addressed the sex stereotype of women as lesser citizens than men, the Court did reject the government's argument that a gender distinction was necessary "in order to preserve the male orientation of the society."[24]

The Guatemalan government, following the *Morales de Sierra* decision of the Inter-American Commission on Human Rights,[25] has taken steps to propose amendments to their Civil Code to eliminate sex role stereotypes in some of the impugned provisions, but the amendments have yet to be approved by Congress.[26] Of particular note, is the establishment of the Maria Eugenia Morales Aceña de Sierra Foundation for Dignity (FUNDADIG). Morales de Sierra waived the financial compensation that the Inter-American Commission had recommended she receive, because "her cause was to win recognition of women's dignity."[27] In exchange for the waiver, the State has agreed to help establish FUNDADIG.[28]

The judiciary, like the executive and the legislature, is an organ of the state and therefore subject to the obligations under the Women's Convention. Court decisions and practices can be means of perpetuating or eliminating stereotypes of women.[29] Decisions and procedures deny the rights of the individual woman who is before the court; but they also degrade similarly situated women by perpetuating wrongful stereotypes about them. Court decisions that perpetuate gender stereotypes thus create individual and collective harms, and court decisions that expose, dismantle, and eliminate stereotypes benefit the individual concerned but also similarly situated people.

The judiciary must refrain from gender stereotyping in its reasoning and practices. Judges are not immune from bias. They can impose generalizations about women that do not necessarily relate to women's actual capabilities, needs, and circumstances. As Justice L'Heureux Dubé explained, "Myths and stereotypes are a form of bias because they impair the individual judge's ability to assess the facts in a particular case in an open-minded fashion. In fact, judging based on myths and stereotypes is entirely incompatible with keeping an open mind, because myths and stereotypes are based on irrational predisposition and generalization, rather than fact. They close one's mind to both truth and reality. . . . Impartiality is, therefore, an invaluable goal for which judges must strive because it obliges us to recognize myths and stereotypes by confronting our unconscious preconceptions of other peoples' perceptions and realities."[30] It will be recalled that in her concurring opinion in the *Ewanchuk* case, Justice L'Heureux Dubé explained how the Canadian Parliament amended the Criminal Code to eradicate stereotypical assumptions about women.[31] She cautioned that these assumptions should not be permitted to resurface through the stereotypical reasoning of courts.[32]

In contrast to Justice L'Heureux Dubé's concurring opinion in the *Ewanchuk* case, the U.S. Supreme Court missed an opportunity in *Miller v. Albright*[33] to expose and condemn the operative sex role stereotypes in the Immigration and Nationality Act of 1994.[34] The impugned provision of the Act required unmarried American fathers, but not unmarried American mothers, to acknowledge their parenthood before their child reaches the age of majority in order for that child to gain U.S. citizenship. Lorelyn Miller, daughter of a Filipino mother and an unwed American father, challenged this acknowledgment requirement under the Equal Protection clause of the Fourteenth Amendment of the U.S. Constitution, in pursuit of her U.S. citizenship. Miller's complaint was rejected because her father acknowledged his paternity only after she had reached the age of majority.

The sex role stereotype that was embedded in the acknowledgment requirement is that unmarried mothers are responsible for their children, while unmarried fathers can evade responsibility except through acknowledgment. The majority failed to reject governmental reliance on interests that depend upon sex role stereotypes. In a dissenting opinion, Justice Breyer, joined by Justices Souter and Ginsburg, explained that "Since either men or women may be caretakers, and since either men or women may be 'breadwinners,' one could justify the gender distinction only on the ground that more women are caretakers than men, and more men are 'breadwinners' than women. This, again, is the kind of generalization that we have rejected as justifying a gender-based distinction in other cases."[35] In failing to overthrow gender-based stereotypes "independent of their truth or falsehood in particular contexts,"[36] the Court in *Miller* limited its ability to discredit governmental interests that rely on sex role stereotypes, and thus "the field of cognizable stereotypes and the operational impact of cognizing them."[37]

Sometimes court decisions can dismantle and perpetuate stereotypes simultaneously, in part due to the confusion in thinking about whether the stereotype is true or false, or descriptive, false, or prescriptive in nature. For example, in *Muojekwu v. Ejikeme* the Nigerian Court of Appeal ruled that certain Ili-ekpe and Nrachi customs were repugnant to natural justice, equity, and good conscience.[38] Under the Ili-ekpe custom, if a man dies without a male heir, his land and belongings would revert to the closest male relative. The Nrachi custom was designed to avoid the consequences of the Ili-ekpe custom. It "enables a man to keep one of his daughters unmarried [in this case, Virginia] perpetually under his roof to raise issues, more especially males for the father to succeed him."[39] A son born to a married daughter would be entitled to inherit through her husband and his family, but not her father. Therefore, in order to ensure inheritance from her father, the son would have to be born while she was unmarried.

Judge Tobi of the Nigerian Court of Appeal in his concurrence reasoned that these customs were contrary to section 42 of the Constitution of Nigeria of 1999 that prohibits sex discrimination, and article 5 of the Women's Convention. He explained that in "my humble view, Virginia is a victim of the prejudices anticipated in Article 5. In view of the fact that Nigeria is a party to the Convention, courts of law should give or provide teeth to its provisions. That is one major way of ameliorating the unfortunate situation Virginia found herself, a situation where she was forced to rely on an uncouth custom not only against the laws of Nigeria but also against nature."[40] By characterizing the custom as "uncouth,"

Judge Tobi presumably meant the harm of requiring a daughter to stay unmarried in order to be used as a reproductive vessel to beget a male heir for her father, and the articulation of a patriarchal ideology in customary law that denies women equal inheritance rights with men.

Judge Tobi's reasoning was not entirely free of stereotypical reasoning. He explained that because "A woman who has no husband generally has more freedom to involve in sexual practices than one who is married. In such a situation indiscriminate sexual practices would result in promiscuity and prostitution."[41] In relying on the offensive sexual stereotype of unmarried women as inherently promiscuous to nullify the custom, it has been explained that the judge was more concerned with the custom's anti-social effect than its discriminatory effect of denying women inheritance through customary laws.[42] It could also be said that Judge Tobi was relying on a false stereotype not a descriptive stereotype of unmarried women.

Before the adoption of the Women's Convention, Justice Brennan exposed and dismantled the sex role stereotype of women in the U.S. Supreme Court case of *Frontiero v. Richardson*.[43] This case concerned military wives' rights to create automatic entitlements for their husbands that military husbands already could create for their wives. Justice Brennan recognized that laws that restrict women's rights have historically been rationalized as benign protections of women, in that wives were afforded protections of their husbands' support that wives could not afford their husbands. He explained that the nation's "long and unfortunate history of sex discrimination" was "Traditionally . . . rationalized by an attitude of 'romantic paternalism' which, in practical effect, put women not on a pedestal, but in a cage."[44] Due to notions of benign paternalism, he explained, "our statute books gradually became laden with gross, stereotyped distinctions between the sexes and, indeed, throughout much of the 19th century, the position of women in our society was, in many respects, comparable to that of blacks under the pre-Civil War slave codes."[45]

Another example of judicial identification of stereotypical thinking is the opinion of Judge Thomas of the New Zealand Court of Appeal in the case of *W. v. New Zealand [A.G.]*.[46] In that case, Judge Thomas exposed how "the law relating to recent complaint evidence is based on discredited male-driven assumptions and is irremediably at odds with the behaviour of women who have been raped or sexually abused."[47] In his reasoning, he carefully analyzed why the Court of Appeal should admit into evidence a victim's complaint of sexual abuse that had occurred while she was in foster care, despite the fact that the harmful effects of the abuse were realized only after the statute of limitations had expired. He explained: "The fact of the matter is that, faced with a situation in which there is no clearly applicable precedent, the Courts have forgone the fresh consideration of the issue to which sexually abused women are entitled in favour of adhering to an obdurate orthodoxy. But for this misplaced adhesion, there is no reason why the Courts could not have held, and could not still hold, that the test for determination whether the cause of action has accrued in the case of a sexually abused woman is an essentially subjective test."[48] In deciding to apply a subjective test to enable women to testify, Judge Thomas essentially rejected the false stereotype of women as noncredible complainants of sexual abuse unless they complain at the first opportunity.

(b) The obligation to protect

The general obligation to protect requires States Parties to take appropriate measures to address violations by non-state actors, [49] such as the family, the community, and the market.[50] The obligation to protect women against wrongful forms of gender stereotyping by non-state actors includes undertaking ongoing awareness-raising regarding biases and prejudices against women, applying sensitizing, preventive, and other appropriate legislation, policies, or programs, introducing effective procedures in response to complaints against non-state actors, and implementing appropriate remedies that redress wrongful forms of gender stereotyping. The Committee on Economic, Social and Cultural Rights, in its explanation of how the obligation to protect builds on the language of article 5(a) of the Women's Convention, explains that States Parties are obligated "to take steps aimed directly at the elimination of prejudices, customary and all other practices that perpetuate the notion of inferiority or superiority of either of the sexes, and stereotyped roles for men and women."[51]

The distinction between state and non-state actors is often blurred. Non-state actors include public corporations and other agencies sponsored by government that function independently or at arm's length from government, and private corporations that discharge functions delegated by government, such as private hospital corporations that operate within publicly funded health insurance schemes. Sometimes violations of the right to equality are perpetrated by both state and non-state actors, and take place in both the public and private spheres. The Committee on Economic, Social and Cultural Rights recognizes this blurred nature by specifically requiring states to monitor and regulate conduct by non-state actors "in cases where public services have been partially or fully privatized."[52]

An example of the combined involvement of state and non-state actors in a violation of women's rights is child marriage. The facilitation of child marriage takes place in the private sphere of the family, where girls are prepared prematurely for marriage by being stereotyped into subordinate, subservient roles, and where they are required to submit to arranged marriages, and in the public sphere of a town hall, where marriage licenses are usually issued and marriages may be registered.[53] In such cases, the state is obligated to take appropriate measures to address wrongful gender stereotyping perpetrated by both the family and the local government.

(c) The obligation to fulfill
The obligation to fulfill women's rights to be free from wrongful gender stereotyping requires States Parties to take positive measures to abolish gender stereotypes that constitute discrimination,[54] and to take positive measures that are appropriate to actually modify the social and cultural patterns of conduct that derive from stereotypical prejudices about women's inferior capacities and/or roles.[55] It is an established principle of international human rights law that States Parties must do more than merely refrain from interfering with human rights; they must also adopt positive measures to ensure that those rights are guaranteed and observed in practice, such as enacting legislation allowing for punishment of rapists violating the right to private life of mentally handicapped girls.[56]

This obligation requires States Parties to establish the legal, policy, and programmatic frameworks to understand, name, eliminate, and remedy wrongful gender stereotypes. The obligation to fulfil might require States Parties to

- facilitate the elimination of wrongful gender stereotypes by taking positive measures to name them and show how they operate to women's detriment in specific sectors;
- provide appropriate measures that break stereotypes, such as to provide and require baby diaper-changing tables in men's public washrooms as well as women's, to deinstitutionalize and challenge the stereotype that only women take care of infant children and to enable men to care for their infant children when away from home; or,
- promote awareness of wrongful gender stereotypes through education and training programs for public officials, including judges.

Some jurisdictions, such as the state of Michigan in the United States, have examined how gender stereotypes have influenced judges to the disadvantage of women in disputes over custody of their children. The record shows that judges often granted custody to minimally interested fathers even when the mothers had been the primary caregivers for years, characterizing mothers who focus on their careers as less fit parents than fathers who do the same and evaluating women's social interests and finances more critically than they do men's.[57] Legal clinics in law schools, such as at the Ateneo University Law School in the Philippines, have taken the lead to develop "bench books" for the judiciary analyzing how the Women's Convention has been applied in domestic court decisions.[58] Building on this model, bench books in other countries could be developed that analyze how judicial reasoning in court decisions has perpetuated or dismantled gender stereotypes and how such stereotypes could be dismantled more effectively in future decisions.

Other countries, such as Brazil, Jamaica, and Venezuela, through their governmental offices of women's affairs, train the judiciary about "stereotypes that discriminate against women and how to be more respectful of and sensitive to women when they turn to the courts for protection of their rights."[59] Training programs for judges could examine the ways in which women are disadvantaged within the judicial process,[60] especially through negative stereotypical depictions of women in certain areas of the law such as divorce.[61] Training programs could invite judges to analyze how wrongful gender stereotypes have become embedded in court decisions, and how such stereotypes have been or can be dismantled and remedied. Training programs could also explore the development of ethical guidelines for lawyers who are engaged in litigation, analyze rules of evidence so as to prevent the application of wrongful gender stereotypes, and formulate judges' instructions to juries, where jury systems exist, cautioning jurors against the reliance on gender stereotypes.[62]

Where legislation already exists that contains gender stereotypes, the legislature must take positive measures to change that legislation. For example, the South African Parliament is obligated under the Women's Convention to amend the Sexual Offences Act of 1957 that constructs the crime of prostitution as concerning only the prostitute (usually a woman), while not making the customer (usually a man) equally liable for conviction under this Act. It took the judiciary, albeit in dissent in *Jordan v. S.*, to identify the unfairness of making the prostitute solely responsible for the offence against morality under the Sexual Offences Act, as the one "soliciting for purposes of prostitution."[63] The male clients might only be charged for a morally neutral public disorder offence under the Riotous Assemblies Act of 1856. Regrettably, the majority of the Constitutional Court of South Africa chose to perpetuate the sexual stereotype of women as immoral temptresses implicit in the Sexual Offences Act, and therefore making them solely responsible under that Act.[64]

Where wrongful gender stereotypes are embedded in customary laws, such as those that bar widows' or women's inheritance of land,[65] or those that permit polygyny, which allows men but not women, to marry several spouses,[66] the legislature is obligated under the Women's Convention to change such laws. Where legislatures fail, the judiciary is obligated to find a violation of women's right to be free from all forms of discrimination, and apply the resources of the legal system to neutralize or minimize the effects of such discrimination.

*   *   *

Whether one is dealing with an obligation to respect, protect, or fulfil human rights prohibiting wrongful gender stereotyping, attributing legal responsibility to a State Party for the wrong depends on the identification of the actors responsible for perpetuating the gender stereotypes. If the actors are state agents or officials, or acting under the delegated authority of the state, the acts are considered state acts. If the violations are caused by non-state actors, and the state fails to take reasonably available measures to restrain, condemn, and remedy those violations, it becomes possible to attribute responsibility to the state for its derogation of duty.[67] In such cases, attributing legal responsibility to a State Party depends on the existence of a legal link between that State Party's acts and/or failures to act and the imposition of a discriminatory form of gender stereotype by a non-state actor. A legal link could arise through positive facilitation of the stereotyping action, for instance by accommodating it, or by failure of due diligence to identify and redress that stereotype or stereotypes of that nature.

Eliminating Gender Stereotyping by Government

States Parties are obligated to take measures that are appropriate to transform wrongful gender stereotypes that are applied by their executive, legislative, and judicial institutions. All branches of government must refrain from gender stereotyping, and when appropriate take positive measures to eliminate such stereotypes. The measures that States Parties must take to eliminate wrongful gender stereotyping will vary according to a particular sector, such as education, employment, or health. The purpose of this section is to explore which measures might be appropriate under articles 2(f), 5(a), and 12 of the Women's Convention for the branches of government to take in the health sector.

The executive, through its ministries of health, welfare, and education, might raise its self-awareness and sensitivity by identifying how its policies and programs might be premised upon gendered assumptions about women's sexuality, sex roles, and compounded traits, for instance regarding age, marital status, and cultural background. The process of naming gender stereotypes is important because health care providers are often unaware, or only partially aware, that they are stereotyping. In addition to naming the gender stereotypes, executive agencies need to explain how gender stereotypes operate to the detriment of women's health in general, and reproductive health in particular.

The next step is to determine how these different forms of gender stereotypes discriminate against women and impede the realization of their substantive equality. Wrongful gender stereotypes often impede women's access to essential, evidence-based reproductive information and to health services. Especially prejudicial are prescriptive and false stereotypes. Prescriptive stereotypes prescribe certain roles and behaviors to women, even when they have not freely chosen those behaviors or roles. A common prescriptive stereotype of women is that they should be mothers. This stereotype may be used to justify denying them access to reproductive health information[68] and services[69] so that they will be more liable to initiate and continue pregnancies.

False stereotypes, which ascribe attributes to individual women that are untrue, are pervasive in the reproductive health sector. A common form of false stereotype, often linked to socioeconomic stratification, is that of women as promiscuous and immoral, who therefore have to be disciplined or punished for their allegedly errant ways.[70] The punishment has taken different forms, and has been known to include manifesting disrespectful and patronizing attitudes of health care staff,[71] withholding anesthesia from women during abortion procedures,[72] or denying women access to the procedure itself.[73]

The false stereotype of women as incapable of making rational decisions is persistent in the health sector. This stereotype can result in women being sterilized without their consent, especially subgroups of women who are further marginalized because of their ethnicity.[74] Law, policies, and practices that are based on this stereotype often require that women have the authorization of their husbands or, if women are unmarried, their fathers or brothers in order to obtain health services.[75] It is the indignity of having to ask others' permission, and not being able to decide for themselves that infantilizes and therefore harms women. This stereotype is especially harmful where reproductive health services are concerned, since women may forgo necessary gynecological care rather than explain to their male relatives what care they require.

Another false stereotype is one of women as weak and vulnerable to the influences and persuasion of allegedly directive health care providers, and therefore requiring a law to protect against giving consent to an "inappropriate" medical procedure.[76] Gender-paternalistic stereotypes have enabled the development of the women-protective rationale for limiting access to therapeutic abortion.[77] It has been explained that these rationales are substantiated by narrative and empirical evidence. The narrative evidence includes stories of women who have been led unknowingly into having abortion. The empirical evidence has included reports of psychological distress following the abortion, known as post-abortion syndrome.[78] This evidence, however specious and incorrect, has been used to buttress false stereotypes of women as weak and in need of protection.

Women are often used instrumentally by the state or by religious hierarchies to protect or advance the values of men endowed with superior or revealed wisdom. That is, prejudice that women only have instrumental value, and not inherent value like men, allows them to be treated as secondary to the interests and rights of others. For example, health professionals try to invoke their rights of conscience in ways that deny women their own rights of conscience and often their rights to equal access to health care.[79] They also use their rights of conscience to deny women the choice of abortion where it is legal such as in cases of rape,[80] or when the procedure is in their own health interests.[81]

Hostile gender stereotypes that limit women's self-determination tend to emerge when women have gained some measure of autonomy through, for example, the enactment of liberal abortion laws. It is not uncommon to find court cases initiated to limit women's autonomy in countries that have liberalized their abortion laws. These cases include attempts by partners to limit women's access to abortion through requirements of partner authorization,[82] and attempts by health care providers to exercise their rights of conscience in ways that prevent women from accessing lawful reproductive health services.[83] Most recently, a case limited the availability of medically indicated abortion, where life itself is not endangered, in order to "protect" women from making decisions they might later regret.[84] The pattern or practice of using hostile or demeaning gender stereotypes to limit legal reforms to enhance reproductive rights and justice for women is pervasive. Similarly, hostile gender stereotypes often emerge to downplay women's competence when their competencies and capabilities become evident.

By identifying the predominant gender stereotypes that operate in the reproductive health sector and mapping their consequences, executive agencies of government are well situated to determine what measures might be appropriate to address them. A health ministry, for instance, might produce guidelines naming predominant gender stereotypes that operate in the health sector, explaining how they depict women as somehow inferior or deficient, or use women as instruments of ideologies, and showing how they impair women's access to services. Guidelines might help to educate health personnel about the need to correct prescriptive and/or false assumptions about women or subgroups of women. They might also identify how hostile stereotypes are used to create backlash to limit the effects of newly enacted liberal laws, for instance by misrepresenting the reasons why women seek contraception or sterilization. Guidelines might also provide examples of how gender stereotypes fail to take account of women's actual situations in ways that harm their rights of choice, agency, and dignity. Such guidelines, and their use in training health care providers, would be an appropriate measure for health ministries to take to meet their obligations under the Women's Convention to identify and eliminate wrongful gender stereotyping that impedes women's fulfillment of their reproductive health needs and their entitlement to sexual intimacy free from the fear of unwanted pregnancy.

Legislators must refrain from enacting laws that are based on wrongful gender stereotypes, and take positive measures to ensure that legislation is respectful of women's rights, including their right to be free from wrongful gender stereotyping. In addition to examining existing or proposed laws that are based on gendered assumptions that degrade women in the clinical setting or infringe or deny their access to reproductive health services, legislators should examine laws beyond the health system that might exacerbate women's ill health. For example, legislators must not stereotype women into childbearing and childrearing roles, such as through differential age legislation that enables women to marry earlier than men. Such legislation is based on gendered assumptions that women do not need the same number of years to prepare for marriage and build their families. States Parties have been put on notice by human rights treaty bodies, such as the Committee on the Rights of the Child,[85] to change such differential legal ages of marriage, in part because they stereotype women into childbearing and unpaid or low-paid service roles at an early age, which can disproportionately prejudice their health.[86]

States Parties are as responsible under international law for human rights violations committed by their courts as for the misconduct of other branches of government. Judges are obligated to implement international human rights law, even when they enjoy personal immunity from liability within certain national legal systems. Court decisions can be a means of perpetuating gender stereotypes. Such decisions not only deny the rights of the individual woman who is before the court, but also degrade similarly situated women by perpetuating wrongful gender stereotypes of the subgroup of women to which they belong. Stereotypes of this nature thus create individual and collective harms and defeat the judicial commitment to justice.

The U.S. Supreme Court, as recently as 2007, relied on a sex stereotype of women as vulnerable and in need of protection to justify in part the prohibition of a particular method of late term abortion.[87] Justice Kennedy, writing for the majority, reasoned that it is permissible to outlaw a certain method of late term abortion, even if indicated to promote women's health, on the ground that, if women could use such a method, they would come to regret their decision: "Whether to have an abortion requires a difficult and painful moral decision. While we find no reliable data to measure the phenomenon, it seems unexceptional to conclude some women come to regret their choice to abort the infant life they once created and sustained. Severe depression and loss of esteem can follow."[88]

The dissent, written by the only female justice on the Court at the time, Justice Ginsburg, challenged the paternalistic reasoning of the majority as a basis for denying women their agency and autonomy.

Revealing in this regard, the Court invokes an antiabortion shibboleth for which it concededly has no reliable evidence: Women who have abortions come to regret their choices, and consequently suffer from "[s]evere depression and loss of esteem." Because of women's fragile emotional state and because of the "bond of love the mother has for her child," the Court worries, doctors may withhold information about the nature of the . . . procedure. The solution the Court approves, then, is *not* to require doctors to inform women, accurately and adequately, of the different procedures and their attendant risks. Instead, the Court deprives women of the right to make an autonomous choice, even at the expense of their safety. This way of thinking reflects ancient notions about women's place in the family and under the Constitution—ideas that have long since been discredited.[89]

Justice Ginsburg compared past decisions that perpetuate stereotypes of women with others that dismantle them.[90] For decisions perpetuating gender stereotypes, she cited decisions limiting women's hours of work[91] and prohibiting them from becoming members of the bar[92] to protect the "proper" discharge of their maternal functions. For decisions dismantling stereotypes, she referred to a decision overturning a law preventing women from attending an all-male military institute, because it relied on overbroad generalizations about the talents, capacities, or preferences of women that have impeded women's progress toward full citizenship.[93] She also referred to a decision overturning a gender-based social security classification, because it relied on "archaic and overbroad generalizations" such as assumptions as to women's dependency.[94] Justice Ginsburg's dissent is especially powerful because it names and rationally condemns the stereotypical thinking implicit and explicit in the majority's reasoning, and guided them to past decisions where stereotypical thinking was identified and dismantled.

Like Justice Ginsburg's opinion, court opinions can be an important means of dismantling wrongful stereotypes of women. By identifying the gender stereotypes implicit in the reasoning of past decisions, and exploring their historical and ideological contexts, dissenting, concurring, and majority opinions can assist in dismantling gender stereotypes, and thus prevent their legal perpetuation. An example of a majority opinion that dismantled a gender stereotype is that of Justice Araújo Rentería and Justice Vargas Hernández of the Colombian Constitutional Court in their 2006 abortion decision.[95] Their majority opinion, which liberalized Colombia's restrictive abortion law, explained that there are certain limits on the legislative power in criminal matters, including limits on violating individuals' fundamental right to dignity, and the right to free development of the individual, even when the legislature aims to protect other constitutional values, such as life. The Justices reasoned that "when the legislature enacts criminal laws, it cannot ignore that a woman is a human being entitled to dignity and that she must be treated as such, as opposed to being treated as a reproductive instrument for the human race. The legislature must not impose the role of procreator on a woman against her will."[96] In naming the sex role stereotype of women "as a reproductive instrument for the human race," the Justices articulated the harmful assumption about women that had been embedded in the criminal law.

Eliminating Gender Stereotyping by Non-State Actors

States Parties are obligated to eliminate wrongful gender stereotyping by both state and non-state actors. Article 2(e) of the Women's Convention requires the adoption of "all appropriate measures to eliminate discrimination against women by any person, organization or enterprise." Under this provision, a State Party, in addition to being legally responsible for the acts or omissions of its own agents, can be held legally responsible for its failure to act with due diligence to prevent, investigate, deter, punish, and remedy wrongful gender stereotyping by non-state actors.[97]

There is such a wide range of non-state actors that grouping them into categories might assist in the application of article 2(e). Since no one approach to categorizing non-state actors will necessarily work in all circumstances, thought needs to be given to which categories are best applied in particular contexts. To open the discussion, this chapter will group non-state actors into the family, the community, and the market.[98]

- The family: non-state actors in this category include family members who engage in or are parties to domestic violence,[99] child abuse,[100] "honor" killing[101] or, for example, who facilitate forced[102] or child marriage,[103] and the trafficking of girl children.[104]

- The community: non-state actors in the community include religious, traditional, educational, and comparable institutions that create or perpetuate modesty, chastity, or obedience codes that inhibit or prevent women from developing their own codes of conduct in a manner that suits their perceptions of their individual best interests and circumstances, or exercising their political freedoms.[105]
- The market: non-state actors in the market are typified by companies, including multinational corporations, whose advertising flaunts images of women's bodies, perhaps provocatively positioned to attract consumer demand, or whose hiring practices perpetuate wrongful gender stereotypes, such as that only women can perform secretarial functions, and/or that women cannot be placed in charge of male colleagues.[106]

There are acts by non-state actors that might fall into two or three of these categories. For instance, tribal councils, which punish males' misconduct by ordering sexual or other assaults on their female family members[107] fall into the first two categories. Privately armed groups that commit crimes, including mass crimes against women such as gang rapes[108] or abduction of girls and women,[109] might fall into all three categories. That is, men who join private militias might facilitate the abduction of one of their female relatives, or be armed through a religious group, which might be paid for by a private company or organization to advance its commercial interests, such as in acquisition of political influence or drug trafficking.

The obligation of states regarding non-state actors, whatever their category, is especially important because non-state actors can be instrumental in creating, perpetuating, and institutionalizing wrongful stereotypes of women, thereby establishing and/or entrenching gender hierarchy. One need only look at how the cinema and the television industries have perpetuated wrongful stereotypes of particular subgroups of women such as nannies of particular races and ethnicities,[110] and how stereotypical thinking is perpetuated through jokes based on demeaning characterizations of certain subgroups of women, such as "dumb blondes."

In determining the appropriateness of measures to eliminate wrongful gender stereotyping by non-state actors, states will need to weigh such measures against rights that individuals who apply gender stereotypes can legitimately claim, such as to freedom of thought and expression.[111] Individuals are entitled to their own opinions that may include stereotypical generalizations about women. A distinction might usefully be made between measures to influence stereotypical thinking, for instance by educational means, and measures to prevent the actual imposition of a gender stereotype in a way that precludes a benefit or imposes some form of burden. Appropriate measures might, for example, condemn gender stereotyping by non-state actors that denies a benefit to a qualified woman, such as preventing access to employment.

The exact nature of the obligations of States Parties to prevent and remedy wrongful gender stereotyping by non-state actors will evolve over time as the Women's Committee applies the Women's Convention in different contexts. As one authoritative report has explained, the critical question is "what constitutes 'appropriate measures' in a particular context. Some guidance can be gained from the jurisprudence that has emerged around the concept of 'due diligence' in human rights law (though in certain circumstances, the standard of appropriateness may be higher than the standard of conduct required by 'due diligence'). The jurisprudence which has developed in relation to the obligation to *protect* dimensions of rights may also provide additional resources for interpreting this phrase."[112]

It needs to be emphasized that, although the due diligence standard of state involvement has evolved in relation to violence against women,[113] it is applicable to all rights falling within the scope of the Women's Convention.[114] For example, where there is evidence of a pattern or practice of violence against women, it raises the question whether a State Party meets the due diligence standard[115] by taking all appropriate preventive measures and exposing and countering negative and subservient stereotypes of women that might condition and condone the practice.

The Women's Committee might develop a test to determine how to engage the responsibility of States Parties for wrongful gender stereotyping by non-state actors. Examples of such tests include the "but for" test and the "real prospect" test. The "but for" test requires the complainant to show that, but for the failure of state authorities to address the stereotype and its oppressive application, women would not have been denied a benefit, such as employment, or would not have had some indignity or burden imposed upon them, such as being trafficked into prostitution. The European Court of Human Rights applied the alternative "real prospect test" for determining the responsibility of states for non-state actors: "The test . . . does not require it to be shown that 'but for' the failing or omission of the public authority ill-treatment would not have happened. A failure to take reasonably available measures which could have had *a real prospect of altering the outcome or mitigating the harm* is sufficient to engage the responsibility of the State."[116] That is, States Parties are responsible when they fail to take reasonably available measures to address wrongful gender stereotyping by non-state actors "which could have had a real prospect of altering the outcome or mitigating the harm."[117]

Reasonably available measures that might be appropriate for States Parties to take to eliminate wrongful gender stereotyping by religious institutions that could have "a real prospect of altering the outcome or mitigating the harm" include circumscribing the manifestation of religion, protecting women's equal right to freedom of religion, which includes freedom from involuntary compliance with others' religion, and challenging a religious practice as a form of discrimination against women.

There have been several court decisions circumscribing manifestation of religion when it wrongs women. The European Court of Human Rights held in effect that it was justifiable for the state to limit the right of pharmacists to manifest their religion when acting in their professional capacity, when such manifestation denied women access to emergency contraception.[118] The European Commission on Human Rights decided that the refusal of a Jewish husband to give his wife a letter of repudiation of marriage ("a gett"), which finalizes divorce in Jewish law and allows the former wife to remarry in religious form, does not constitute the manifestation of religious observance or practice.[119] Similarly, the Supreme Court of Canada ordered a Jewish man to pay damages for the harms to his ex-wife due to his refusal to issue the letter that repudiates their marriage, required under religious law for his ex-wife to manifest her religion on remarriage.[120]

Courts have protected women's equal right to freedom of religion. For instance, the Supreme Court of Israel guaranteed women's right to pray at the sacred site of the Western Wall in Jerusalem,[121] and to participate in religious councils on an equal basis with men,[122] thus helping to dismantle stereotypes of women as subordinate in religious observance and institutions. Legal cases challenging the religious practice of women's ineligibility to become religious ministers on the same basis as men as constituting a wrongful form of gender stereotyping, have yet to be successful. This is in part due to courts deferring to religious institutions' defences of freedom of religion.[123]

Some institutions that engage in stereotyping women as incapable of holding religious or holy office, such as ordained ministry, do not present "a real prospect of altering"[124] their practices. However, the state should acknowledge that, although institutional leaders are free to manifest their religions through discriminatory practices against women, discriminatory religious institutions do not merit state privileges, such as charitable status accompanied by tax exemptions. Like noncharitable institutions, discriminatory religious institutions should not be awarded the public subsidy of relief from payment of local or municipal taxes, but should pay tax, like others, for the municipal services they receive. Similarly, governments could make them liable to pay tax on their income, including income from voluntary gifts and payments for goods and services. Likewise, governments could deny their contributors tax relief for charitable donations. States that privilege non-state actors that violate individuals' human rights may be considered complicit in the violation.

Religious institutions will not immediately abandon their fundamental doctrines for mercenary reasons, so that denial of public subsidies by withdrawal of tax exemption will not directly cause them to alter their practices of stereotyping. However, there is a real prospect that public demonstration that stereotyping practices are uncharitable and offensive to human rights principles will serve to educate the public that discriminatory gender stereotyping, even when embedded in doctrines of religious institutions, do not warrant privilege or protection.

What Are the Obligations of States Parties to Remedy Gender Stereotyping?

Devising effective remedies for wrongful gender stereotyping is essential for its eradication. Ineffective remedies fuel a climate of disregard, disrespect, and devaluation of women in all sectors of society. When societies fail to recognize their prejudices against women, and the gender stereotypes on which prejudices are based, that failure exacerbates impunity of agencies and individuals that violate women's rights. Impunity enables prejudices and wrongful gender stereotypes to fester, aggravating the devaluation of women and the diminishment of justice throughout society. Remedies would be more effective if they were based on a diagnosis of the gender stereotype, its form, the nature of its wrong, its origins and contexts, and its means of perpetuation and means of elimination.

The Women's Convention requires States Parties to remedy wrongful gender stereotyping. While the Convention does not specifically address remedies, it is clear through interpretation of its overall object and purpose that remedies are required to eliminate all forms of discrimination against women that States Parties do not prevent. Article 2(b) requires States Parties "to adopt appropriate legislative and other measures, including sanctions where appropriate, prohibiting all discrimination against women." Sanctions are a form of prospective remedy, in that, while not necessarily correcting a wrong that was committed, they provide deterrents to its repetition or its continuation. Whatever form the remedy takes, States Parties are obligated under international human rights law to provide *effective* remedies, not remedies that are illusory.[125]

Where States Parties have not met their obligation "to address prevailing gender relations and the persistence of gender-based stereotypes that affect women not only through individual acts . . . but also in law and legal and societal structures and institutions,"[126] they are obligated to remedy their violation. Accordingly, effective remedies will need to contain both individual and structural dimensions. Individual remedial measures are often devised in terms of compensating the victim for the material harm of the application, enforcement, or perpetuation of the wrongful gender stereotype. This approach to remedies is modeled on tort law that aims to restore the wronged parties to the position in which they would have been if not wronged.

Remedying the structural nature of wrongful gender stereotyping is prospective in nature and more complex. Structural remedies for such stereotyping attempt to deinstitutionalize gender stereotypes from the laws, policies, and practices of States Parties so that their application can no longer wrong women in the future. Structural remedies for such stereotyping might be more akin to remedies for violations of socio-economic rights. It has been explained that "socio-economic rights may require more complex remedies such as declarations or injunctions that invite or require positive governmental action. They also raise difficult tensions between achieving corrective justice for the individuals before the court as opposed to distributive justice for larger groups not before the court. In addition, there are also tensions between ordering compensation for past violations and ensuring compliance in the future with related tensions between achieving instant remedies that correct discrete violations as opposed to the commencement of much more drawn out and uncertain process of systemic reform."[127]

Eliminating and remedying wrongful gender stereotyping will not happen instantly, and it will need both individual relief and systemic reform. A remedy, whether aimed at the individual or structural level, will be more effective if it targets the operative gender stereotype that has been exposed, and redresses the harms that a woman, or a subgroup of women, suffered as a result of the stereotype's application, enforcement, or perpetuation.

Clarifying the reasons why a gender stereotype has been applied, enforced, or perpetuated can also help in the crafting of effective remedies. For example, it will be recalled that people stereotype for the sake of simplicity or predictability, to assign difference based on assumptions that may be false, or to prescribe identities. Courts and human rights treaty bodies may base their reasoning, for instance, on what they consider to be descriptive stereotypes, but often they fail to understand that they are adopting false or prescriptive stereotypes.[128] To remedy descriptive or statistical stereotypes, it is important that courts and human rights treaty bodies craft remedies that aim to correct misperceptions relating to the relevance of the description or the statistical "fact."[129]

An appropriate remedial course for false stereotypes involves correcting the factual misunderstanding underpinning the gender stereotype.[130] In order to address prescriptive stereotypes effectively, we must reshape prevailing social norms.[131] Reshaping does not necessarily mean that social norms should be eliminated. It might require, for instance, broadening and/or redefining norms to ensure that all individuals are valued.[132]

Remedies for gender stereotyping are more likely to be effective in dismantling false, descriptive or prescriptive stereotypes and in discrediting stereotypical thinking, when stereotype-disconfirming information is provided. Such information shows how stereotypes can be dysfunctionally inaccurate, inefficient, and unjust. "Considerable research indicates that the effects of gender stereotypes are *nullified* or 'swamped' when perceivers have access to unambiguous or highly diagnostic individuating information,"[133] meaning information that exposes the fallacy of a gender stereotype in an individual case.

REMEDYING GENDER STEREOTYPING OF THE INDIVIDUAL

Remedies for violations of human rights aim to place individuals or groups of individuals in the position they would have occupied had the violation of their rights not occurred. In the context of wrongful gender stereotyping, this means that remedies should aim to place a woman or a group of women where they should have been if not stereotyped through the application of laws, policies, or practices of their State Party. In order to effectively address such stereotyping, remedies must target the operative gender stereotype. An effective remedy for gender stereotyping is also one that addresses the specific ways in which the application, enforcement, or perpetuation of a gender stereotype affects a particular woman, including how it has harmed her. Crafting a remedy that specifically addresses the nature of the gender stereotype and its harm is essential for that remedy to be effective.

In the case of *Yilmaz-Dogan*,[134] for instance, the employment contract of Ms. Yilmaz, a Turkish national residing in the Netherlands, was terminated due to how her employer understood her absenteeism. The Race Committee found a violation of her equal right to work in a textile factory, because she was discriminated against on grounds of her ethnic Turkish status. The explanation for termination noted: "When a Netherlands girl marries and has a baby, she stops working. Our foreign women workers, on the other hand, take the child to neighbours or family and at the slightest setback disappear on sick leave under the terms of the Sickness Act. They repeat that endlessly. Since we all must do our utmost to avoid going under, we cannot afford such goings-on."[135]

In its views, the Race Committee found a violation of Yilmaz's right to work because she was discriminated against on grounds of her ethnic Turkish status. By way of remedial measures, the Race Committee urged the Dutch government to ascertain whether Yilmaz currently was gainfully employed and, if she was not, to "use its good offices to secure alternative employment for her and/or to provide her with such other relief as may be considered equitable."[136] The Race Committee essentially limited its remedy to recommending the reinstituting of suitable employment for Yilmaz. Had the Race Committee engaged in a careful analysis of gender stereotyping in its reasoning, it might have devised a more effective remedy, specifically a remedy that targeted the specific wrongs Yilmaz suffered as a result of being stereotyped by her employer.

The Race Committee might have identified that the operative gender stereotype was compounded by Yilmaz's status as an immigrant, working mother of Turkish origin. The Race Committee might have explained that she was stereotyped as an inferior mother because she had to combine her roles as both mother and contributing breadwinner in an impoverished immigrant household. The Race Committee might have clarified that Yilmaz was a member of a group previously excluded from working in the country, and as such was subject to hostile gender stereotyping. The Race Committee might have explained that she was degraded through the subordination of her dignity that lowered her personal or professional reputation in her community. Had the Race Committee suggested that the government

- issue a declaration specifically recognizing how the compounded gender stereotype wronged Yilmaz; and
- require the textile factory that stereotyped her to pay symbolic damages to at least acknowledge the wrong, even though such damages could not compensate for it,

then the Race Committee would have raised awareness about the degrading and discriminatory nature of the compounded gender stereotype.

Remedying the Structural Nature of Gender Stereotyping

Each society has to determine how women as a group are constructed differently than men as a group, and how gender stereotypes contribute to those gender differences in ways that wrong women.[137] Each society will need to assess how gender stereotypes are formed in different sectors, and how they work to create gender hierarchies and operate to marginalize women.[138] In other words, understanding and articulating how societies use gender stereotypes to stratify and subordinate women is key to devising an effective structural remedy.

Designing measures to remedy the structural nature of wrongful gender stereotyping is challenging because understanding of how societies use gender stereotypes to subordinate women is still evolving. At a minimum, States Parties are obligated to deinstitutionalize gender stereotypes from their laws, policies, and practices, and to adopt appropriate measures aimed at modifying the social and cultural patterns of conduct of men and women. For example, where a wrongful gender stereotype is entrenched into the structure of the law, as in the *Morales de Sierra* case,[139] it should be eradicated through legal reform, ideally followed by legal literacy programs that educate communities on the importance of the reform. When courts and human rights treaty bodies hold that a law based on a gender stereotype was a form of unlawful discrimination, or a form of degrading treatment, that holding benefits individuals that had been the subject of discriminatory or degrading treatment, and similarly situated individuals and groups, because it signals that such gender stereotyping should be prevented in the future. Reform by legislation or judicial findings of unconstitutionality or other illegality also have a structural dimension because it eradicates the wrongful gender stereotype from the law, and thus from future application.

One form of structural harm that may prove especially challenging to remedy is the imposition of subordinate identities through gender stereotyping. This is particularly true of stereotypes that degrade women in a way that affects the status of an entire group of women. These kinds of stereotypes affect "hearts and minds in a way unlikely to be ever undone."[140] Even though it might be difficult to design remedial measures to undo the psychological harm arising from the imposition of subordinate identities on a group of women, it is essential to expose and articulate the harm.

In the case of Yilmaz, the very articulation of how the application of the compounded stereotype degraded her status and dignity would have helped to advance understanding of and raise consciousness about the prejudice against other Turkish immigrant female workers. Had the Race Committee recommended that the State Party issue a formal apology for its failure to address the prejudices and hostile stereotyping that contributed to the wrong, it would have had a powerful effect on the self-esteem of immigrant women workers. Such apologies have been known to be combined with more enduring gestures, such as the naming of a memorial park, square, or street.[141]

Where a gender stereotype is socially pervasive and persistent, that fact suggests that conditions for social stratification and subordination of women exist. As a result, remedies to correct the structural nature of the stratification and subordination will be that much more difficult to devise. At a minimum, it will require sustained leadership and programs in all sectors of society to raise consciousness about the structural nature of stereotyping. Had the facts been presented in the *Yilmaz-Dogan* case to show that the compounded stereotype of Turkish women workers was socially pervasive and persistent, the Race Committee might have suggested that the government devise some structural remedies. The Race Committee might have suggested the establishment of an ombudsman system to enable the government to investigate and learn from the wrongs of the application of the compounded gender stereotype and devise means to prevent its perpetuation. The Race Committee might have also suggested that the government take temporary special measures to address the subordination of immigrant women workers as a group in the textile industry.

TEMPORARY SPECIAL MEASURES

Temporary special measures, sometimes called "affirmative action," might well be appropriate for States Parties to adopt, in order to accelerate the elimination of customs and practices and stereotypical attitudes and behaviors that disadvantage women. Article 4(1) of the Women's Convention explains that "temporary special measures aimed at accelerating de facto equality between men and women shall not be considered discrimination as defined in the present Convention." This article goes on to explain that such measures "shall in no way entail . . . the maintenance of unequal or separate standards; these measures shall be discontinued when the objectives of equality of opportunity and treatment have been achieved." Temporary special measures are "time-limited positive measures intended to enhance opportunities for historically and systemically disadvantaged groups, with a view to bringing group members into the mainstream of political, economic, social, cultural and civil life."[142]

Building on article 4(1) of the Convention, in its General Recommendation No. 25 the Women's Committee has explained that such measures are not an exception to the norm of nondiscrimination; in its view, they "are part of a necessary strategy by States parties directed towards the achievement of de facto or substantive equality of women with men in the enjoyment of their human rights and fundamental freedoms."[143] This means that, although temporary special measures may result in nonidentical treatment of men and women, such differential treatment may be justified to improve women's de facto position. This view that these measures shall not be considered a form of discrimination, while the position of women remains inferior to that of men, is also taken, for example, by the Human Rights Committee,[144] the Committee on Economic, Social and Cultural Rights,[145] and the Inter-American Commission on Human Rights.[146]

Temporary special measures might be appropriate in the period following a reform of a law that removes wrongful gender stereotypes, such as a law that grants women equal rights with men "in respect of the ownership, acquisition, management, administration, enjoyment and disposition of property."[147] Temporary special measures might include means to educate communities about the purpose of the law, their rights under the law, and in the event of a violation of women's newly established rights, a prompt, effective and public remedy. Such measures are needed until such time as there is widespread understanding and acceptance of the new law, in part in order to avoid a backlash through the use of hostile stereotyping that could undermine the acceleration of "de facto equality between men and women."[148] When such equality has been secured, the special measures should be ended, perhaps accompanied by the satisfaction in its achievement to which a truly just society is entitled.

Temporary special measures might be especially appropriate for eliminating the structural nature of wrongful gender stereotyping. Such measures might include preferential admission of women to educational, professional, and comparable institutions, to preferential funding of sporting and recreational facilities for girls and women, and to requiring gender parity in appointments to public office.

In the case of *Yilmaz-Dogan*, [149] the Race Committee might have explored the use of temporary special measures to change the compounded stereotype of foreign female workers in the textile industry as inferior until such time as those stereotypes are dismantled. The Race Committee might have also considered temporary special measures to encourage both immigrant and Dutch fathers to take parental leave and otherwise share the responsibility of child rearing. Such measures might have helped to transform the social value attached to childcare to include men's roles. This transformation would have ensured that the Netherlands was compliant with article 5(b) of the Women's Convention that recognizes that childrearing is the common responsibility of men and women.

What Are the Obligations of States Parties to Withdraw Their Reservations Regarding Gender Stereotyping?

A State Party is permitted to limit the scope of its legal obligations under the Women's Convention through a reservation, provided it is not "incompatible with the object and purpose" of the Convention.[150] A reservation is "a unilateral statement, however phrased or named, made by a State, when signing, ratifying, accepting, approving, or acceding to a treaty, whereby it purports to exclude or to modify the legal effect of certain provisions of the treaty in their application to that State."[151] Reservations that are considered to exceed the object and purpose of the Women's Convention are impermissible.[152] The object and purpose is to eliminate all forms of discrimination against women with a view to achieving substantive equality.[153]

In its General Recommendation No. 25, the Women's Committee stated explicitly that combating wrongful gender stereotyping is central to States Parties' efforts to eliminate all forms of discrimination against women.[154] CEDAW Committee member Indira Jaising has echoed this statement by observing that "While the CEDAW Convention is an international treaty wholly devoted to the human rights of women in every sphere, its essence lies in articles 2(f) and 5 because they capture the concern expressed in the Preamble that only change in traditional roles of men and women can bring about genuine equality between the sexes."[155] Reservations that purport to protect the practice of wrongful gender stereotyping thus appear prima facie incompatible with the object and purpose of the Women's Convention, and, for this reason, should be treated extremely seriously.[156]

Several States Parties have nevertheless sought to limit their normative obligations to eliminate wrongful forms of gender stereotyping. One group of States Parties has sought to limit their obligations by entering reservations to articles 5(a) and/or 2(f) of the Women's Convention.[157] The governments of the Cook Islands and the Federated States of Micronesia on behalf of their states have reserved, for example, the right not to apply these articles to the inheritance of, or succession to, certain customary and traditional titles and offices. The United Kingdom has a similar reservation concerning succession to the monarchy. The Federated States of Micronesia has also reserved the right not to apply these articles "to marital customs that divide tasks or decision-making in purely voluntary or consensual private conduct." The Government of India has conditioned its compliance with article 5(a) on its policy of noninterference in personal affairs,[158] while Malaysia has indicated that Islamic Sharia (law) and its federal constitution preclude its compliance with this article. As well, with regard to family relations, Niger has said that it cannot comply with article 5 immediately, as it is "contrary to existing customs and practices which, by their own nature, can be modified only with the passage of time and the evolution of society."

A second group of States Parties has sought to limit its normative obligations to eliminate wrongful gender stereotyping, through entry of reservations to other provisions of the Women's Convention, underscoring the connections between articles 2(f) and 5(a) and those provisions. For example, although the government of Israel has not reserved its obligations under article 5(a) of the Convention, it has entered a reservation to article 7(b) with respect to the appointment of female judges to religious courts. The reservation reads: "The State of Israel hereby expresses its reservation with regard to article 7(b) of the Convention concerning the appointment of women to serve as judges of religious courts where this is prohibited by the laws of any of the religious communities in Israel. Otherwise, the said article is fully implemented in Israel, in view of the fact that women take a prominent part in all aspects of public life." This reservation relies on the sex role stereotype of only men as religious decision-makers. The stereotype discriminates against women because it prevents them from serving as religious judges, and reinforces their inferior status by implying that they are not worthy of assuming such roles within their particular religious communities in Israeli society.[159]

Some States Parties have developed a practice of formulating objections to other Parties' reservations that they consider incompatible with the object and purpose of the Women's Convention. For example, the Government of France objected to the reservations made by Niger to articles 2(f) and 5, as well as to articles 2(d) (state obligations), 15(4) (the right to choose residence and domicile), 16(1)(c) (rights and responsibilities during marriage and at its dissolution), 16(1)(e) (the right to decide freely on the number and spacing of children), and 16(1)(g) (personal rights as husband and wife). These reservations, France explained, seek "to ensure that domestic law, and even domestic practice and the current values of society, prevail in general over the provisions of the Convention. The provisions in question concern not only family relations but also social relations as a whole." For this reason, France asserted that Niger's reservations are "manifestly contrary to the object and purpose of the Convention" and "completely vitiate the undertaking of the Republic of the Niger and are manifestly not authorized by the Convention."[160] In addition to registering a State Party's belief in the incompatibility of another's reservation to the specific right under the Convention, objections reinforce the normative value of the right in question,[161] and, in some cases, occasion the reserving State Party's withdrawal or modification of its reservation.

The Women's Committee has routinely noted its concern with respect to the number, scope and validity of reservations to the Women's Convention,[162] including those purporting to limit States Parties' obligations to eliminate wrongful gender stereotyping. For example, the Women's Committee in its General Recommendation No. 21 noted its concern that many of the States Parties that have lodged reservations to article 16 on family and marriage relations, justified their decisions on the basis of wrongful sex role stereotypes. The Committee elaborated that "Many of these countries hold a belief in the patriarchal structure of a family which places a father, husband or son in a favourable position. In some countries where fundamentalist or other extremist views or economic hardships have encouraged a return to old values and traditions, women's place in the family has deteriorated sharply."[163]

The Women's Committee has developed a practice of regularly questioning States Parties about their reservations during the periodic reporting process.[164] For instance, in its Concluding Observations on Israel's periodic reports, the Women's Committee has noted its concern regarding the maintenance of Israel's reservations to articles 7(b) and 16 of the Women's Convention. In particular, it has expressed regret that women are unable to become religious judges, and that the religious laws governing family relations discriminate against women in a significant way.[165] As well, the Committee expressed its particular concern "at the State party's statement that such reservations are 'unavoidable at this point in time' and its position that laws based on religious values cannot be reformed."[166] Taking into account its concerns, the Committee has urged the government of Israel to withdraw its reservations, which the Committee has deemed incompatible with the object and purpose of the Convention.[167] The effect of the Committee's questions has been to require States Parties like Israel, to reassess the need for and validity of their reservations, including those reservations that entrench discriminatory gender stereotypes.

The Women's Committee has also asked reserving States Parties to include information in their periodic reports on: reservations and declarations to the Convention, explaining the specific article to which they refer, why their maintenance is considered necessary, and their precise effect in terms of national law and policy; their plans to limit the effect of reservations and declarations; and reservations and declarations entered to similar obligations in other international human rights instruments.[168] The Human Rights Committee has also explained that reservations must be specific and transparent, "so that the Committee, those under the jurisdiction of the reserving State and other States parties may be clear as to what obligations of human rights compliance have or have not been undertaken."[169]

Entry into force of the Optional Protocol has provided the Women's Committee with further opportunities to determine whether it will apply the entire Convention to a State Party, despite its reservations. The Committee has explained that "the determination of the permissibility of a reservation falls within its functions in the examination of an individual communication."[170] In *Constance Ragan Salgado v. United*

Kingdom of Great Britain and Northern Ireland,[171] the complainant alleged, *inter alia*, a violation of article 9(2) of the Convention, which provides for equality regarding the nationality of children. The United Kingdom argued that the complaint should be declared inadmissible because of the United Kingdom's reservation to article 9(2). The Committee chose not to address that claim, since it held the complaint inadmissible on other grounds. Had the Committee found the complaint admissible,[172] it would have had to address the severability of the reservation. The European Court of Human Rights[173] and the Human Rights Committee[174] tend to treat incompatible reservations as nullities, and hold the reserving States Parties bound by the entire treaty, including the provision the State Party attempted to reserve. This is consistent with general international practice that states not intending to be bound by treaties do not ratify them.

Chapter 4

Gender Stereotyping as a Form of Discrimination

The Convention on the Elimination of All Forms of Discrimination against Women ("Women's Convention" or "Convention"; see Appendix A) obligates States Parties to eliminate all forms of discrimination against women. It will be recalled that article 1 of that instrument defines "discrimination against women" as "any distinction, exclusion or restriction made on the basis of sex which has the effect or purpose of impairing or nullifying the recognition, enjoyment or exercise by women, irrespective of their marital status, on a basis of equality of men and women, of human rights and fundamental freedoms in the political, economic, social, cultural, civil or any other field."[1] As explained in Chapter 3, article 2(f) of the Convention obligates States Parties "to take all appropriate measures, including legislation, to modify or abolish existing laws, regulations, customs and practices which constitute discrimination against women." Thus, where "laws, regulations, customs and practices" are based on discriminatory forms of gender stereotypes, States Parties are obligated to "modify or abolish" them.

It is significant that the obligation to eliminate all forms of discrimination against women has been interpreted to include those forms of discrimination that are rooted in gender stereotypes. The Women's Committee has explained in its General Recommendation No. 25 that the obligation to eliminate wrongful forms of gender stereotyping is one of three general obligations central to States Parties' efforts to eliminate all forms of discrimination against women, the other two being to eliminate direct and indirect discrimination and to improve the de facto position of women in society.[2] The Committee has further explained that discrimination against women on the basis of sex includes those differences of treatment that exist "because of stereotypical expectations, attitudes and behaviour directed towards women which are based on the biological differences between women and men," and that exist "because of the generally existing subordination of women by men."[3] In adopting the Women's Convention's definition of discrimination against women in its General Comment No. 16 on equality, the Committee on Economic, Social and Cultural Rights has affirmed that "Discrimination on the basis of sex may be based on the differential treatment of women because of their biology, such as refusal to hire women because they could become pregnant; *or stereotypical assumptions*, such as tracking women into low-level jobs on the assumption that they are unwilling to commit as much time to their work as men."[4]

Consistent with the article 1 definition of discrimination against women, discrimination may occur when a distinction, exclusion, or restriction is made on the basis of a gender stereotype that has the purpose of impairing or nullifying the recognition, enjoyment, or exercise by women, irrespective of their marital status, on a basis of equality of men and women, of their human rights and fundamental freedoms.[5] Discrimination against women may also occur when a law, policy, or practice is facially neutral, but has the effect of impairing or nullifying the recognition, enjoyment, or exercise by women, irrespective of their marital status, on a basis of equality of men and women, of their human rights and fundamental freedoms because it perpetuates a gender stereotype.[6] Yet not all differences of treatment based on a gender stereotype will constitute a form of discrimination prohibited in the Women's Convention.[7] This is because not every form of discrimination in practice will be characterized in law as a form of discrimination. Gender stereotyping might, for example, be justified in circumstances where the State Party pursued a legitimate purpose and the means it chose to attain that purpose were both reasonable and proportionate. Gender stereotyping might also be justified where the harm is not sufficiently significant to warrant legal protection.

When differences in treatment are based on prejudices and stereotypical practices that do not constitute discrimination, they might offend article 5(a) of the Women's Convention. That is, where States Parties have not taken appropriate measures to "modify the social and cultural patterns of conduct of men and women, with a view to achieving the elimination of prejudices and customary and all other practices which are based on the idea of the inferiority or the superiority of either of the sexes or on stereotyped roles for men and women,"[8] they might be held responsible under article 5(a) of the Women's Convention. When gender stereotyping does not constitute a form of discrimination, it might constitute a form of degrading treatment or violate women's other human rights and fundamental freedoms,[9] which States Parties are obligated under the Convention to eliminate.

Efforts to eliminate discriminatory forms of gender stereotyping, pursuant to article 2(f), are contingent on the ability to identify when the application, enforcement, or perpetuation of a gender stereotype in a law, policy, or practice constitutes a form of discrimination against women. This first requires the identification of operative gender stereotypes and their forms, the uncovering of their harms and injustices, and an explanation of States Parties' obligations to eliminate wrongful gender stereotyping. Having done this, it is then possible to determine whether the application, enforcement, or perpetuation of operative gender stereotypes in laws, policies, or practices constitutes a form of discrimination against women.

This chapter explores how States Parties might be held responsible for discriminatory forms of gender stereotyping. Building on the definition of discrimination against women in article 1 of the Women's Convention, one approach to the question of whether a law, policy, or practice has discriminated against a woman on the basis of a gender stereotype is to ask:

- Did a law, policy, or practice make a difference in treatment on the basis of a gender stereotype?
- Did a law, policy, or practice impair or nullify any of a woman's human rights or fundamental freedoms?
- Was the application, enforcement, or perpetuation of a gender stereotype in a law, policy, or practice justified?

As with the naming process, there may be different ways that one might determine whether the application, enforcement, or perpetuation of a gender stereotype discriminated against a woman. For this reason, and also taking into account jurisdictional differences in understanding of equality and nondiscrimination, the approach presented here is intended to illustrate the types of considerations that might be helpful in carrying out a discrimination analysis of gender stereotyping. States Parties, as well as regional and international human rights treaty bodies, might find this approach helpful in assessing a claim of discrimination based on gender stereotyping.

To demonstrate how these questions might assist in determining whether there is discrimination against women on the basis of a gender stereotype, this chapter will further draw on the cases of *Morales de Sierra*[10] and *Hugo*.[11] It will be recalled that the first of these cases concerned a challenge to several provisions of Guatemala's Civil Code, which enforced sex role stereotypes in defining spousal roles and responsibilities in marriage. The *Hugo* case concerned a constitutional challenge to a pardon issued by President Nelson Mandela, remitting the sentences of certain categories of prisoners, including mothers who had children younger than twelve and had been convicted of nonviolent crimes, but excluding similarly situated fathers.

This chapter will also consider *Nevada Department of Human Resources v. Hibbs*[12] ("the *Hibbs* case"). The *Hibbs* case concerned sex role stereotyping in the provision of family-care leave to employees. Mr. Hibbs, a Nevada Department of Human Resources employee, was granted leave under the Family and Medical Leave Act of 1993 to care for his wife, who had been seriously injured in a car accident. However, the department later informed him that his leave had been exhausted and that he must report to work. When Hibbs failed to report by the specified date, the department terminated his employment. Hibbs subsequently sued the Nevada Department of Human Resources, seeking damages and injunctive and declaratory relief for alleged violations of the Act.

On appeal, Chief Justice Rehnquist, writing for the U.S. Supreme Court, upheld the validity of the Family and Medical Leave Act, and found that state employees are able to recover monetary damages in federal court in relation to a state's noncompliance with that Act's family-care provisions.[13] In reaching this decision, Chief Justice Rehnquist explained that the Act had been enacted to remedy persistent sex and gender discrimination in the workplace, including gender stereotyping.[14] Moreover, he linked states' infrequent provision of family-care leave to fathers to the sex role stereotype of women as primarily caregivers and the sex role stereotype of men as primary breadwinners, which presumes a corresponding lack of domestic responsibilities for men, and that reinforces the unequal distribution of labor in marriage and family relations.[15]

Does a Law, Policy, or Practice Make a Difference in Treatment on the Basis of a Gender Stereotype?

In order to establish a claim of discrimination against women under article 2(f) of the Convention, it must first be shown that a law, policy, or practice makes a distinction, exclusion, or restriction on the basis of a gender stereotype. To satisfy this limb of the discrimination test, it must be shown that

- a law, policy, or practice makes a difference in treatment of men and women (i.e., a distinction, exclusion, or restriction); and
- the difference in treatment is based on a gender stereotype.

DISTINCTION, EXCLUSION, OR RESTRICTION

Based on the definition of discrimination in article 1 of the Women's Convention, a difference in treatment may take the form of any distinction between men and women, any exclusion of women, or any restriction of women's human rights and fundamental freedoms.

A law, policy, or practice that fails to treat similar interests of men and women in the same way, or that fails to treat a significantly different interest between them in a way that adequately respects that difference, creates a *distinction between men and women* in violation of article 1 of the Women's Convention. For instance, health services should treat men and women equally by reference to incidence levels of diseases in populations. For health expenditures to be equal, they have to be proportionate to the incidence. The Women's Committee has explained: "States parties should allocate adequate budgetary, human and administrative resources to ensure that women's health receives a share of the overall health budget comparable with that for men's health, taking into account their different health needs."[16] The Women's Convention accordingly obligates States Parties not only to ensure formal (*de jure*) equality, meaning equal treatment of equal cases, but also substantive (*de facto*) equality, meaning treatment that pays equal regard to the differences.[17]

Laws, policies, and practices that have been found to create impermissible distinctions between men and women include

- an employment policy that prohibits the hiring[18] or promotion[19] of married women, but that imposes no similar prohibition on married men;
- a law, policy, or practice that permits or condones the neglect of healthcare that only women need, for example, during pregnancy and childbirth;[20]
- a regulation that establishes different conditions for the reimbursement of moving expenses for married male and female teachers;[21] and
- a law that provides that fathers, but not mothers, shall have the right of final decision in the exercise of parental rights and duties.[22]

These laws, policies, and practices were found to create impermissible distinctions between men and women either because they failed to treat the similar interests of men and women in the same way, or because they failed to treat their significantly different interests in ways that adequately respected those differences.

In the *Hugo* case, all members of the Constitutional Court of South Africa agreed that, in remitting the sentences of certain categories of prisoners, President Mandela created a distinction between mothers and fathers. President Mandela elected to remit the sentences of nonviolent mothers with children under the age of twelve, but he did not remit the sentences of similarly situated fathers. Owing to the distinction that President Mandela made between mothers and fathers, Hugo was denied the opportunity to be released from prison in order to resume his childcare responsibilities. Had he been a mother, his sentence would have been remitted. (See discussion in Chapter 3.)

In the *Hibbs* case, Chief Justice Rehnquist explained that many states had created impermissible distinctions between the provision of family-care leave to male and female employees. In particular, he explained that "Many States offered women extended 'maternity' leave that far exceeded the typical 4- to 8-week period of physical disability due to pregnancy and childbirth, but very few States granted men a parallel benefit: Fifteen States provided women up to one year of extended maternity leave, while only four provided men with the same. . . ."[23]

A law, policy, or practice that purports to *exclude* women, while including men, offends the definition of discrimination against women in article 1 of the Women's Convention. If States Parties are "to ensure the full development and advancement of women,"[24] women must be included in all fields on a basis of equality with men. A law, policy, or practice that seeks to exclude women—for example, by denying them benefits, opportunities, or entitlements provided to men—does not enable their full development and advancement; rather, it violates their rights to equality and nondiscrimination.

Laws, policies, and practices that impermissibly exclude women include

- a law that prohibits women from entering certain occupations or professions;[25]
- a law that prohibits women from performing jury duty;[26] and
- a law, policy, or practice that excludes women from military service,[27] prohibits them from performing certain duties within military service (e.g., engaging in direct combat),[28] or denies them access to educational institutions that provide training to join the military.[29]

Each of these laws, policies, and practices purports to exclude women; that is to say, they each seek to prevent women from entering and participating in certain political, social, economic, and/or cultural fields. Moreover, they exclude women from even being considered for positions within these fields.

In the *Morales de Sierra* case, the legislature sought to exclude married women, including Morales de Sierra, from family responsibility by enacting a Civil Code that denied them legal capacity in matters related to the representation of the marital union, the administration of marital property, and the representation of children of the union. In finding this denial discriminatory, the Inter-American Commission on Human Rights explained that the exclusion of a married woman from the representation of the marital union deprived her of the legal capacity necessary to invoke judicial protection.[30] It further explained that "the fact that the law vests exclusive authority in her husband to represent the marital union and their minor child creates a disequilibrium in the weight of the authority exercised by each spouse within their marriage—an imbalance which may be perceived within the family, community and society. While the victim, as a parent, has the right and duty to protect the best interests of her minor child, the law strips her of the legal capacity she requires to do that."[31]

In order to guarantee substantive equality, it is not sufficient merely to enact or initiate laws, policies, and practices that establish women's human rights and fundamental freedoms. The Women's Convention requires States Parties to ensure, through the adoption of laws and other measures, the practical realization of substantive equality.[32] Laws, policies, and practices that impose *restrictions* on the human rights and fundamental freedoms of women, but not men, impede the realization of substantive equality and, in so doing, violate the Convention's guarantee of nondiscrimination.

Laws, policies, and practices can restrict women's human rights and fundamental freedoms when, for example, they limit or impose conditions on the exercise or enjoyment of those rights or freedoms. They can also restrict women's human rights and fundamental freedoms when they burden women in ways that prevent them from fully exercising and enjoying their legally guaranteed rights and freedoms, such as in cases involving forced motherhood. Laws, policies, and practices that have been found to impose unlawful restrictions on women include

- a law that provides that a mother can function as a guardian of a minor child only after the death of the father;[33]
- a law, policy, or practice that restricts women's access to health care services;[34]
- a law that restricts a female immigrant's husband from joining her while a male immigrant's wife can automatically join him;[35] and
- a practice of failing to act with due diligence in matters involving gender-based violence against women.[36]

In the *Morales de Sierra* case, Guatemala's Civil Code made Morales de Sierra's right to work conditional on her role as mother and homemaker, as well as on the consent of her husband.[37] In the view of the Inter-American Commission on Human Rights, this restriction denied her the right to equality in employment.[38] The restriction on Morales de Sierra's rights derived from the unjustifiable infringement on her personal sphere; it was not dependent on her husband's opposition to her work outside of the marital home. The Inter-American Commission explained that "The mere fact that the husband of María Eugenia Morales de Sierra may oppose that she works, while she does not have the right to oppose this in his case, implies a discrimination. . . . As a married woman, the law does not accord her the same rights or recognition as other citizens, and she cannot exercise the same freedoms they do in pursuing their aspirations."[39]

One approach to determining whether there is a difference in treatment of men and women might be to ask: Does a law, policy, or practice create distinctions between men and women by failing to treat their similar interests in the same way, or by failing to treat significantly different interests in ways that adequately respect those differences?[40] Does it purport to exclude women by failing to recognize certain human rights or fundamental freedoms, or by preventing women from exercising or enjoying those rights and freedoms? Does it restrict women's human rights and fundamental freedoms by imposing limits or conditions on their exercise or enjoyment, or by burdening women? Ultimately, the question of whether a law, policy, or practice makes a difference in treatment of men and women will need to be determined with due regard to the facts and context of a particular case.

On the Basis of a Gender Stereotype

In circumstances where it can be shown that a distinction, exclusion, or restriction relied on, or is connected to, a gender stereotype, it becomes possible to make a legal finding of discrimination resulting from that particular form of stereotyping. Identifying and articulating this connection is central to showing that an application, enforcement, or perpetuation of a gender stereotype in a law, policy, or practice is a form of discrimination against women. In the absence of an established connection, there is no legal basis upon which to make such a finding. It must be shown that the difference in treatment was based on a gender stereotype,[41] either because it applied, enforced, or perpetuated that stereotype.

Individual men and women may embrace gender stereotypes, and they may take steps to structure their lives, attitudes, and relationships accordingly. However, the rights to nondiscrimination and equality prohibit states from adopting laws, policies, or practices that make distinctions, exclusions, or restrictions based on gender stereotypes.[42] Although tolerated in the past,[43] a law, policy, or practice that applies, enforces, or perpetuates gender stereotypes is today understood to violate these rights.[44] While a State Party, through its executive, legislative, and/or judicial branch of government, might have a preference for how men and women should behave or which roles they should perform in society, the rights to nondiscrimination and equality prevent it from imposing those preferences on individual men and women through its laws, policies, or practices.[45] These rights require that states' laws, policies, and practices respect and honor the choices that men and women make about their own lives, including what it means for them to be a man or a woman; laws, policies, and practices should not confine men and women to a rigid understanding of masculinity or femininity or deny them their diversity.[46]

Determining whether a difference in treatment was based on a gender stereotype requires an explicit connection to be drawn between a distinction, exclusion, or restriction made in a law, policy, or practice and the operative gender stereotype that was earlier identified in the naming process. While this may result in overlap with the naming process (see Chapter 2), it is important to rearticulate this link as part of the discrimination analysis. One might seek to establish and underscore the connection between the differential treatment and the operative gender stereotype by again asking: does a law, policy, or practice apply, enforce, or perpetuate a gender stereotype? It will be recalled that in some circumstances, it may be obvious that a law, policy, or practice applies, enforces, or perpetuates a gender stereotype, but it is still important to publicly articulate that connection. In other circumstances, it might be helpful to look for symptoms or indicators of the cognitive processes that give rise to stereotyping. It might also be helpful to ask the "woman question." In this connection, it might be asked: what are the assumptions that a law, policy, or practice makes about men and/or women?

In the *Morales de Sierra* case, the Inter-American Commission on Human Rights was explicit that the impugned provisions of Guatemala's Civil Code created distinctions between married men and women based on "stereotyped notions of the roles of women and men."[47] Married men, but not married women, were granted authority to represent the marital union, to administer marital property, and to represent the children of the union and administer their property, because they were stereotyped as breadwinners with the responsibility to protect and provide for their families. Responsibility for the care of minor children within the marital home was bestowed upon married women, not married men, because they were stereotyped as mothers, homemakers, and caregivers. Moreover, Guatemala's Court of Constitutionality had entrenched these sex role stereotypes when it upheld the impugned provisions as constitutional.

In the *Hibbs* case, Chief Justice Rehnquist was explicit that the distinctions made by states in the provision of family-care leave to male and female employees were based on sex role stereotypes of women as caregivers and of men as breadwinners. He explained that "This and other differential leave policies were not attributable to any differential physical needs of men and women, but rather to the pervasive sex role stereotype that caring for family members is women's work."[48] He further explained that the sex role stereotype of women as caregivers was reinforced by the parallel sex role stereotype of men as breadwinners, which presumed a corresponding lack of domestic responsibilities for men. "These mutually reinforcing stereotypes," he said, "created a self-fulfilling cycle of discrimination that forced women to continue to assume the role of primary caregiver, and fostered employers' stereotypical views about women's commitment to work and their value as employees."[49]

In the *Hugo* case, the Constitutional Court of South Africa concluded that the differential treatment of mothers and fathers in the remission of sentence arose out of President Mandela's application of sex role stereotypes of women as homemakers and primary caregivers, and of men as breadwinners. It explained, for example, that "The reason given by the President for the special remission of sentence of mothers with small children is that it will serve the interests of children. To support this, he relies upon the evidence of Ms. Starke that mothers are, generally speaking, primarily responsible for the care of small children in our society. . . . This statement, of course, is a generalisation."[50] President Mandela remitted the sentences of imprisoned mothers with children under age twelve because of the stereotypical belief that mothers, and not fathers, bear or should bear primary responsibility for childcare. He did not remit the sentences of imprisoned fathers with children of a similar age, even where they were primary caregivers. Hugo was thus treated differently because of a stereotype that women, and not men, are caregivers.[51]

In order to determine whether the difference of treatment of men and women on the basis of a gender stereotype constitutes a form of discrimination against an individual woman, it is necessary only to consider the impact of the gender stereotype on her.[52] How she was treated matters more than whether she was treated differently than a man. For example, it has been explained that "stereotyping of women as caregivers can by itself and without more be evidence of an impermissible, sex based motive."[53] While evidence of a male comparator might strengthen a claim of sex or gender discrimination, it is not essential that such evidence be adduced.[54]

That a male comparator is not essential for a finding of discriminatory treatment based on a gender stereotype is significant for the achievement of substantive equality. The principle of substantive equality requires that women be liberated to be all that they can be; not just in relation to men. In sum, it requires States Parties to "ensure the full development and advancement of women."[55] Understanding how gender stereotypes devalue female-associated attributes, characteristics, or roles, and exploring how law can be most effectively framed to give those attributes, characteristics, or roles meaning are just some of the challenges of eliminating all forms of discrimination against women, and of realizing the goal of substantive equality.

Did a Law, Policy, or Practice Impair or Nullify Any of a Woman's Human Rights or Fundamental Freedoms?

In order to establish that gender stereotyping rises to the level of discrimination that States Parties are obligated to eliminate under article 2(f), it must also be shown that the differential treatment resulting from the application, enforcement, or perpetuation of a gender stereotype had the purpose or effect of impairing or nullifying the recognition, enjoyment, or exercise by women, irrespective of their marital status, on a basis of equality of men and women, of human rights and fundamental freedoms.[56]

PURPOSE OR EFFECT

Direct discrimination may occur when a law, policy, or practice has the purpose or intent of creating distinctions between men and women, excluding women from entitlements or opportunities, or restricting their human rights and fundamental freedoms.[57] In the context of gender stereotyping, direct discrimination may occur when a law, policy, or practice has the purpose or intent of impairing or nullifying women's human rights and fundamental freedoms on the basis of a gender stereotype.

In the *Morales de Sierra* case, the purpose of Guatemala's Civil Code was that married women be mothers, homemakers, and caregivers, unlike their husbands. Its purpose was also that married men, and not married women, be primary breadwinners, decision-makers, and heads of households. The impugned provisions were designed in such a way that men and women were obligated to conform with traditional sex roles; legally, men and women could not diverge from these roles, except in exceptional circumstances.

In the *Hugo* case, it was intended that mothers, not fathers, should be primary caregivers. While the overarching purpose of President Mandela's pardon was to ensure the adequate care of children, only nonviolent mothers with children under the age of twelve had their sentences remitted. The sentences of nonviolent fathers who were primary caregivers were not remitted unless they applied for remission on an individual basis. As Justice Kriegler pointed out in his dissenting opinion, the purpose of the pardon was prescriptive in nature; in remitting the sentences of mothers, and not fathers, President Mandela was not only saying that women *are* primary caregivers in South African society; he was also saying that women, and not men, *should be* primary caregivers. Sex roles were imposed on "men and women, not by virtue of their individual characteristics, qualities or choices, but on the basis of predetermined, albeit time-honoured, gender scripts."[58]

As well, in the *Hibbs* case, states' more generous provision of family-care leave to women was intended to enforce traditional sex roles within the family. Although women require a period of leave to recover from the physical act of giving birth, the granting of additional family-care leave only to mothers was intended to confine women to caregiving roles. The infrequent provision of such leave to fathers, on the other hand, was meant to confine men to breadwinning roles and to prevent them from assuming caregiving roles.[59] Thus, like in the *Morales de Sierra* and *Hugo* cases, the states were seeking to impose a preference for which roles men and women should perform in society, in violation of the principles of equality and nondiscrimination.

Indirect discrimination may occur when a law, policy, or practice is sex or gender-neutral on its face, but it has a detrimental effect on women when implemented.[60] In the context of gender stereotyping, indirect discrimination may occur when a law, policy, or practice does not explicitly contain gender stereotypes, but it has the effect of perpetuating gender stereotypes when implemented in practice.[61] For example, laws that permit health care professionals to refuse to provide medical care on grounds of conscience may be sex neutral. However, when health care professionals rely on conscientious objection laws to deny women, and not men, essential medical treatment, or when they more frequently invoke grounds of conscience with respect to the treatment of women, because of sex role stereotypes of women as mothers, such stereotypical practices have a detrimental effect on women.[62]

The effect of a law, policy, or practice may be ascertained through an examination of its impact on women. Examining the context within which a law, policy, or practice operates is central to identifying if it has the effect of perpetuating gender stereotypes when implemented in practice. In this connection, it might be helpful to ask: how does a law, policy, or practice affect women's needs, interests, and experiences in their day-to-day lives? For example, does a sex or gender-neutral law, policy, or practice unintentionally perpetuate the consequences of past discrimination? Is a sex- or gender-neutral law, policy, or practice "inadvertently modelled on male lifestyles and thus fail[s] to take into account aspects of women's life experiences which may differ from those of men?"[63]

As none of the cases examined so far in this chapter deal with indirect discrimination on the basis of a gender stereotype, it is helpful to consider *Jordan v. S.*[64] ("the *Jordan* case"), concerning a constitutional challenge to a provision of the Sexual Offences Act of 1957 that criminalizes the conduct of sex workers[65] but not their clients. The majority judgment, written by Justice Ngcobo of the Constitutional Court of South Africa, found that as the provision penalized "any person" engaging in sex for reward, it applied equally to female and male sex workers and, therefore, did not amount to direct discrimination under the South African (Interim) Constitution of 1993.[66] Nor, according to Justice Ngcobo, did the provision amount to indirect discrimination on grounds of sex or gender. Justice Ngcobo explained that the distinction between sex workers and their clients reflected the legislature's intention in this provision to outlaw the offer for sale, but not the purchase, of commercial sexual services. Justice Ngcobo saw a "qualitative difference" between sex workers, who repeatedly engage in sex for reward, and clients who only occasionally seek the services of a sex worker,[67] even though they, too, are liable to punishment under the Riotous Assemblies Act of 1856.[68] Justice Ngcobo acknowledged that sex workers are negatively stereotyped (i.e., "sex workers are more blameworthy than their clients"), but considered that this was a result of social attitudes rather than the law itself.[69] Justice Ngcobo was therefore unwilling to find indirect discrimination on the basis that it is women, and not men, who constitute the overwhelming majority of sex workers.[70] In other words, Justice Ngcobo did not acknowledge that sex work is sex identified in practice.

Writing for the minority, however, Justices O'Regan and Sachs concluded that by constructing sex workers as primary offenders, the legislature had reinforced a pattern of sexual stereotyping in violation of the principle of equality.[71] Engaging in a contextual analysis of the sex work industry, Justices O'Regan and Sachs reasoned that in criminalizing only the conduct of sex workers, most of whom are women, the Sexual Offences Act indirectly and unfairly discriminated against women on the basis of sexual stereotypes. Male patrons, they explained, are regarded as "having given in to temptation, or as having done the sort of thing that men do," whereas female sex workers are deemed to be "beyond the pale."[72] While they conceded that sex workers' clients were elsewhere liable to punishment, they asserted that the primary crime and stigma attached to engaging in sex for reward, rather than its purchase.[73] They therefore disagreed with Justice Ngcobo's assessment that the law played no role in stigmatization of sex workers. For Justices O'Regan and Sachs, the criminalization of the conduct of sex workers indirectly reinforced and perpetuated degrading stereotypes of female sex workers in violation of the equality provision of the constitution[74]: "The inference is that the primary cause of the problem is not the man who creates the demand but the woman who responds to it: she is fallen, he is at best virile, at worst weak."[75]

Underlying Justice Ngcobo's "qualitative" distinction between the sex worker and the customer was the stereotypical view that women, and not men, should be chaste. As a result, women's promiscuity is morally blameworthy, while male promiscuity is seen as an indication of male virility.[76] Justice Ngcobo entrenched stereotypes of improper female sexuality, further stigmatizing female sex workers. While the Sexual Offences Act was sex neutral in principle, Justice Ngcobo missed an opportunity to explain how the law should address work that is identified in practice with women. Justice Ngcobo's differentiated view of female and male promiscuity exacerbated the harmful effects of the sexual stereotypes underlying the Act, and left unexamined their discriminatory impact.

For the reason that gender stereotypes are often "deeply embedded in our unconscious, even while they inform our conscious reasoning processes,"[77] a law, policy, or practice may not intend to discriminate against women on the basis of a gender stereotype.[78] Yet, as cases like *Jordan* demonstrate, the unintentional perpetuation of gender stereotypes may nevertheless result in discrimination against women. Where a law, policy, or practice is sex or gender-neutral, vigilance must therefore be applied in order to identify the gender stereotypes that might be at work in practice; the unconscious or unintended perpetuation of gender stereotypes must not be allowed to discriminate against women.[79]

IMPAIRMENT OR NULLIFICATION OF WOMEN'S HUMAN RIGHTS AND FUNDAMENTAL FREEDOMS

The Women's Committee has identified the elimination of gender stereotyping as one of three obligations that are central to the realization of substantive equality.[80] As a result, it is important that an expansive approach is adopted in determining whether a gender stereotype has impaired or nullified a woman's human rights or fundamental freedoms. Of particular importance is the need to "take into account the intent and spirit of the Convention";[81] that is to say, to take account of the need

118   Chapter Four

to eliminate all forms of discrimination against women and ensure the realization of women's de jure and de facto equality.[82] According to this approach, domestic courts and human rights treaty bodies have a special role to play in ensuring the elimination of gender stereotypes that impede the realization of substantive equality. They must "be broad in [their] interpretation and recognition of the violations of women's right to equality, going beyond the obvious consequences of discriminatory acts and recognizing the dangers of ideology and norms that underpin such acts."[83]

Pursuant to the definition of discrimination in article 1, the differential treatment of men and women that is based on a gender stereotype will constitute a form of discrimination when it has the purpose or effect of *impairing or nullifying* the recognition, enjoyment, or exercise by women of human rights and fundamental freedoms. Where a law, policy, or practice makes a difference in treatment on the basis of a gender stereotype that has the purpose or effect of impairing or nullifying women's equal human rights and fundamental freedoms, it is a form of discrimination that article 2(f) of the Convention obligates States Parties to eliminate. The obligation to abolish discriminatory laws, customs, and practices under article 2(f) might be read in combination with the obligation to eliminate discrimination in education under article 10(c) and, for example, civil matters under article 15.

An analysis of gender stereotyping jurisprudence reveals that, in general, courts and human rights treaty bodies have been willing to find an impairment or nullification of women's human rights and fundamental freedoms, on a basis of equality of men and women, where women are disadvantaged because of the application, enforcement, or perpetuation of a gender stereotype in a law, policy, or practice. For example, segregating students into single-sex schools with curricula differences that reflected sex role stereotypes of men as breadwinners and women as homemakers, and that limited girls' future choices, was found to discriminate.[84] Analysis also suggests that courts and human rights treaty bodies are willing to find an impairment or nullification of human rights and fundamental freedoms where women are treated as men's inferiors or subordinates on account of a gender stereotype. For example, the treatment of women as men's property has been found to offend the rights to equality and nondiscrimination.[85] In contrast, the jurisprudence suggests that adjudicative bodies have been more reluctant to find discrimination based on a gender stereotype in cases pertaining to dress and appearance standards, such as where women, and not men, have been required by an employment policy to wear makeup at their place of work.[86]

How the Women's Convention will be applied to address stereotyping harms deemed to impair or nullify women's human rights and fundamental freedoms will evolve with experience. Having regard to the object and purpose of the Convention, one approach to determining whether there is an impairment or nullification of women's human rights is to ask: Does the application, enforcement, or perpetuation of a gender stereotype in a law, policy, or practice deny women a benefit? Does the stereotype impose a burden on women? Or, does it degrade women, diminish their dignity, or otherwise marginalize them? (see Chapter 2)

In the *Morales de Sierra* case, the Inter-American Commission on Human Rights found that Morales de Sierra's right to equal protection of and before the law, right to equality in marriage, and right to dignity and private life had been either impaired or nullified. Regarding the right to equal protection of and before the law, the Inter-American Commission found that, by requiring married women to depend on their husbands to represent the marital union, Guatemala's Civil Code "mandate[d] a system in which the ability of approximately half the married population to act on a range of essential matters [was] subordinated to the will of the other half."[87] It explained that in denying Morales de Sierra her legal autonomy, the Civil Code nullified her legal capacities and reinforced systematic disadvantage, thereby impairing her ability to exercise other human rights and fundamental freedoms.[88]

Regarding the right to equality in marriage, the Inter-American Commission explained that, in establishing distinct roles for each spouse, Guatemala's Civil Code institutionalized imbalances in spousal rights and duties.[89] "The fact that the law vests a series of legal capacities exclusively in the husband," it explained, "establishes a situation of *de jure* dependency for the wife and creates an insurmountable disequilibrium in the spousal authority within the marriage."[90] The enforcement of sex role stereotypes in the impugned provisions perpetuated the discriminatory treatment of women, and prevented Morales de Sierra from exercising her human rights and fundamental freedoms within marriage on a basis of equality of men and women.[91]

Taking into account these and other violations, the Inter-American Commission found Guatemala in breach of its obligations to respect and ensure the rights guaranteed in the American Convention on Human Rights, as well as its obligation to adopt necessary domestic measures to give effect to those rights.[92] In this connection, it explained that gender discrimination impairs or nullifies women's ability to freely and fully exercise their rights.[93] The discriminatory provisions, the Inter-American Commission said, can also contribute to other violations, such as gender-based violence against women.[94]

In determining whether the application, enforcement, or perpetuation of a gender stereotype impairs or nullifies a woman's human rights and fundamental freedoms, it is important to consider the historical patterns of women's systematic disadvantage, women's position in society, and the effect on them of the stereotyping. If it can be shown that women have been historically disadvantaged vis-à-vis a particular right or freedom, or that they are vulnerable on account of past discrimination, it is more likely that the differential prejudicial treatment of women on the basis of a gender stereotype will be found to have impaired or nullified women's human rights and fundamental freedoms.

In the *Hibbs* case, Chief Justice Rehnquist was careful to emphasize historical patterns of enforcing and perpetuating gender stereotypes in laws, policies, and practices, when finding that states discriminated between male and female employees in the provision of family-care leave.[95] Evidence before Congress, he explained, suggested that sex role stereotypes concerning the allocation of caregiving responsibilities remained firmly rooted, and that states systematically discriminated against employees in the workplace on the basis of those impermissible stereotypes, particularly in relation to the administration of leave benefits.[96] There was also evidence that the provision of parental leave to fathers was rare, and that even where there existed policies granting fathers leave, men were frequently discriminated against in their requests for such leave. The provision of leave to women, on the other hand, frequently extended beyond the period of time needed to recover from the physical act of giving birth.[97] Moreover, Chief Justice Rehnquist noted that, even in the absence of discriminatory laws, states discriminated between male and female employees in practice on the basis of impermissible stereotypes.[98]

In determining in the *Hugo* case whether the remission of sentence of only mothers impaired Hugo's right to nondiscrimination, the majority of the Constitutional Court of South Africa considered the historically disadvantaged position of each of the categories of prisoners pardoned. The fact that mothers of young children had been victims of discrimination in the past—in large part, because of the sex role stereotype of women as primary caregivers—had a significant impact on the majority's finding that the discriminatory treatment of fathers was constitutionally compliant.[99] Justice Goldstone, writing for the majority, explained that "the task of rearing children is a burdensome one. . . . For many South African women, the difficulties of being responsible for the social and economic burdens of child rearing, in circumstances where they have few skills and scant financial resources are immense. The failure by fathers to shoulder their share of the financial and social burden of child rearing is a primary cause of this hardship. The result of being responsible for children makes it more difficult for women to compete in the labour market and is one of the causes of the deep inequalities experienced by women in employment."[100]

Justice Goldstone identified the sex role stereotype of women as primary caregivers as a root cause of women's disadvantage in South African society, and explained that reliance on this stereotype to disadvantage women would constitute a form of discrimination against them. However, he concluded that President Mandela had not disadvantaged women in this case; rather, in relying on this sex role stereotype of women, President Mandela had afforded women an advantage in the form of early release from prison. In his view, women's disadvantage in South African society derived not from President Mandela's reliance on this sex role stereotype, but from the inequality that results from women's role as primary caregivers.[101]

While Justice Goldstone viewed the elimination of gender stereotyping as an important goal, he, along with Justice O'Regan, recognized the challenges presented by the reality of women's childcare responsibilities and the impossibility of immediately erasing problematic gender conventions. In particular, they recognized the need to encourage fathers to play a more active role in childcare and the need to alleviate women's disproportionate childcare burden. As has been explained, they "recognise (albeit implicitly) that the long term objective of gender equality will be enhanced if men are encouraged to participate in child care."[102] But Justices Goldstone and O'Regan also acknowledged "that in the short term, measures designed to help women may not always be able to serve the longer term purpose of encouraging men to share the burden."[103] Yet, as Justices Goldstone and O'Regan make clear, this does not necessarily invalidate those measures, as alleviating women's immediate disadvantage is also an important goal.[104]

Although the Constitutional Court succeeded in situating the operative sex role stereotypes within the context of the disadvantages faced by women in South African society, it missed an opportunity to situate those stereotypes within the context of the complainant's reality as a single father. It has been explained, for example, that "The Court assumed that only mothers have been historically disadvantaged with regard to child care responsibilities. The Court briefly looks at fathers as a group and notes the failure of fathers to take financial and social responsibility for child care. There is no recognition of the complexities of the issues where fathers are primary caregivers. The Court seems unable to see Hugo as both part of an advantaged group of fathers, and as distinct from that group, because of his location with the sub-group of disadvantaged fathers or the group of primary care-giver parents."[105] Situating the operative sex role stereotypes within the context of the complainant's reality as a single father as well as within the context of the disadvantages faced by women would have helped the Constitutional Court to better understand how the differential treatment impaired Hugo's right to be free from discrimination based on stereotypical beliefs about fathers' proper childrearing roles.

In his dissenting opinion, Justice Kriegler disputed Justice Goldstone's finding that the pardon afforded mothers an advantage and explained that President Mandela's application of this stereotype relegated women "to a subservient, occupationally inferior yet unceasingly onerous role."[106] "The benefits in this case," he said, "are to a small group of women—the 440 released from prison—and the detriment is to all South African women who must continue to labour under the social view that their place is in the home."[107] In Justice Kriegler's view, then, the human rights and fundamental freedoms of women had been impaired through the perpetuation of sex role stereotypes that he characterized as a root cause of women's inequality. He also acknowledged the broader social harm caused "when society imposes roles on men and women, not by virtue of their individual characteristics, qualities or choices, but on the basis of predetermined, albeit time-honoured, gender scripts."[108]

It is significant that in finding discrimination, Justice Kriegler took into account the prescriptive or normative elements of President Mandela's enforcement of sex role stereotypes. Unlike Justice Goldstone, who did not believe the pardon to be discriminatory because it reflected the statistical reality of women's disproportionate childcare burden, Justice Kriegler believed that President Mandela's pardon imposed on men and women his executive preference for how roles and responsibilities should be distributed between men and women. In remitting the sentences of mothers, and not fathers, President Mandela was not only saying that women *are* primary caregivers; he was also saying that they *should be* primary caregivers. Men, on the other hand, *should not be* primary caregivers; according to President Mandela, they *should be* primary breadwinners. In Justice Kriegler's view, this amounted to a nullification of Hugo's rights to nondiscrimination and equality. It could be argued that, by focusing only on the statistical basis of President Mandela's enforcement of sex role stereotypes, Justice Goldstone failed to recognize the full extent of the harm of sex role stereotyping on women in this case. Simply put, he failed to recognize the discriminatory nature of President Mandela's actions because he was unable to see that President Mandela, through his pardon, had prescribed roles for men and women in South African society.

Was the Application, Enforcement, or Perpetuation of a Gender Stereotype in a Law, Policy, or Practice Justified?

It will be recalled that not all distinctions, exclusions, or restrictions made on the basis of a gender stereotype will be considered discrimination against women, in violation of articles 1 and 2(f) of the Women's Convention. In certain circumstances, discrimination against women on the basis of a gender stereotype might be legally justified. For example, a comparative analysis of gender stereotyping jurisprudence reveals that, at times, courts and human rights treaty bodies have found such discrimination to be justified where the application, enforcement, or perpetuation of a gender stereotype in a law, policy, or practice served a legitimate purpose and the means chosen to attain that purpose were both reasonable and proportionate. It also shows that courts and human rights treaty bodies have sometimes been willing to accept that discrimination against women on the basis of a gender stereotype is justified because the harm or harms that resulted from its application, enforcement, or perpetuation were too insignificant to warrant legal protection (*de minimis non curat lex*).

Using existing jurisprudence as a guide, in deciding whether discrimination against women on the basis of a gender stereotype is or was justified, it might be asked:

- Does the application, enforcement, or perpetuation of a gender stereotype in a law, policy, or practice serve a legitimate purpose, and were the means chosen to attain that purpose reasonable and proportionate?
- Does the harm of gender stereotyping warrant legal protection?

Questions that will need to be determined on a case-by-case basis are which justifications for gender stereotyping will withstand scrutiny under the Women's Convention, in what contexts, and in what ways. These questions need to be addressed having regard to the definition of discrimination against women in article 1, and the principles of state responsibility in article 2, especially States Parties' obligation to eliminate discriminatory forms of gender stereotyping as specified in article 2(f) of the Convention. As well, regard will need to be paid to the Convention's overarching object and purpose of eliminating all forms of discrimination against women and achieving substantive equality.

LEGITIMATE PURPOSE AND PROPORTIONATE RESPONSE

Some states have sought to justify discrimination against women by arguing that the application, enforcement, or perpetuation of gender stereotypes in laws, policies, or practices served a legitimate purpose and that the means chosen to attain that purpose were both reasonable and proportionate. A legitimate purpose is one that has an objective and reasonable goal.[109] A reasonable and proportionate response requires that the means chosen to achieve the legitimate purpose not be excessive; that is, the benefits of the differential treatment that result from gender stereotyping should outweigh its negative effects. Which purposes are legitimate, and which means are proportionate, vary depending on the facts and the context in which they operate; what might be a legitimate purpose or a proportionate response in one context, may not be so in another.

States' arguments in support of gender stereotyping have ranged from the need to ensure adequate care for young children,[110] the need to "protect" women in their capacity as wives and mothers, and the need for certainty and juridical security in spousal roles.[111] In one case, it was argued that legislation abrogating or abolishing states' immunity from suit in federal court was justified having regard to states' widespread and discriminatory enforcement of sex role stereotypes in the administration of family-care leave.[112] The purpose of this section is to consider, in more detail, the nature and validity of those arguments, with a view to elaborating when and in what contexts discrimination on the basis of a gender stereotype might be justified.

In her concurring opinion in the *Hugo* case, Justice Mokgoro found that President Mandela's reliance on sex role stereotypes was legally justified under the interim constitution, as it served a legitimate purpose and the means chosen to achieve that purpose were both reasonable and proportionate. According to Justice Mokgoro, there could be no doubt that the aim of *ensuring adequate care for young children* was legitimate. The real controversy, she explained, centered on whether President Mandela's decision to remit the sentences of mothers, and not fathers, was a proportional response to this aim.[113] Put differently, the central issue for determination was whether the means chosen by President Mandela to ensure adequate care for young children was reasonable and proportionate. Faced with the choice of releasing only mothers, or releasing no parents at all, Justice Mokgoro reasoned that "every possible opportunity" should be taken to ease the plight of South African children. She thus concluded that "The temporary denial of parenthood to fathers" was justified "with reference to the interests of the children whose mothers were released";[114] the means chosen, in other words, were both reasonable and proportionate to the aim pursued.

In the *Morales de Sierra* case, the Inter-American Commission on Human Rights concluded that the reasons advanced by the Court of Constitutionality for upholding the impugned provisions—*the need to "protect" women in their capacity as wives and mothers, and the need for certainty and juridical security in spousal roles*—could not be legally justified under the American Convention on Human Rights. The Inter-American Commission reasoned that the Court of Constitutionality made no effort to examine the validity of these claims or to consider alternative positions. Moreover, it was unclear that the differential treatment of married men and women was even compatible with those aims. Considering the denial of married women's right to represent the marital union, the Inter-American Commission explained that this "neither contributes to the orderly administration of justice, nor does it favor her protection or that of the home or children. To the contrary, it deprives a married woman of the legal capacity necessary to invoke the judicial protection which the orderly administration of justice and the American Convention require be made available to every person."[115]

The *Hibbs* case differs from the previous cases. Here, the Nevada Department of Human Resources did not argue that it was justified in discriminating between men and women in the provision of family-care leave on the basis of sex role stereotypes. Rather, it challenged the validity of the Family and Medical Leave Act in abrogating states' immunity from suit in federal court. In upholding the validity of that abrogation of immunity, Chief Justice Rehnquist explained that the abrogation was justified having regard to states' widespread and discriminatory enforcement of sex role stereotypes in the administration of family-care leave.[116] He also explained that states' justification for discriminatory treatment "must not rely on overbroad generalizations about the different talents, capacities, or preferences of males and females."[117] He further explained that states' justifications for discrimination in the employment context, in particular in the administration of leave benefits, must not rely on sex role stereotypes of men and women.

A number of other arguments to justify discrimination on the basis of gender stereotypes have been advanced in domestic, regional, and international jurisprudence. In the *Jordan* case, for example, a majority of the Constitutional Court of South Africa found that the *prohibition of commercial sex* was "an important and legitimate constitutional purpose,"[118] and that the criminalization of the conduct of sex workers was a reasonable and proportionate response to achieve that purpose. The majority suggested that there is a "qualitative" difference between a sex worker, who regularly engages in sex for reward, and a patron, who might or might not regularly pay for sex. Targeting sex workers through criminal sanctions to achieve the provision's legitimate purpose of outlawing commercial sex was therefore justified.[119] In contrast, the minority asserted that it was unclear how the criminalization of the conduct of sex workers, and not their patrons, facilitated the purpose of outlawing commercial sex. It reasoned that the government's purpose may have been more effectively achieved had it criminalized the patron's conduct in the same way as that of sex workers and had it regularly prosecuted patrons.[120] Since the state had not argued that the discriminatory impact of the impugned provision served an important purpose, and given that the provision perpetuated harmful sexual stereotypes of sex workers, the minority concluded that the discrimination could not be legally justified.[121]

In *Abdulaziz, Cabales and Balkandali v. United Kingdom*,[122] the European Court of Human Rights accepted the *protection of a domestic labor market* as a legitimate purpose for the differential treatment of men and women, but found that the means chosen to attain that purpose were disproportionate.[123] The case concerned the United Kingdom Immigration Act of 1971 and its related rules, which permitted lawfully settled husbands to have their foreign wives join them in the United Kingdom without restriction but which did not extend the same rights to wives with respect to their foreign husbands. The state submitted that the differential treatment was justified by the need to protect its domestic labor market at a time of high unemployment.[124] Relying on sex role stereotypes of men as breadwinners and women as homemakers, it reasoned that male immigrants were more likely to have a greater impact on the market than female immigrants.[125] Although the European Court of Human Rights accepted the protection of the domestic labor market as a legitimate purpose, it concluded that it was an insufficient reason to justify the differential treatment of men and women.[126] It thus characterized the state's response as disproportionate and concluded that the differential treatment could not be legally justified.[127]

Some states have sought to justify gender stereotyping on the ground that it serves the legitimate purpose of ensuring *national security*. In *Alice Miller v. Ministry of Defense*,[128] for example, the Government of Israel argued that its policy of excluding women, including Alice Miller, from the air force's prestigious pilot training course was justified on grounds of planning considerations. More specifically, it argued that granting women access to the course, which would enable women to qualify as pilots, would prejudice the army's ability to plan for combat. It based this argument on the fact that women serve shorter terms in the army than men and are eligible for exemptions from service because of their traditional sex roles as mothers and wives. In her concurring opinion, Justice Dorner found the army's planning considerations to be a legitimate purpose. However, she concluded that the measure chosen to realize that purpose, namely the exclusion of women from the pilot training course, was disproportionate and therefore discriminatory. She explained that "closing the aviation course to women violates their dignity and degrades them."[129]

Another argument advanced in support of gender stereotyping has been that of *administrative efficiency*. Several members of the Constitutional Court of South Africa raised administrative efficiency arguments in the *Hugo* case. In that case, Justice Mokgoro explained that "it would have been virtually impossible to release all men and women with children under twelve, because of the sheer numbers involved."[130] Moreover, she said, "there would have been great administrative inconvenience in engaging in a case-by-case evaluation for each mother and father as to whether they were the primary care giver for their child."[131] However, as Justice Kriegler rightly pointed out, there was no evidence before the Court to verify the degree of administrative inconvenience that might be caused by evaluating on a case-by-case basis whether a mother or father was a family's primary caregiver.[132]

Some states have sought to justify gender stereotyping by arguing that it is essential to preserve, or because it accurately reflects, the "*natural*" *order of gender relations.*[133] For example, in 1872 in *Bradwell v. Illinois*,[134] Justice Bradley justified his decision to deny Myra Bradwell entry into the legal profession by explaining that the sex role stereotype of women as homemakers was in accordance with the proper nature of sex roles and gender relations. There he observed:

the civil law, as well as nature herself, has always recognized a wide difference in the respective spheres and destinies of man and woman. Man is, or should be, woman's protector and defender. The natural and proper timidity and delicacy which belongs to the female sex evidently unfits it for many of the occupations of civil life. The Constitution of the family organization, which is founded in the divine ordinance as well as in the nature of things, indicates the domestic sphere as that which properly belongs to the domain and functions of womanhood. The harmony, not to say identity, of interest and views which belong, or should belong, to the family institution is repugnant to the idea of a woman adopting a distinct and independent career from that of her husband.[135]

It is significant, however, that a large number of courts and human rights treaty bodies have long since discredited such attempts at justifying discrimination.[136] Discriminatory gender practices or gender hierarchies can no longer be relied upon as legitimate justifications for the impairment or nullification of the recognition, enjoyment, and exercise by women, on a basis of equality of men and women, of human rights and fundamental freedoms.

Because the purposes of gender stereotyping that will be characterized as legitimate, and the means chosen to achieve those purposes that
will be deemed to be proportionate, will vary depending on the context within which such stereotyping occurs, it may be useful for States
Parties to develop guidelines to assist in ensuring compliance with the
rights to nondiscrimination and equality. In this connection, it might
be asked: under what circumstance is it legitimate to apply, enforce, or
perpetuate a gender stereotype in a law, policy, or practice? When are
the means chosen to attain a legitimate purpose of gender stereotyping
considered both reasonable and proportionate?

Building on the definition of discrimination against women in the
Women's Convention, a starting proposition might be that:

- A *legitimate purpose* is one that has an objective and reasonable goal.
  On this basis, it might be argued, for example, that gender stereotyping that seeks to alleviate women's immediate disadvantage
  is in pursuit of a legitimate purpose, since it aims to address the
  consequences of past discrimination against women. However, gender stereotyping that seeks to create or maintain existing gender
  hierarchies is not a legitimate purpose; it is not legitimate as it is
  antithetical to the Women's Convention's overarching object and
  purpose of eliminating all forms of discrimination against women
  and ensuring substantive equality.
- A *reasonable and proportionate response* requires that the means chosen
  to achieve the legitimate purpose not be excessive. Gender stereotyping that results in the impairment or nullification of the recognition, enjoyment, or exercise by women, on a basis of equality of
  men and women, of human rights and fundamental freedoms, will
  be characterized as excessive (i.e., not proportionate) and, therefore, cannot be justified under articles 1 and 2(f) of the Women's
  Convention.

Degree of Harm Warranting Legal Protection

Gender stereotyping leaves an imprint on all aspects of our lives, beginning from the time we are born and ending only after we die. We
see evidence of this in the way that newborn girls are dressed in pink
and given dolls as presents, while newborn boys are dressed in blue and
given trucks to play with. We also see evidence of this in the way that
women are subordinated to men or are burdened with gender-based
violence. Yet it is one thing to dress boys and girls in different colors,
and another thing entirely to subordinate women to men through the
application, enforcement, or perpetuation of gender stereotypes. As law

cannot address all differences of treatment between men and women that result from gender stereotyping, it intervenes only in cases of gender stereotyping that involve significant harm.[137] It is for this reason that some forms of gender stereotyping, such as those that associate the color pink with girls and blue with boys, might be found to be legally inconsequential, while others, like those that result in the subordination of women, are likely to be found to constitute an unacceptable form of discrimination against women.

States have sometimes sought to justify the application, enforcement, or perpetuation of gender stereotypes in laws, policies, and practices by arguing that the resulting harm was not sufficiently significant to warrant legal protection. In the *Hugo* case, Justice Goldstone, writing for the majority, found that while President Mandela's pardon had denied fathers the same release advantage that it afforded women, the harm to fathers was not sufficiently significant to warrant legal protection under the guarantee of nondiscrimination in the South Africa (Interim) Constitution. Justice Goldstone based this decision on the fact that the rights or obligations of fathers had not in any way been permanently restricted or limited by President Mandela's stereotype-based pardon.[138] Fathers' rights, he explained, had been curtailed on account of their conviction, and not as a result of the president's pardon. According to Justice Goldstone, the effect of the pardon was merely to disqualify fathers from an early release from prison to which they had no legal entitlement. Imprisoned fathers were still eligible to apply on an individual basis for remission of sentence. Moreover, he explained that while the pardon denied men an opportunity afforded to women, it did not do so in a way that fundamentally impaired their rights to equality and dignity.[139]

Justice Mokgoro disagreed with Justice Goldstone's finding regarding the harm to fathers. In her concurring opinion, she explained that President Mandela's reliance on the sex role stereotype of men as breadwinners signaled to society that men are less capable caregivers than women. She explained that this ignored "the equal worth of fathers who are actively involved in nurturing and caring for their young children" and treated them "as less capable parents on the mere basis that they are fathers and not mothers."[140] She also elaborated how this stereotype has been used to deny fathers the opportunity to carve out identities as caregivers and to actively participate in childrearing.[141] Nevertheless, she reasoned that because fathers could still apply for an individual remission of sentence, their rights had not been significantly infringed, and therefore the differential treatment of mothers and fathers was legally justified.[142]

Determination of which harms of gender stereotyping will be sufficiently significant to attract legal protection under the Women's Convention will evolve over time. Answers will need to be determined on a case-by-case basis, having regard to the context at hand. Building on the definition of discrimination against women in the Women's Convention, a starting proposition might be that those harms of gender stereotyping that impair or nullify the recognition, enjoyment or exercise by women, on a basis of equality of men and women, of human rights and fundamental freedoms, cannot be justified under articles 1 and 2(f). Put differently, a State Party to the Convention is not justified in gender stereotyping where the application, enforcement, or perpetuation of a gender stereotype in a law, policy, or practice impairs or nullifies the recognition, enjoyment, or exercise of a woman's human rights and fundamental freedoms.

Chapter 5

The Role of the Women's Committee in Eliminating Gender Stereotyping

What Is the Mandate of the Women's Committee?

With the thirtieth anniversary of the adoption of the Convention on the Elimination of All Forms of Discrimination against Women[1] ("Women's Convention" or "Convention"; see Appendix A) in 2009, there is much to celebrate. Understanding about gender stereotyping and how it wrongs women has grown, and an international consensus is beginning to emerge on the importance of securing its elimination.[2] Notwithstanding such important strides, however, gender stereotyping persists, significantly compromising the elimination of all forms of discrimination against women, and women's exercise of other human rights and fundamental freedoms. As we move toward the Convention's fiftieth anniversary, it is thus important that the Women's Committee articulates norms and standards that address the ways in which this phenomenon enables the exploitation and suppression of women, and the maintenance of gender hierarchies. The purpose of this chapter is to provide an overview of the Committee's mandate under the Convention and the Optional Protocol to the Convention on the Elimination of All Forms of Discrimination against Women ("Optional Protocol"; see Appendix B),[3] and to consider how, through that mandate, the Committee can strengthen its articulation of norms and standards related to gender stereotyping.[4]

The Women's Committee was established in 1982 to monitor States Parties' compliance with the Convention.[5] In this role, the Committee monitors compliance through the reporting procedure, under which States Parties are required to submit periodic reports, every four years, "on the legislative, judicial, administrative or other measures" adopted to give effect to the Convention, as well as "on the progress made in this respect."[6] Typically, these reports address measures undertaken to eliminate discrimination against women, as well as any factors or difficulties affecting implementation of the Convention.[7]

The Committee considers periodic reports at each of its sessions in a process known as "constructive dialogue" with States Parties. This process consists of Committee members posing a series of questions about the content of a State Party's report and its compliance with the Convention, followed by the State Party's responses. The Committee then issues Concluding Observations in which it identifies strengths and weaknesses in the State Party's compliance with the Convention, and also presents recommendations for overcoming obstacles impeding the elimination of all forms of discrimination against women and the realization of substantive equality. These observations not only provide an expert assessment of a State Party's compliance with the Convention, but also elaborate the nature and scope of States Parties' normative obligations to eliminate all forms of discrimination against women.

In describing the significance of the reporting procedure for the enforcement of women's rights, one commentator has noted that "ratification of CEDAW, with the prime obligation of reporting, makes states accountable by international standards and subjects them to international scrutiny. This makes the CEDAW convention and its reporting process a potent tool not only in the international arena but also in the domestic struggle for the advancement of women. The reporting process provides the opportunity to assess the conformity of domestic guarantees for equal rights for women with the international framework, to develop baseline data concerning the factual position of women, and to identify obstacles to the implementation of CEDAW."[8]

More specifically, the reporting procedure has proven to be an important mechanism for identifying and naming gender stereotypes in the laws, policies, and practices of States Parties. The process of preparing periodic reports, and considering and responding to the Women's Committee's questions, has helped States Parties to evaluate how their own laws, policies, and practices apply, enforce, and perpetuate gender stereotypes.[9] For example, participating in the reporting procedure enabled the government of Thailand to acknowledge that male characters were overrepresented in its school textbooks, suggesting that men were ascribed a superior status to women, and that its students were taught that men and women have different and unequal roles to play in Thai society. It also allowed the Thai government to recognize that its school textbooks "present men as the leader or administrators in the community, and as family breadwinners. Women are generally presented as housewives, cooks and child carers, and as supplementary income earners in poorer families."[10]

The reporting process has also caused States Parties to reflect on the adequacy of their steps undertaken to address wrongful forms of gender stereotyping. For example, having recognized the inadequacy of past measures to eliminate gender stereotyping in education, the Thai gov-

ernment reported that it had directed its Department of Curriculum
and Instruction Development to review its school textbooks, and that it
was working to improve the situation of gender stereotyping in the education sector. The government explained in its report that "It hope[d]
to work with text preparation teams, including writers and illustrators,
and expert advisers, to increase their sensitivity to gender issues and
ha[d] recommended the establishment of an on-going supervisory system to oversee the production of all future new texts."[11]

Facilitating a constructive dialogue on gender stereotyping, and the
subsequent adoption of Concluding Observations, has enabled the
Committee to foster understanding of the socially pervasive and persistent forms of gender stereotyping that are implicit and explicit in different societies. It has also allowed the Committee to identify obstacles
that States Parties face in eliminating gender stereotypes and to make
recommendations on how they might seek to overcome those obstacles.
In addition, the Committee has been able to use its Concluding Observations to explain States Parties' normative obligations to eliminate
different and compounded forms of gender stereotyping.[12]

For instance, in 2006, in its Concluding Observations for the Democratic People's Republic of Korea, the Women's Committee noted its
concern regarding

the persistence of traditional and stereotyped assumptions and attitudes in respect of the roles and responsibilities of women and men, which are discriminatory against women and have a pronounced impact, particularly in the areas of
education and employment as well as in other areas of their lives. For example,
the Committee is concerned at the stereotyping of women, which perceives
them exclusively as caregivers and homemakers and assigns them to areas such
as education and employment on the basis of spheres suitable to their "characteristics." The Committee is concerned that such expectations of women have
serious consequences, preventing them from accessing rights and entitlements
on an equal basis with men and creating a dependency on men, husbands and
family for housing, food entitlements and other services. It is also concerned
that in times of economic crisis, as in the current situation of the country,
women's prescribed roles and lesser entitlements intensifies their hardship and
amounts to multiple discrimination.[13]

Taking into account its concerns regarding wrongful gender stereotyping, the Women's Committee called on the State Party to "address stereotypical attitudes about the roles and responsibilities of women and
men, including the hidden patterns that perpetuate direct and indirect
discrimination against women and girls in the areas of education and
employment and in all other areas of their lives, in accordance with articles 2(f) and 5(a) of the Convention. Those efforts should include educational measures at all levels, beginning at an early age; the revision

of school textbooks and curricula; and awareness-raising campaigns directed at both women and men to address stereotypes regarding the roles of women and men."[14]

Under the Convention, the Women's Committee is also responsible for formulating General Recommendations, which interpret the nature and scope of the normative obligations enumerated in the Convention and guide States Parties in the discharge of their periodic reporting duties.[15] Key recommendations include General Recommendations Nos. 19 (violence against women),[16] 21 (marriage and family relations),[17] 23 (political and public life),[18] 24 (women and health),[19] 25 (temporary special measures),[20] and 26 (women migrant workers).[21] From its inception, the Committee has used its General Recommendations to voice concerns regarding gender stereotyping, and States Parties' failure to adequately address this phenomenon.[22] For example, in one of its earliest General Recommendations, the Committee noted that "although the [periodic] reports have come from States with different levels of development, they present features in varying degrees showing the existence of stereotyped conceptions of women, owing to socio-cultural factors, that perpetuate discrimination based on sex and hinder the implementation of article 5 of the Convention."[23]

As the nature and scope of General Recommendations have evolved, the Committee has begun to highlight States Parties' obligations to eliminate the different and compounded forms of gender stereotyping that minimize women's equal enjoyment of human rights and fundamental freedoms. In General Recommendation No. 23 (political and public life), for example, the Committee explained how women have typically been confined to the private sphere, with responsibility for the bearing and rearing of children—sex roles often characterized as inferior—whereas men have been allowed to dominate the respected spheres of political and public life.[24] The Committee attributed women's exclusion from political and public life to, among other factors, cultural values, religious beliefs, and men's failure to share domestic responsibilities. In all nations, the Committee said, "cultural traditions and religious beliefs have played a part in confining women to the private spheres of activity and excluding them from active participation in public life."[25] That is, sex role stereotypes of women as mothers and homemakers, and of men as breadwinners and leaders, have impeded women's participation in political and public life, while, at the same time, entrenching traditional sex roles.

Responding to these and other concerns related to gender stereotyping, the Women's Committee called on States Parties to adopt measures designed to achieve an equitable balance in the participation of men and women in political and public life. It urged States Parties to include in their periodic reports information on any reservations entered to articles 7 (political and public life) and 8 (representation) of the Convention,[26] explaining whether those reservations reflect gender stereotypes, and the steps undertaken to ensure their elimination.[27] The Committee also encouraged States Parties to adopt measures aimed at alleviating women's domestic burden and economic dependency, with a view to facilitating their access, on a basis of equality of men and women, to political and public life.[28]

Perhaps most significantly, the Committee has used one of its most recent General Recommendations to underscore the importance of combating wrongful gender stereotyping to achieve the goals of eliminating all forms of discrimination against women and of realizing substantive equality. It will be recalled that in General Recommendation No. 25 of 2004, the Committee characterized the elimination of wrongful gender stereotyping as one of three general obligations central to States Parties' efforts to eliminate all forms of discrimination against women.[29] Thus, in its expert view, eliminating gender stereotyping is not only a fundamental goal in its own right, but also an essential precondition for States Parties' compliance with the Convention and the achievement of substantive equality.

The entry into force of the Optional Protocol,[30] in December 2000, significantly expanded the mandate of the Women's Committee. Developed directly in response to calls to improve the international protection of women's rights,[31] the Optional Protocol introduced two new mechanisms—a communication procedure and an inquiry procedure—with a view to strengthening enforcement of the Convention. Under the communication procedure, the Committee has the responsibility to determine communications (i.e., complaints) submitted by individuals or groups of individuals or, alternatively, persons acting on their behalf, alleging violations by a State Party of the Convention.[32] The inquiry procedure enables the Women's Committee to undertake inquiries into reliable information concerning grave or systematic violations by a State Party.[33]

Since the Optional Protocol's entry into force, the Committee has issued decisions on admissibility and views on the merits of communications in a small but growing body of jurisprudence. The Committee has also undertaken and issued findings in one inquiry. Many of these decisions, views, and findings, including in *Cristina Muñoz-Vargas y Sainz de Vicuña v. Spain*,[34] have, in varying degrees, addressed the phenomenon of gender stereotyping.[35] *Karen T. Vertido v. The Philippines*,[36] a communication concerning allegations of rape and gender stereotyping that is currently pending before the Women's Committee, promises to be a significant decision on gender stereotyping.

The *Cristina Muñoz-Vargas y Sainz de Vicuña* case concerned the complainant's right, as a Spanish citizen and first-born child of the "Count of Bulnes," to succeed to her father's title of nobility. Under the Decree on the Order of Succession to Titles of Nobility then in effect, a first-born child was entitled to inherit a title of nobility, except in cases where the first-born child was female and had a younger brother. In such circumstances, the Decree provided that the male child be given primacy in the ordinary line of succession. When, upon the Count's death, the complainant's younger brother inherited the title of nobility, the complainant initiated domestic legal proceedings claiming that her rights to nondiscrimination and equality, as protected in article 14 of the Constitution of Spain of 1978 and articles 2(c) (obligation to establish equal protection of the law) and (f) (obligation to abolish discriminatory laws, customs and practices) of the Women's Convention, had been violated. The complainant's claim was dismissed, however, on grounds that the primacy afforded to male children was compatible with the principles of nondiscrimination and equality, and because the brother's succession had occurred prior to the entry into force of the Spanish Constitution. Several appeals were also dismissed.

The complainant subsequently submitted a communication to the Women's Committee alleging discrimination on the basis of sex, in violation of articles 2(c) and (f) of the Women's Convention. A slim majority of the Committee declared the communication inadmissible on account of the brother succeeding to the title of nobility prior to the international entry into force, and to Spain's ratification, of both the Convention and its Optional Protocol.[37] Several Committee members justified their finding of inadmissibility on the basis that a title of nobility was of a purely symbolic and honorific nature, devoid of any legal protection under the Convention.[38]

In a well-reasoned dissenting opinion, Committee member Shanthi Dairiam determined that the communication should have been declared admissible and found to show a violation of the Convention. According to Dairiam, although the facts predated the relevant entry into force of the Convention, their effects—namely, denial of the complainant's right to succeed and entrenchment of male primacy in the order of succession—continued after its entry into force. Moreover, she found that although a title of nobility is not a fundamental human right, "when Spanish law, enforced by Spanish courts, provides for exceptions to the constitutional guarantee for equality on the basis of history or the perceived immaterial consequence of a differential treatment, it is a violation, *in principle*, of women's right to equality."[39] In reaching this conclusion, Dairiam identified an implicit sex stereotype in the impugned legislation that women, by virtue of their physiology alone, are unworthy of succeeding to the title of honor, and that men, owing to their distinctive biology, should be afforded primacy in such matters. On this view, any man has a higher claim to noble status than any woman. She also identified the sex role stereotype of men, and not women, as nobles. According to Dairiam, each of these stereotypes had directly contributed to the denial of the complainant's right to succeed to her father's title.

In fulfilling its mandate under the Convention and the Optional Protocol, the Women's Committee has played an important normative role in efforts to eliminate gender stereotyping. Notwithstanding, owing to the resilience of gender stereotyping, and its ongoing impairment and nullification of the recognition, enjoyment, and exercise by women of equal human rights and fundamental freedoms,[40] more must be done to combat this wrongful practice. While the Committee is but one of many actors that can influence the effectiveness of efforts to eliminate this injustice, since it is the treaty body responsible for monitoring States Parties' compliance with the Convention, it is well positioned to take a leading role in this endeavor. The remainder of this chapter will consider how the methodology advocated in this book could be applied to strengthen the Committee's contributions to the elimination of gender stereotypes.

What Is the Role of the Women's Committee in Eliminating Gender Stereotyping Through the Reporting Procedure?

The Women's Committee has addressed wrongful gender stereotyping in a number of its General Recommendations and Concluding Observations. However, even with the thirtieth anniversary of the Convention, the Committee has yet to fully elaborate in a General Recommendation or a Concluding Observation the nature and scope of States Parties' normative obligations to eliminate wrongful gender stereotyping. As the Committee moves forward, it is important that it consider how to use its General Recommendations and Concluding Observations to strengthen its approach to gender stereotyping, including articulating the corresponding normative obligations of States Parties.

One approach for the Women's Committee is the crafting of a General Recommendation on articles 2(f) and 5(a) of the Convention.[41] Another approach is to ensure that, where appropriate, new General Recommendations on other issue-specific provisions of the Convention, such as article 10 on education, articulate States Parties' obligations to eliminate wrongful gender stereotyping as they pertain to those provisions. For instance, States Parties might be urged to name and eliminate gender stereotypes that are perpetuated through government-sponsored abstinence-only sex education programs.[42] A third approach is to encourage States Parties to make wrongful gender stereotyping a central focus of their periodic reports, and to make certain that the Committee's Concluding Observations squarely address gender stereotyping.

Measures such as these would clarify and provide an authoritative interpretation of the meaning of States Parties' normative obligations to eliminate gender stereotyping, and help States Parties to better understand and fulfil those obligations. Significantly, they would also guide States Parties in the discharge of their periodic reporting duties. Concluding Observations allow the Committee to apply its normative analysis of gender stereotyping at the state level, where it can be given concrete meaning and practical effect. Significantly, Concluding Observations also provide an important opportunity to highlight facts and contextual information that States Parties can use to disconfirm the gender stereotypes that their laws, policies, or practices apply, enforce, or perpetuate.

The purpose of the following section is to consider some of the key elements that the Committee might include in a General Recommendation on articles 2(f) and 5(a) of the Convention. Should the Committee decide to craft a General Recommendation on these provisions, it might include the following elements.

NAMING GENDER STEREOTYPING

A General Recommendation on articles 2(f) and 5(a) might begin by exploring the meaning of the term "gender stereotype," as applied specifically to women. By way of illustration, the Women's Committee might note that the term is an overarching concept that refers to a generalized view or preconception of the attributes or characteristics that are or should be possessed by, or the roles that are or should be performed by, men and women. It might further note that the concept encompasses sex, sexual, sex role, and compounded stereotypes. Drilling down further, it might explore each of these different forms of gender stereotypes. For example, the Committee might explain that the term "sex stereotype" refers to a generalized view or preconception of the physical attributes or characteristics possessed by men or women, whereas the term "sexual stereotype" refers to a generalized view or preconception of sexual characteristics or qualities that are, or should be, possessed by men and women respectively. The Committee might further explain that the term "sex role stereotype" describes a normative view or preconception of appropriate roles or behavior for men and women respectively, while the term "compounded stereotype" refers to a gender stereotype that coincides with another type of stereotype, for example one that relates to race, age, and/or disability (see Chapter 1). The Committee might decide to open up the discussion even further, uncovering and elaborating other forms of gender stereotyping.

The Women's Committee might also encourage States Parties to consider the different reasons why people stereotype. In this encouragement, the Committee might explain that understanding the reasoning behind gender stereotyping can help States Parties uncover and dismantle assumptions about women that underlie their laws, policies, and practices. The Committee might further explain that understanding such reasoning can enable States Parties to determine how different stereotypes should be approached and what kind of remedial response should be pursued.[43] To instigate the discussion, the Committee might explain that sometimes people stereotype to maximize simplicity and predictability, while at other times, they stereotype to assign difference or, for instance, to script identities (see Chapter 1).

A General Recommendation on articles 2(f) and 5(a) might encourage States Parties to name and describe in their periodic reports, as well as more generally, the gender stereotypes that operate in their laws, policies, and practices. As a first step, the Committee might recommend that States Parties undertake a review of existing laws, policies, and practices to determine whether they apply, enforce, or perpetuate gender differences based on stereotypes. It might further recommend that States Parties establish monitoring bodies to ensure that proposed laws do not embody gender stereotypes. Next, the Committee might encourage States Parties to: identify the different forms of operative gender stereotypes (e.g., sex, sexual, sex role, or compounded); describe the contexts (individual, situational, or broader) within which they operate; and, analyze their means of perpetuation and means of elimination.

In a General Recommendation on articles 2(f) and 5(a), the Committee might articulate some of the ways in which gender stereotypes can operate to harm women, including through the denial of a benefit or the imposition of a burden, or by degrading women, diminishing their dignity or otherwise marginalizing them. The Committee could draw upon the experience of reviewing States Parties' periodic reports to illustrate unacceptable gender stereotypes, and show what reported measures have been used to dismantle them. The Committee might encourage States Parties to be cognizant of the full range of harmful effects of gender stereotyping. Significantly, it might call on States Parties to identify in their periodic reports the different ways in which women have been harmed by the application, enforcement, or perpetuation of gender stereotypes, and the remedial measures they have taken to redress that harm (see Chapter 2).

State Obligations to Eliminate Gender Stereotyping

It will be recalled that, in General Recommendation No. 25, the Women's Committee characterized the elimination of wrongful gender stereotyping as one of three obligations central to States Parties' efforts to give full force and effect to the Convention.[44] In a General Recommendation on articles 2(f) and 5(a) of the Convention, the Committee could explain more fully why the elimination of wrongful gender stereotyping is central to the elimination of all forms of discrimination against women, the realization of substantive equality, and the exercise of human rights and fundamental freedoms. In this connection, the Committee could highlight how gender stereotyping can impair and nullify women's human rights and fundamental freedoms across a range of sectors and over time, illustrated by its Concluding Observations on different States Parties' periodic reports.

A General Recommendation on articles 2(f) and 5(a) could clarify the general and specific nature of States Parties' obligations to eliminate wrongful gender stereotyping. Such a General Recommendation should not only articulate normative obligations as they relate to articles 2(f) and 5(a), but also articles 1 and 10(c) (education) of the Convention. In this context, it might be helpful for the Committee to clarify the different nature of the obligations in article 2(f) "To take all appropriate measures, including legislation, to modify or abolish existing laws, regulations, customs and practices which constitute discrimination against women," and in article 5(a) "To modify the social and cultural patterns of conduct of men and women, with a view to achieving the elimination of prejudices and customary and all other practices which are based on the idea of the inferiority or the superiority of either of the sexes or on stereotyped roles for men and women." A General Recommendation could also articulate the linkages between States Parties' obligations in articles 1, 2(f), and 5(a), and the other issue-specific provisions set forth in the Convention (see Chapter 3).

Often it is non-state actors, such as the family, the community and/or the market, that are responsible for applying, enforcing, or perpetuating gender stereotypes. Accordingly, in a General Recommendation on articles 2(f) and 5(a) of the Convention, the Committee should not only articulate States Parties' obligations with respect to its own agents and officials, but also express their obligations to take all appropriate measures to address gender stereotyping by non-state actors (see Chapter 3).

The Committee could also elaborate the nature of States Parties' obligations to remedy gender stereotyping. It could explain, for instance, that States Parties are obligated to provide individual relief to women where they have been wronged on account of gender stereotypes. It might further explain that States Parties are also obligated to adopt all appropriate measures to deinstitutionalize gender stereotypes from their laws, policies, and practices, with a view to addressing the structural nature of gender stereotyping.[45] The Committee could illustrate what States Parties may do, and have done, to eliminate gender stereotypes from laws, policies, and practices so that they no longer wrong women. The Committee could, for example, highlight some of the different approaches that States Parties have adopted to sensitize their judiciaries to the wrongs of gender stereotyping,[46] and the need to ensure that individual judges do not apply, enforce, or perpetuate gender stereotypes in their reasoning (see Chapter 3).

The Women's Committee might specify a test for determining the responsibility of States Parties for violations of the Convention's provisions on wrongful gender stereotyping. The Committee might decide, for instance, to adopt a "but for" test or a "real prospect" test. Should the Committee decide to adopt a "but for" test, it might explain that the test requires that it be shown that, but for the failure of state authorities to address the operative gender stereotype and its oppressive application, women would not have been discriminated against nor have any of their other human rights and fundamental freedoms violated. Should the Committee adopt a "real prospect" test, it might explain that this test provides that States Parties will be held legally responsible under the Women's Convention where they fail to take reasonably available measures that could have had a real prospect of altering the outcome or mitigating the harm of wrongful gender stereotyping (see Chapter 3).

GENDER STEREOTYPING AS A FORM OF DISCRIMINATION

Should the Women's Committee adopt a General Recommendation on articles 2(f) and 5(a) of the Convention, it could outline for States Parties the circumstances in which the adoption, enforcement, or perpetuation of a gender stereotype would rise to a form of direct or indirect discrimination against women. Building on the definition of "discrimination against women" in article 1, and noting States Parties' obligations to eliminate discriminatory forms of gender stereotyping in article 2(f), the Committee could set forth a discrimination test that States Parties can apply in determining whether their laws, policies, or practices discriminate against women on the basis of gender stereotypes. Of particular importance is the need to identify when a gender stereotype will impair or nullify the recognition, enjoyment, or exercise by women, on a basis of equality of men and women, of human rights and fundamental freedoms.[47] Also important is the need to articulate the reasons why gender stereotyping might be justified with reference to articles 1 and 2(f) of the Convention (see Chapter 4).

* * *

The scope of this chapter does not allow for a separate analysis of how the Committee could address wrongful gender stereotyping in its Concluding Observations or in General Recommendations on other issue-specific provisions of the Convention, such as article 10 on education. However, many of the same considerations discussed with respect to a General Recommendation on articles 2(f) and 5(a) will be relevant to Concluding Observations and/or General Recommendations on other issue-specific articles of the Women's Convention.

What Is the Role of the Women's Committee in Eliminating Gender Stereotyping Through the Communication Procedure?

Under the communication procedure, the Women's Committee considers communications submitted by individuals, groups of individuals or, alternatively, persons acting on their behalf, alleging violations by a State Party of the Convention.[48] Before proceeding to an examination of the merits of a communication, the Committee must first determine whether the communication satisfies the Optional Protocol's admissibility criteria. Failure to comply with these criteria will render a communication inadmissible, and will prevent the Committee from evaluating its substantive claims. For a communication to be declared admissible, it must be in writing, cannot be anonymous, and must concern allegations against a State Party,[49] meaning a state that has ratified, and acceded or succeeded to, both the Convention and the Optional Protocol. In addition, the complainant must establish that

- all available domestic remedies have been exhausted;[50]
- the same matter has not already been examined by the Committee or by another procedure of international investigation or settlement;[51]
- the facts occurred after the Optional Protocol's entry into force for the State Party;[52] and,
- the communication is compatible with the Convention,[53] is not manifestly ill-founded or insufficiently substantiated,[54] and is not an abuse of the right to submit a complaint.[55]

Should a communication be declared admissible, the Committee can examine its merits, determining whether the State Party has fulfilled its normative obligations under the Convention.[56] The Committee's decision will be issued in the form of views, together with any recommendations.[57] The Committee may also decide to follow up on its recommendations through the reporting procedure.[58]

The communication procedure is significant as it enables individual women and groups of individual women to seek redress where they have been discriminated against because of a gender stereotype. Because the communication procedure provides an important avenue of international redress for women, it is important that the Committee take steps to ensure that gender stereotyping does not impede women's access to this procedure, either at the admissibility or merits stage of proceedings. The purpose of the following section is to consider how the Committee has already applied the communication procedure to address gender stereotyping, and how it might apply the procedure to combat practical and doctrinal barriers to recourse to the procedure arising from gender stereotyping.

EXHAUSTION OF DOMESTIC REMEDIES

For a communication to be declared admissible it must be shown that all available domestic remedies have been exhausted;[59] that is, that domestic remedies that are available and offer a reasonable prospect of redress for alleged violations of the Convention have been sought.[60] International law requires that states be afforded opportunities to remedy wrongs before they can be considered by international human rights treaty bodies. Abstract, obscure, or extraordinary domestic remedies need not be exhausted.[61] The Committee may waive the exhaustion of domestic remedies requirement in circumstances where domestic remedies have been unreasonably prolonged ("justice delayed is justice denied") or are unlikely to bring effective relief to the victim.[62] There is no requirement to exhaust domestic "remedies" where they do not practically exist.

The Women's Committee had to address the exhaustion of domestic remedies requirement in *A.T. v. Hungary*,[63] a case concerning allegations of domestic violence. Ms. A.T. alleged that her former common-law husband, Mr. L.F., had subjected her to ongoing domestic violence and threats, and that Hungary had neglected its positive obligations under the Convention to stop that violence.[64] In finding the communication admissible, the Committee observed that there was no remedy available to A.T. in the Hungarian legal system that would have effectively protected her against her former partner's domestic violence. The Committee explained that a delay in domestic proceedings exceeding three years was unreasonable, especially considering that A.T. had "been at risk of irreparable harm and threats to her life" because of the absence of temporary protection measures, as well as Hungary's failure to detain L.F.[65] Moreover, although domestic proceedings were ongoing, the Committee noted that their final outcome was unlikely to bring A.T. effective relief with respect to her life-threatening situation of domestic violence.[66] While Hungary questioned whether A.T. had made effective use of the domestic remedies available to her, it conceded that its remedies were ineffective as they were incapable of providing her with immediate protection against domestic violence.[67] Thus, although Hungary did not raise any preliminary objections to the admissibility of A.T.'s communication, the Committee's observations make it clear that, had it chosen to do so, there was no effective remedy available in Hungary that A.T. was required to exhaust.

A challenge for the Women's Committee when assessing compliance with the requirement of exhaustion of domestic remedies concerns how best to address the ways in which gender stereotyping might impede the availability, accessibility, and effectiveness of domestic remedies. Where, for example, a gender stereotype is socially pervasive or persistent, such as in rules of legal admissibility of evidence that reduce the credibility of women's testimony, a State Party might have difficulty in identifying the gender stereotype and recognizing the different ways in which it impairs or nullifies the recognition, enjoyment, or exercise by women, on a basis of equality of men and women, of human rights and fundamental freedoms. In such circumstances, a State Party might also have difficulty in understanding the need to provide remedies that address the problem of gender stereotyping. For example, in denying Cristina Muñoz-Vargas y Sainz de Vicuña the right to succeed to her father's title of nobility, the Spanish courts were unable to identify the gender stereotypes in the Decree on the Order of Succession to Titles of Nobility, recognize the wrongs that they inflicted on the complainant, or understand the need to remedy this injustice.[68]

Even where States Parties have provided domestic remedies in principle, gender stereotypes might prevent women from accessing them. For instance, in cases involving sexual assault, sexual stereotypes about women's chastity and modesty might deter women from successfully pursuing and accessing relevant domestic remedies. Moreover, where States Parties have provided domestic remedies for violations of human rights and fundamental freedoms, compounded stereotypes might operate to deny different subgroups of women access to those remedies. For instance, lesbians might be unable to access domestic remedies where a law prevents same-sex partners from founding a family through adoption, because the law enforces sexual stereotypes concerning the heterosexual family.[69]

The stereotypical reasoning of judges might also influence the effectiveness of remedies granted to women in domestic legal proceedings

and, in some circumstances, their reasoning can entrench and perpetuate wrongful gender stereotypes. For example, one commentator has
insightfully explained that judges often penalize women in divorce proceedings for their failure to conform to prescriptive sex role stereotypes,
such as the "good housewife." "While those women who remain within
their traditional stereotypes of good wives and mothers are treated with
protective paternalism," she observed, "women who venture outside
those boundaries and attempt to assert themselves apart from their husbands, for instance as career women, are punished by lack of recognition of status or financial hardship. In the divorce cases sampled, there
are suggestions that certain white middle-class women who can be categorized as mothers/homemakers are rewarded by the judges for this,
while the women who fall outside this categorization, either by virtue of
their class or career status, are disadvantaged."[70]

Considering the multifaceted ways in which gender stereotypes can
impede the availability, accessibility, and effectiveness of domestic remedies, it is important that the Women's Committee have regard to the
possibility of gender stereotyping when determining whether a complainant has satisfied the requirement of exhaustion of domestic remedies. If women are to achieve substantive equality, the Committee must
remain aware that gender stereotyping at the domestic level may present
the illusion but not the reality that domestic procedures afford women a
fair hearing and remedy. The communication procedure was designed
to provide women with a means of redress where the domestic system
has failed or would fail to adequately protect and remedy violations of
human rights and fundamental freedoms.

NONDUPLICATION OF PROCEDURES

The Women's Committee is required to declare a communication inadmissible where "The same matter has already been examined by the
Committee or has been or is being examined under another procedure
of international investigation or settlement."[71] For a communication to
be declared inadmissible on this ground, the State Party must demonstrate that the same complainant has previously submitted the same
complaint to the Committee or to another procedure of international
investigation or settlement. It is not sufficient to point to a similar communication concerning a different complainant.[72]

Individuals could potentially submit communications alleging gender
stereotyping to a wide range of procedures of international investigation
or settlement. In addition to the Women's Convention, the Convention
on the Rights of Persons with Disabilities,[73] the Protocol to the African
Charter on Human and Peoples' Rights on the Rights of Women in Af-

rica,[74] the Inter-American Convention on the Prevention, Punishment and Eradication of Violence against Women ("Convention of Belém do Pará"),[75] and the Inter-American Convention on the Elimination of All Forms of Discrimination against Persons with Disabilities[76] all contain provisions obligating States Parties to address stereotyping. Moreover, international[77] and regional[78] human rights treaty bodies and domestic courts[79] are also beginning to interpret the rights to nondiscrimination and equality as requiring the elimination of wrongful gender stereotyping. This means that women now have the opportunity to submit complaints concerning gender stereotyping to a broader range of courts and human rights treaty bodies. The Committee will need to consider the nature of any complaints about stereotyping on a case-by-case basis in order to determine whether they concern a matter that has already been addressed by another international procedure.

In *Rahime Kayhan v. Turkey*,[80] a communication concerning the termination of employment of a Turkish schoolteacher for wearing a headscarf at her place of employment, the Committee had to consider whether the European Court of Human Rights had previously considered the same matter in *Leyla Şahin v. Turkey*.[81] The Committee found that the communication considered by the European Court did not preclude the Women's Committee's examination of the communication in *Rahime Kayhan v. Turkey*. Unlike the *Rahim Kayhan* communication, the one in *Leyla Şahin* concerned the right of a university student to wear a headscarf at her educational institution. Moreover, the individuals responsible for submitting the respective communications were different.[82] Thus, in the Committee's expert view, the fact that both communications concerned headscarves in educational settings was insufficient to render the communication inadmissible. The same matter had not already been examined under another international procedure. However, as the complainant had not satisfied the requirement of exhaustion of domestic remedies, the Committee found the communication inadmissible.

Had *Rahime Kayhan v. Turkey* ultimately been found admissible, the Women's Committee might have illuminated the prescriptive sex role stereotype that Muslim women should wear headscarves in order to show deference to their religion. In this connection, the Committee might have analyzed the tension between a woman's right to equality, her right to freedom of thought, conscience, and religion, and her right to freedom of opinion and expression. Religious codes,[83] such as the dress code that prescribes that Muslim women wear headscarves, can be a positive manifestation of one's religion, but when these codes are enforced in a way that penalizes a woman for her decision to wear or not to wear a headscarf, they can assume a hostile and unjust form.

By Reason of Time

The Women's Committee is required to declare communications inadmissible where the facts that are the subject of the complaint occurred prior to the Optional Protocol's entry into force for the State Party concerned. An exception is made where the facts or their effects continued after the date of the Protocol's entry into force.[84] In *A.T. v. Hungary*, the Committee observed that although, with one exception, the reported incidents of domestic violence against A.T. took place prior to the Optional Protocol's entry into force for Hungary, the facts demonstrated a clear continuum of regular violence that had "uninterruptedly characterized the period beginning in 1998 to the present."[85] The fact that A.T. remained at risk of domestic violence following the Optional Protocol's entry into force was significant in this respect. In the Committee's expert opinion, it helped to substantiate A.T.'s claim regarding the continuous and regular nature of the gender-based violence against her.[86] Notably, it is accepted that a "battered woman" suffers from continuous fear of violence and even death.[87]

In determining whether a communication that alleges gender stereotyping satisfies the *ratione temporis* ("by reason of time") requirement, it is important that the Committee consider how the social and cultural patterns of conduct of men and women sustain practices of devaluation and subordination of women over time. This is especially important in the case of communications that allege that a law, policy, or practice applied, enforced, or perpetuated a socially pervasive or persistent gender stereotype.

The case of *Haines v. Leves*[88] demonstrates how the perpetuation of a gender stereotype can have an ongoing effect on the recognition, enjoyment, or exercise by women, on a basis of equality of men and women, of human rights and fundamental freedoms. In discussing the limitations that were placed on Ms. Leves's choice of elective school curriculum subjects because of sex role stereotyping, Chief Justice Street illuminated the long- and short-term impact on her human rights and fundamental freedoms. Besides preventing Leves from enrolling in the elective subjects of her choice, he explained "that the qualification open to pupils at the boys' high school provided competence for tertiary [e.g., university] studies superior to the qualification open to Melinda Leves. It was also established that the employment prospects of those successfully completing the curriculum available at the boys' high school were superior to the employment prospects of those successfully completing the curriculum available to Melinda Leves at the girls' high school."[89] In addition, the Equal Opportunity Tribunal of New South Wales cautioned that limiting girls' educational choices on the basis of sex role stereotypes would likely become a self-fulfilling prophecy, since it would entrench girls' "domestic" aspirations and, in turn, affect expectations of women and girls.[90]

Considering that the facts in the case of *Haines v. Leves* occurred prior to the entry into force of the Convention and its Optional Protocol, had this case come before the Committee, it would have been important for it to consider, as did the judges in this case, the ongoing effects of the violations of Leves's rights to nondiscrimination and equality. Taking into account the long-term impact on Leves's educational and employment prospects, as well as the identity burden imposed on her in terms of her life goals and aspirations, it could be argued that it would have been open to the Committee to find the communication admissible *ratione temporis*.

A pragmatic reason for the Women's Committee to be accommodating in recognizing the wrongs of persistent gender stereotyping is that it allows the Committee to address injustices at the soonest moment, rather than wait while another victim, similarly situated to the complainant, spends time and resources exhausting domestic remedies before submitting a communication to the Committee.

By Reason of Subject Matter

Communications will be found inadmissible under the Optional Protocol if they are incompatible with the provisions of the Convention; that is, if they are in conflict with or not accommodated within the Convention's substantive provisions and its object and purpose of eliminating all forms of discrimination against women.[91] As one commentator has explained, incompatibility "implies that the substantive rights implicated by the facts underlying the claim are not guaranteed by the Convention or that the claim seeks a result that conflicts with the overarching objectives of the Convention itself."[92] Thus, in order for a communication concerning gender stereotyping to be declared admissible by reference to this criterion, it must allege a violation that is compatible with the Convention, especially articles 2(f) and/or 5(a), as well as the Convention's overarching object and purpose of eliminating all forms of discrimination against women and of ensuring substantive equality between men and women.

The question of a communication's compatibility with the Convention arose in the *Cristina Muñoz-Vargas y Sainz de Vicuña* case. It will be recalled that a slim majority of the Committee found the communication, which concerned the complainant's succession to a title of nobility, inadmissible because the facts of the communication predated the Optional Protocol's date of entry into force for Spain.[93] While agreeing with the majority's conclusion, several members of the Committee took a different legal route in their joint concurring opinion, finding instead that the communication was inadmissible on the ground of incompatibility.[94] They noted that the title of nobility "is of a purely symbolic and honorific nature, devoid of any legal or material effect."[95] On the basis of this reasoning, they concluded that "claims of succession to such titles of nobility are not compatible with the provisions of the Convention, which are aimed at protecting women from discrimination which has the effect or purpose of impairing or nullifying the recognition, enjoyment or exercise by women on a basis of equality of men and women, of human rights and fundamental freedoms in all fields."[96]

Although conceding that a title to nobility is not a fundamental right protected under the Convention,[97] Committee member Dairiam argued, in dissent, that the facts of the communication concerned "a violation, in principle, of women's right to equality."[98] Dairiam explained that the Committee "must be broad in its interpretation and recognition of the violations of women's right to equality, going beyond the obvious consequences of discriminatory acts and recognizing the dangers of ideology and norms that underpin such acts."[99] Since the denial of the complainant's right to succeed was founded on the sex role stereotype of men as nobles and the sex stereotype that women are unworthy of priority to any male in succeeding to titles of honor, thus offending the definition of discrimination, Dairiam concluded that the communication was admissible and in violation of the Convention.[100] In Dairiam's expert opinion, for the purpose of declaring the communication admissible, it did not matter that the right to succeed to a title of nobility was not afforded specific protection under the Convention; it was enough that the denial of the complainant's right to succeed rested on discriminatory forms of gender stereotyping.

The Women's Committee's decision in this case raises important questions regarding the kinds of communications that will be deemed compatible with the Convention. With the exception of Dairiam, other members of the Committee missed an opportunity to show how this communication implicated sex and sex role stereotypes of men and women. The missed opportunity is all the more incongruous considering the Committee's own recognition that the elimination of wrongful gender stereotyping is central to States Parties' efforts to eliminate "all forms" of discrimination against women,[101] which would seem to include discriminatory forms of succession to hereditary titles of honor.

In considering whether a communication is compatible with the Convention, it is important that the Committee have regard to the existence of wrongful gender stereotyping. For example, could a communication that might otherwise have been declared inadmissible be declared admissible because, as in the *Cristina Muñoz-Vargas y Sainz de Vicuña* case, the facts underlying the claim concerned gender stereotyping? The ability to apply States Parties' obligations under articles 2(f) and 5(a) to concrete cases, and to provide individual and structural relief against gender stereotyping, is dependent on the Committee declaring admissible such communications as the *Cristina Muñoz-Vargas y Sainz de Vicuña* case, which rest on gender stereotypes.

MANIFESTLY ILL-FOUNDED, INSUFFICIENTLY SUBSTANTIATED, OR ABUSE

The Women's Committee is required to declare inadmissible communications that are manifestly ill-founded, insufficiently substantiated,[102] or an abuse of the right to submit a communication.[103] A communication is manifestly ill founded if, for example, it "relies on a plainly erroneous interpretation of the Convention, or alleges facts that unquestionably indicate that the State Party's act or omission is consistent with the obligations imposed by the Convention."[104] Communications that fail to provide sufficient factual information and legal argument to render a complaint against a State Party credible will be found insufficiently substantiated. A communication may be deemed an abuse of the right to submit a complaint in circumstances where, for example, it is made with malicious intent, is vindictive, or is unjustly self-serving.[105]

A challenge for the Committee will be to decide in what circumstances a communication alleging wrongful gender stereotyping can be declared sufficiently substantiated. The Committee will need to decide on a case-by-case basis whether the information submitted in a communication substantiates a claim that a law, policy, or practice wronged a woman through the application, enforcement, or perpetuation of a gender stereotype. While the Committee might rely on a range of different sources in determining whether a communication is sufficiently substantiated, it is important that the Committee's deliberations are informed by the overarching object and purpose of the Convention.

Where the application, enforcement, or perpetuation of gender stereotypes in laws, policies, or practices is explicit, substantiating a claim that a woman was wronged on the basis of that stereotype might be more straightforward than when the gender stereotype is implicit. In such circumstances, it might be possible to point to statements of state agents or officials as evidence of gender stereotyping. In the *Hugo* case,[106] for example, President Mandela admitted in his affidavit that he had relied on sex role stereotypes of men and women within the family when deciding which prisoners should have their sentences remitted. This affidavit was then used by the Constitutional Court of South Africa to substantiate Hugo's claim that sex role stereotyping had occurred. In the *Ewanchuk* case,[107] Justice L'Heureux-Dubé looked to the statements of the trial judge and Justice McClung of the Alberta Court of Appeal in order to establish that the case was not about implied consent, but rather myths and stereotypes concerning sexual assault.

To substantiate a claim of wrongful gender stereotyping in cases where that stereotyping is explicit in legislation, it might be sufficient to name the operative gender stereotypes, identify the provisions within which they have been applied, enforced, or perpetuated, and identify a difference in treatment of men and women. For example, it will be recalled that in the *Morales de Sierra* case,[108] a textual reading of Guatemala's Civil Code revealed that several sex role stereotypes had been explicitly incorporated into the impugned provisions. For the purpose of substantiating Morales de Sierra's claim of discrimination on the basis of sex role stereotyping, it was sufficient that the operative sex role stereotypes of male representation of family interests and control of family property were named, the provisions of the Civil Code that enforced those stereotypes were identified, and a difference in treatment of married men and women was exposed.

In certain circumstances, it might be helpful to rely on statistical information or surveys in order to substantiate a claim of wrongful gender stereotyping. For instance, several surveys have been carried out that reveal the nature, scope, and extent of gender stereotyping in the education sector. Summarizing some of these surveys, one commentator has noted: "School textbooks tend to portray women as staying at home while men are making history. A survey regarding women in primary school textbooks has revealed that in Peru, for example, women are mentioned ten times less than men. In Croatia, a study of secondary school textbooks has shown that sons are the subject of 42 percent of the material on family life, and daughters of only 17%. A study of school textbooks in Tanzania revealed that girls doing domestic chores constituted the favourite topic for explaining to children English and Kiswahili grammar."[109] Surveys such as these, while not essential to substantiate a claim of wrongful gender stereotyping, might help to bolster such claims under the Optional Protocol.

Reports compiled by nongovernmental organizations[110] as well as academic scholarship, both in the legal[111] and social science fields,[112] might also prove helpful in substantiating a claim that a particular law, policy, or practice wronged a woman on the basis of a gender stereotype. For instance, the rich body of legal scholarship examining the connection between sex role stereotypes and continuing bias against mothers in the workforce[113] might help to strengthen a woman's claim that a law, policy, or practice wronged her on the ground that it applied, enforced, or perpetuated a sex role stereotype of women as mothers or, for example, primary caregivers.

In *Price Waterhouse v. Hopkins*,[114] Ann Hopkins relied on expert testimony from psychologist Dr. Susan T. Fiske to help substantiate her claim that sex role stereotyping had contributed to the decision of her corporate employer, Price Waterhouse, to deny her a promotion. Drawing on recent cognitive approaches, Fiske testified to the antecedent conditions that encourage stereotyping, the indicators that expose stereotyping, and the wrongs that arise as a consequence of stereotyping. She also gave testimony regarding possible remedies to prevent wrongful stereotyping in decision-making. While Fiske's testimony was not considered essential to substantiating Hopkins's claim of sex role stereotyping, Justice Brennan, delivering the opinion of the United States Supreme Court, noted that this evidence enhanced Hopkins's case. "Dr. Fiske's expert testimony," he explained, was "icing on Hopkins' cake."[115]

Perhaps one of the more difficult challenges for the Women's Committee concerns how to determine whether a communication alleging wrongful gender stereotyping is sufficiently substantiated where the operative gender stereotype is only implicit in the law, policy, or practice. Communications alleging a wrong on the basis of implicit gender stereotypes may necessitate some creative thinking. In certain circumstances, it might be possible to point to indicators or signposts of gender stereotyping as a means of substantiating a communication at the admissibility stage of proceedings. For example, where there is information that a greater availability of selective boys' schools than girls' schools has resulted in higher entrance test score requirements for girls, it might be helpful to examine whether there is evidence to show that gender stereotypes are an underlying cause of such differential availability and entrance requirements.[116]

Why, for example, is there a greater number of boys' schools? Is it because girls are discouraged from pursuing an education on account of the sex stereotype that girls' distinctive physiology renders them unsuitable for the rigors of academic life, and that therefore they should be concerned only with the "natural" functions of their sex? Is it because boys' education has been prioritized owing to the enforcement of sex role stereotypes of men as breadwinners and leaders, which requires that men be prepared for the varied work of public and political life?[117] Is it because sex role stereotypes of women as wives, mothers, homemakers, and primary caregivers have been applied to deny or limit women's education and confine them to traditional roles?[118]

Once the operative gender stereotype has been named and described, and its harms have been identified, in order to substantiate a claim it must be shown that the State Party, either through its own agents or officials or its failure to attend to the stereotyping of non-state actors, could reasonably be held to have violated the Convention's prohibitions against wrongful gender stereotyping. That is to say, it is not enough to sufficiently substantiate a communication to expose operative gender stereotypes; it must also be shown that there is a causal relationship between the State Party's exercise of power and the alleged violation of the Women's Convention. If the actors responsible for wrongful gender stereotyping are state agents or officials, the acts are considered state acts for which the State Party can be held legally accountable under the Convention. If non-state actors are responsible for wrongful gender stereotyping, and the state fails to take reasonably available measures to restrain, condemn, and remedy those violations, it becomes possible to attribute responsibility to the State Party for its derogation of duty. In such cases, attributing legal responsibility to a State Party depends on the ability to demonstrate a legal link between that state's acts and/or omissions and wrongful gender stereotyping by a non-state actor. For example, a legal link might be established by demonstrating that the State Party failed to exercise due diligence to identify and redress the gender stereotyping of the non-state actor.

INTERIM MEASURES

At any time after the Women's Committee has received a communication and before it has reached a determination on its merits, the Committee may request the State Party complained against to implement interim measures to "avoid possible irreparable damage to the victim or victims of the alleged violation."[119] Human rights treaties, like the Women's Convention, are unique in that they aim to protect and enforce the human rights and fundamental freedoms of individuals. For this reason, breaches of human rights treaties can impair or nullify those rights and freedoms. Interim measures are intended to protect individuals against such harm *before* it occurs. This is the same principle applied by domestic courts, which may issue interim orders on the unproven assumption that alleged facts are true, to prevent irreparable injury to complainants while the case is being prepared for trial on the merits of evidence. Interim measures might, for example, be applied to prevent the irreparable harm faced by pregnant HIV-positive women in need of treatment before,[120] and after[121] the birth of their children. Interim measures are also intended to ensure that the Committee has sufficient time to engage in a proper determination of the facts, without risk to the woman concerned.

In the context of gender stereotyping, interim measures might be applied to prevent the irreversible impairment or nullification of the human rights and fundamental freedoms of women that can result from the application, enforcement, or perpetuation of gender stereotypes in laws, policies, or practices. The Committee might, for example, request that a State Party adopt interim measures to prevent child[122] or forced[123] marriages that are about to take place because the girls or women in question have been stereotyped into the roles of wives and mothers. In the case of child marriages, the Committee might act to prevent potential complications such as early pregnancy, high maternal mortality and morbidity rates, and increased health complications for adolescent mothers following labor and childbirth. The Committee might also intervene by way of interim measures in cases of threatened "crimes of honor,"[124] where women's lives or physical safety are at risk because of their failure to conform to prescriptive stereotypes that women should be obedient, modest, or chaste.

VIEWS, RECOMMENDATIONS, AND FOLLOW-UP

Once the Women's Committee has declared a communication admissible, it can examine evidence regarding the communication's merits in order to determine whether the State Party has violated any rights protected under the Convention.[125] Once the Committee has reached a decision, members are required to issue "views," in which they must articulate their reasons for finding a State Party in violation of, or in compliance with, the Convention. In cases where the State Party is found in violation of the Convention, the Committee shall issue recommendations on how the State Party might remedy that violation.[126] Recommendations might aim to redress the victim's individual situation, such as in cases of recommendations for reparations.[127] The Committee could also aim to address the underlying causes of the violation, such as by proposing domestic law reform,[128] improved training and public awareness about women's rights,[129] or the implementation of measures designed to eliminate gender stereotypes. The Committee could also recommend temporary special measures, such as vocational training for women until such time as they are employed in equal proportion to men in particular employment sectors.

When a State Party has applied, enforced, or perpetuated a gender stereotype in a law, policy, or practice, it might have violated articles 2, 3, 5(a), and 24 of the Women's Convention. Depending on the context, the State Party might have also violated one or more of the Convention's issue-specific provisions. For instance, where a State Party has discriminated against a woman because it enforced a sex role stereotype in an employment law, in addition to violations under articles 2, 3, 5(a), and 24 of the Convention, it might also have violated article 11 on employment. When considering which articles of the Convention have been violated, it is important that the Committee consider not only whether the State Party has violated articles 2, 3, 5(a), and 24, but also whether it has impaired or nullified a woman's human rights and fundamental freedoms guaranteed in the Women's Convention or "In any other international convention, treaty or agreement in force for that State."[130]

In order to determine whether a State Party has violated the Convention's prohibitions against gender stereotyping, the Women's Committee might apply the "real prospect" test (see Chapter 3 and above). Should the Committee apply this test, it might consider whether there would have been a "real prospect" of altering the wrong that a woman experienced because of gender stereotyping had the State Party taken reasonably available measures to address gender stereotyping. If the application of the test reveals a real prospect of altering the wrong, then the Women's Committee may find the State Party in violation of relevant Convention provisions.

Because the types of remedial actions needed to address gender stereotyping will vary, depending on the factual and legal context within which each communication arises, what might be an effective recommendation in one context might be ineffective in another. When making recommendations, the Committee should carefully consider the operative gender stereotype and the context within which it arises. Even though the Committee might receive separate communications relating to the same application of a gender stereotype, the way that stereotype has wronged one woman may differ from the way in which it has wronged another. For example, a twenty-one year old educated woman might not have been wronged by the application of a gender stereotype in the same way as a woman from a different racial background with the same level of education or a sixty-year-old illiterate woman.

In order to ascertain which recommendations might be most effective with respect to a particular communication, it might be helpful to ask: What measures are needed to redress the consequent wrong that the victim has experienced? For example, what measures are needed to redress discrimination against women, the degradation of women, the diminishing of their dignity, or their marginalization? What measures are needed to address the structural nature of wrongful gender stereotyping? Put differently, what measures are needed to deinstitutionalize the gender stereotype from the impugned law, policy, or practice, from people's minds, and, for example, from common interactions so that the stereotype does not continue to wrong women?

The Women's Committee can follow up on its recommendations made in proceedings under the Optional Protocol by inviting States Parties to submit in their periodic reports information about any measures adopted to implement the Committee's recommendations.[131] Because the elimination of wrongful gender stereotyping is an ongoing goal, which requires longer-term processes designed to achieve structural reform, States Parties should be supported, encouraged, and acknowledged for their advances throughout the process of implementing Committee recommendations.

The communication procedure's follow-up potential enables the Committee to maintain a dialogue with States Parties regarding their efforts to eliminate wrongful gender stereotyping. This allows the Committee to learn of any achievements or obstacles in eliminating gender stereotypes that operate in their laws, policies, and practices. At the same time, the follow-up procedure allows the Committee, through its secretariat, to keep abreast of the nature and extent of wrongful gender stereotyping and enables it to apply pressure on States Parties, as required. The potential for follow-up is not limited to the Committee, however. States Parties, national human rights institutions, courts, tribunals, and civil society have an influential role in naming gender stereotypes, generating debate about their contexts, identifying how they wrong women, raising awareness of obligations not to stereotype, and in requiring appropriate remedial relief.

As the treaty body responsible for monitoring States Parties' compliance with the Women's Convention, the Committee has a unique opportunity to influence jurisprudence on wrongful gender stereotyping. For this reason, it would be helpful that the Committee not only articulate norms and standards on States Parties' obligations to eliminate and remedy gender stereotyping, but that it also engage in a detailed factual and legal analysis of wrongful gender stereotyping, just as it requires other courts and human rights treaty bodies to do. The Committee should identify gender stereotyping in States Parties' laws, policies, and practices, name the gender stereotypes that operate therein, detail the harm to women, explain States Parties' normative obligations to eliminate wrongful gender stereotyping, and elaborate why the application, enforcement, or perpetuation of those gender stereotypes does or does not constitute discrimination against the alleged victim, or prevent her from exercising or enjoying her other human rights and fundamental freedoms. The Committee should also ensure that, where gender stereotyping is identified, it crafts effective recommendations to assist the States Parties in securing its elimination.

While the Committee has touched on gender stereotyping in a series of communications alleging domestic violence,[132] and Committee member Dairiam addressed gender stereotyping in her dissenting opinion in *Cristina Muñoz-Vargas y Sainz de Vicuña*,[133] the Committee has missed valuable opportunities to take a lead role on this issue. For example, while the Committee in *A.T. v. Hungary*[134] is to be celebrated for identifying the link between gender stereotyping and gender-based violence against A.T., it missed an opportunity to more fully address the gender stereotyping phenomenon in Hungary, as it concerns violence against women.

The Women's Committee named gender stereotyping as a wrong in *A.T. v. Hungary* when it noted concerns regarding the "persistence of entrenched traditional stereotypes regarding the role and responsibilities of women and men in the family" and the "traditional attitudes by which women are regarded as subordinate to men."[135] The Committee could have strengthened its analysis by naming the specific sex role stereotypes within the family. For example, it might have named the sex role stereotype that Hungarian *men should be heads of households*, which implies that L.F., the former common law husband of A.T., should have been obeyed and that he should have held ultimate power within the family unit. The Committee might have named the sex role stereotype that Hungarian *women should be homemakers, wives and mothers*, which implies that A.T. ought to attend to the home and care for her children. The Committee might have been more explicit regarding the sex stereotype of *women as men's subordinates*, describing how it required A.T. to obey L.F. and to be disciplined by use of violence if she did not obey him. In discussing the primacy that domestic courts afforded L.F.'s right to property and his right to privacy over A.T.'s right to security of the person,[136] the Committee might have named the sex stereotype relating to *men's "proprietary interest" in women*, which suggests that A.T. is the property of L.F. and that she can be treated by him accordingly.

In order to foster understanding of how A.T. was wronged by these gender stereotypes, the Women's Committee might have analyzed the contexts within which they operated. Since the Committee determined that gender stereotypes were both socially pervasive and persistent in Hungary,[137] it could have described how the stereotypes were integrated into social institutions and meanings and how they facilitated the conditions for the social stratification and subordination of A.T., and Hungarian women in general. In this connection, the Committee could have considered situational factors in sectors such as the family and the criminal justice system. For example, in the context of the criminal justice system, the Committee might have analyzed how the failure of the Ministry of Justice to exercise due diligence to eliminate the entrenched, persistent, and pervasive gender stereotypes enabled their perpetuation. The Committee could have further considered whether the climate of impunity surrounding domestic violence in Hungary enabled the perpetuation of the operative gender stereotypes, since it implied that such violence was not a serious crime from which women required protection, through such measures as injunctive relief or the detainment of abusive spouses. The Committee might have illuminated how a domestic court's finding that L.F.'s rights to property and privacy superseded A.T.'s right to security of the person was reflective of a larger problem of judges perpetuating gender stereotypes through their reasoning.

In its views, the Committee was explicit that the perpetuation of the operative gender stereotypes had harmed A.T. by undermining her right to live free of gender-based violence. It noted, for instance, that "traditional attitudes by which women are regarded as subordinate to men contribute to violence against them."[138] It would have been helpful had the Committee also addressed the dynamic potential of those stereotypes, explaining *how* they enabled domestic violence against her. The Committee could have considered, for example, whether the perpetuation of the sex stereotype that women are men's subordinates enabled domestic violence against A.T. because it required her to obey her male partner and to be disciplined by use of violence if she did not obey. The Committee could have also considered whether the stereotype enabled domestic violence against A.T. because it constructed her as a subordinate being and as a form of property, whom her male partner could direct as he saw fit, including through the means of violence. It would have been helpful had the Committee also explained how the perpetuation of the operative gender stereotypes harmed the dignity of A.T. by failing to recognize and respect her intrinsic worth as a human being, and how the gender stereotypes impaired or nullified other human rights and fundamental freedoms of A.T., such as the right to health.[139]

The Women's Committee could have described more clearly the nature of Hungary's obligations to eliminate the gender stereotypes that facilitated domestic violence against A.T. In particular, the Committee could have elaborated the nature and scope of the obligations to eliminate wrongful gender stereotyping imposed on Hungary's three branches of government under articles 2(f) and 5(a) of the Convention. For example, considering the stereotypical comments made by domestic judges, the Committee could have emphasized the obligation incumbent on Hungary's judiciary to refrain from wrongful gender stereotyping in its reasoning and practices. The Committee could also have elaborated Hungary's due diligence obligations under article 2(e) of the Convention to eliminate gender stereotyping by non-state actors. For instance, the Committee might have urged Hungary to adopt measures to debunk and educate the public about the wrongful effects of the gender stereotypes that facilitated domestic violence against A.T. As well, the Committee might have explained that articles 2(c) and 15 of the Convention, which obligate Hungary to ensure equality of and before the law, requires that it rid the legal system, including its judiciary, of gender stereotypes that impair or nullify women's equal human rights and fundamental freedoms.

It is disappointing that, in its findings, the Committee failed to recognize that the stereotyping of A.T. constituted a form of discrimination against her, which Hungary is obligated, under article 2(f) of the Convention, to eliminate. Drawing on the definition of discrimination against women in article 1 of the Convention, the Committee could have articulated the reasons why Hungary's stereotypical treatment of A.T. resulted in discrimination. For example, the Committee could have explained that the perpetuation of the operative gender stereotypes, which resulted from Hungary's failure to act with due diligence to eliminate them, had the effects of nullifying A.T.'s right to live free of gender-based violence and of impairing her other human rights and fundamental freedoms. It could also have explained that Hungary was not justified in its failure to act to protect A.T. against the wrongs of gender stereotyping. The Committee could have also elaborated its reasoning for finding a violation of article 5(a) of the Convention.

In order to redress the wrongs arising out of the stereotyping of A.T., the Women's Committee could have recommended, among other things, that Hungary

- issue a personal apology to A.T. for its failure to protect her from being stereotyped in a way that allowed her to be subject to ongoing domestic violence; and
- compensate A.T. for the judiciary's stereotyping of her that resulted in the prioritization of L.F.'s rights to property and privacy over her rights to physical and mental integrity.

In order to deinstitutionalize from Hungary's laws, policies, and practices, and to eradicate from the minds of Hungarian men and women, the gender stereotypes that enable gender-based violence against women, the Committee might have recommended that Hungary:

- implement ongoing judicial training to sensitize judges to the issue of gender stereotyping and the wrongs that result when judges incorporate gender stereotypes into their reasoning;
- issue a public statement acknowledging and apologizing for its failure to address widespread gender stereotyping; and

- undertake a review of domestic laws, policies, and practices with a view to eradicating from them the gender stereotypes that enable domestic violence.

What Is the Role of the Women's Committee in Eliminating Gender Stereotyping Through the Inquiry Procedure?

The inquiry procedure enables the Women's Committee to undertake inquiries into reliable information concerning grave or systematic violations by a State Party.[140] The term "State Party" is used here to refer to states that have ratified, and acceded or succeeded to, both the Convention and the Optional Protocol, and that have not opted out of the inquiry procedure.[141] Ms. Ferrer Gómez and Ms. Tavares da Silva, the two Committee members charged with carrying out the first inquiry under the Optional Protocol, have explained that reliability of information is assessed "on the basis of its consistency, corroborating evidence, the credibility of its sources, as well as information from other sources, national or international, official or nonofficial."[142]

The Committee has yet to explicitly determine when gender stereotyping will reach the level of gravity required, or can be characterized as systematic, to initiate an inquiry under the Optional Protocol. Insights can be gained by how the two Committee members have explained these terms in their commentary on the inquiry procedure. They explained that the term "grave violation" refers to the severity of an alleged violation. It "means that a severe abuse of fundamental rights under the Convention has taken place or is taking place."[143] The violation "includes discrimination against women expressed in the abuse of their right to life and security, to their integrity, both physical and mental, or to any other fundamental right protected by the Convention. Severe violence or torture, disappearances or kidnappings, trafficking or killings could certainly be motives for an inquiry under the Optional Protocol."[144]

The term "systematic violation," on the other hand, refers to the scale or prevalence of an alleged violation. It means that "the violation is not an isolated case, but rather a prevalent pattern in a specific situation; one that has occurred again and again, either deliberately with the intent of committing those acts, or as the result of customs and traditions, or even as the result of discriminatory laws or policies, with or without such purpose."[145] Committee members Ferrer Gómez and Tavares da Silva have also explained that "Systematic denial of equal rights for women regarding, for example, nationality or inheritance; laws that permit polygamy or are sex specific in regard to adultery; tolerance of sex tourism, or recruitment of labor under false promises leading to forced prostitution; systematic acceptances of forced marriages; tolerance of violence against women, including the practice of female genital mutilation (FGM) or other traditional harmful practices—all of these could be potential themes for investigation and could well be challenged on the basis of the inquiry procedure."[146]

Assuming that information received under the inquiry procedure is reliable and concerns grave or systematic violations of the Convention by a State Party, the Women's Committee may initiate a confidential inquiry into those allegations.[147] At an inquiry's end, the Committee shall issue its findings to the State Party, together with any comments and recommendations.[148] The Committee may also follow up on its inquiry in order to determine what, if any, measures the State Party has taken in response to its recommendations.[149]

Like the communication procedure, the inquiry procedure enables the Committee to make determinations on alleged violations by a State Party of the Convention. What distinguishes the inquiry procedure from the communication procedure is that it affords the Committee the ability to examine patterns of offending conduct culminating in systematic Convention violations by a State Party. Since the entry into force of the Optional Protocol, the Committee has undertaken one inquiry, namely that into the abduction, rape, and murder of women in Ciudad Juárez, Mexico.[150] The purpose of this section is to consider how the Women's Committee addressed gender stereotyping in that inquiry and how it could apply the inquiry procedure to maximize efforts to combat such wrongful practices in the future.

RELIABLE INFORMATION

Reliability of information is a key consideration in the Women's Committee's decision to initiate an inquiry.[151] It will be a challenge to decide what information meets the reliability threshold to initiate an inquiry into allegations of grave or systematic violations of the Convention that are grounded in gender stereotyping. As with the requirement to sufficiently substantiate alleged violations under the communication procedure, the Committee will need to determine on a case-by-case basis whether reliable information has been submitted. To meet this requirement, it is not sufficient to establish objectively that the information is reliable. The Committee must also be satisfied that the information is reliable as it pertains to allegations of gender stereotyping.

Where the application, enforcement, or perpetuation of gender stereotypes in laws, policies, and/or practices is explicit, satisfying the requirement of reliability might be more straightforward than when the gender stereotype is implicit.[152] When there is an absence of explicit information relating to gender stereotyping, or when it is not immediately obvious that allegations of gender stereotyping are of a grave or systematic nature, it would be useful, once again, to look for indicators or signposts of gender stereotyping, such as differential rates of higher educational, healthcare access, or parliamentary participation. This process must be engaged in not only by the Committee when deciding whether to initiate an inquiry, but also by those initially submitting information under the inquiry procedure. These signposts should be resourcefully scrutinized for what they reveal about gender stereotyping of men and women.

For instance, indicators of sexual stereotypes might exist where reliable information is submitted under the inquiry procedure that a significant number of pregnant girls, but not the boys who impregnated them, have been expelled from school in a three-year period.[153] The question arises whether differential rates of expulsion reflect a widespread policy of punishing girls for their failure to conform to the prescriptive sexual stereotype that "girls should be chaste,"[154] and not boys. In addition, when reliable information is submitted indicating differential literacy rates among boys and girls,[155] the question arises as to whether gender stereotyping is an underlying cause. In such circumstances, it is helpful to examine domestic laws, educational policies, and school practices to determine whether an underlying cause is, for example, a sex role stereotype of women as homemakers who do not require education, or men as breadwinners who must be as skilled as possible.

Once the operative gender stereotype has been named and described, and its harms have been identified, it must be shown—as in the case of sufficiently substantiating a communication (see above)—that there are reasonable grounds to believe that the State Party violated the Convention's prohibitions against wrongful gender stereotyping. That is to say, legal responsibility for the violation or violations of the Women's Convention must be attributed to the State Party. If state agents or officials are responsible through their exercise of power for wrongful gender stereotyping, the State Party can be held legally accountable. If non-state actors are responsible for wrongful gender stereotyping, and the State Party failed to address that stereotyping, it can be held legally accountable for the conduct of the non-state actor.

GRAVE OR SYSTEMATIC VIOLATIONS OF THE WOMEN'S CONVENTION

The inquiry procedure enables the Women's Committee to examine reliable information of a State Party's *grave* or *systematic* violations of rights protected under the Convention.[156] In the context of gender stereotyping, the Committee will therefore need to determine whether allegations of gender stereotyping can be characterized as grave or systematic violations of the Women's Convention.

The Committee has yet to explicitly determine when gender stereotyping will reach the level of gravity required to initiate an inquiry under the Optional Protocol. However, in view of the Committee's characterization of the elimination of wrongful gender stereotyping as one of three obligations central to States Parties' efforts to eliminate all forms of discrimination against women,[157] it seems likely that the Committee will treat any violation of that obligation extremely seriously. The Committee might characterize the application, enforcement, or perpetuation of a gender stereotype as grave when, for example, it denies a woman a benefit, imposes a burden on her, or when it degrades her, diminishes her dignity, or otherwise marginalizes her in society. The Committee might also find gender stereotyping grave when it leads to violations of issue-specific provisions of the Convention with grave consequences for women, such as in cases of gender-based violence, forced sterilization, female genital cutting, or maternal mortality or morbidity.

The Committee has also yet to determine when gender stereotyping might be characterized as systematic. Gender stereotyping that is socially pervasive is likely to be treated as a systematic violation, and therefore as grounds for initiating an inquiry. Gender stereotyping that is socially persistent is also likely to be characterized as systematic, and treated as a valid basis upon which to initiate an inquiry under the Optional Protocol. Sex role stereotypes of women as mothers and homemakers are both socially pervasive[158] and socially persistent. For example, evidence of the enforcement and perpetuation of these stereotypes was apparent in 1872, when, in his concurring opinion in *Bradwell v. Illinois*,[159] Justice Bradley relied in part on the sex role stereotype of women as homemakers to deny Ms. Myra Bradwell entry into the legal profession. More recently, evidence of these sex role stereotypes has reappeared, in cases such as *President of the Republic of South Africa v. Hugo*,[160] *Petrovic v. Austria*,[161] and *Morales de Sierra v. Guatemala*.[162]

FINDINGS, RECOMMENDATIONS, AND FOLLOW-UP

At the conclusion of an inquiry, the Women's Committee issues its findings, in which it describes whether or not the State Party violated the human rights and fundamental freedoms protected under the Convention.[163] When the Committee finds that a State Party has applied, enforced, or perpetuated a gender stereotype in a law, policy, or practice, it might hold that state legally accountable under articles 2, 3, 5(a), and 24 of the Convention. The Committee could find a further violation of an issue-specific provision, such as article 12 on the right to health. Should a violation or violations be found, the Committee shall issue recommendations on how that State Party might redress its noncompliance.[164] The Women's Committee can elect subsequently to follow up on its inquiry in order to determine what, if any, measures the State Party has taken in response to its recommendations.[165] Since the inquiry procedure typically addresses questions that "are broader than individual problems, and not likely to be solved by individual answers, legal or administrative,"[166] any recommendations or follow-up inquiries are likely to be well suited to addressing gender stereotypes that are socially pervasive or persistent, or both.

As with the merits stage of the communication procedure, it is important that the Committee articulate its reasoning for finding a State Party in violation of, or in compliance with, Convention obligations to eliminate wrongful gender stereotyping. Since the inquiry procedure is significantly broader in scope than the communication procedure, it is particularly important that the Committee take advantage of the opportunity to elaborate its reasoning. As the discussion below of the Ciudad Juárez inquiry reveals, it would be helpful for the Committee to: name the operative gender stereotypes; identify their forms, their contexts, means of perpetuation, and means of elimination; describe the ways in which they harm women; articulate States Parties' normative obligations to eliminate gender stereotypes; and identify whether such gender stereotyping constitutes a form of discrimination or otherwise violates human rights and fundamental freedoms.

In order to ascertain whether a State Party has committed a grave or systematic violation of the Women's Convention in the form of gender stereotyping, as with the communication procedure, the Committee might apply the "real prospect" test (see Chapter 3 and above). Should it do so, the Committee might question whether there would have been a "real prospect" of altering the wrong experienced by an individual woman or group of women had the State Party addressed grave or systematic gender stereotyping through the taking of reasonably available measures. If the application of the test reveals a real prospect of altering the wrong, then the State Party may be held legally accountable for violating the Women's Convention.

In determining what recommendations might best address the harms of gender stereotyping, and facilitate the deinstitutionalization of gender stereotypes from the law, policy or practice, it is important that the Committee once again analyze the context or contexts within which a violation took place. Analyzing the individual, situational, and broader factors of violations can be a helpful way to understand what measures States Parties might usefully adopt to eliminate wrongful forms of gender stereotyping. With socially pervasive or socially persistent gender stereotyping, understanding the situational and broader factors, in particular, might provide important insights into measures needed to redress the conditions that have enabled the social stratification or subordination of women over time and across different sectors.

Ciudad Juárez Inquiry

Factual background of the Ciudad Juárez inquiry. The Women's Committee's 2005 report into the abduction, rape, and murder of women in Ciudad Juárez, Mexico, was its first under the inquiry procedure.[167] It followed earlier reports of the Inter-American Commission's Rapporteur on the Rights of Women,[168] Amnesty International,[169] and several United Nations Special Rapporteurs,[170] and that have since resulted in several cases before the Inter-American Commission[171] and the Inter-American Court of Human Rights.[172] A follow-up to the Committee's report occurred in 2006.[173] The events culminating in the inquiry can be traced back to 1993, when violence against women in Ciudad Juárez skyrocketed.[174] Up to 400 women were estimated as having been murdered from 1993 to 2003;[175] one third of these victims were reportedly sexually assaulted.[176] In addition, up to 4,500 women reportedly disappeared.[177] Victims were mostly young, attractive women of humble origins, employed in *maquiladoras* (i.e., assembly factories that produce for export) or local businesses, and/or attending school.[178]

Numerous theories have been advanced to explain the violence, including trafficking, domestic violence, police corruption, and complicity,[179] and the recent growth of *maquiladoras*.[180] Despite the various theories put forward, there is a consensus that the crimes embody gender-based violence;[181] women were, and continue to be, targeted because they are women.[182] One report has explained: "many cases share common features that indicate gender-based violence; that is to say, the gender of the victim seems to have been a significant factor in the crime, influencing the motive, the context, the type of violence suffered by the woman and the way in which the authorities responded to it. Consequently, despite the fact that men, women and children are all affected by the general manifestations of violence . . . by studying the murders and abductions of women, it is possible to detect a pattern of violence against women, in other words, violence that has a clear gender dimension."[183] Yet "it is not just 'being a woman' that is a danger," in Ciudad Juárez, it is also "all of the unstated, attached constructions and assumptions about women's value, worth, and respectability that makes 'being a woman' dangerous in Juárez."[184] That is, gender stereotyping has facilitated the violence.

Although Mexico has taken some steps to address violence against women, its response has been criticized as seriously deficient. Mexico has been blamed for, among other failings, refusing to recognize the gendered nature of these crimes,[185] inadequate investigations and results, evidence tampering, and ill treatment of family members.[186] It has also been criticized for trivializing and deflecting responsibility for the violence, and for blaming victims for their violent encounters, "attributing it to their manner of dress, the place in which they worked, [or] their conduct."[187]

Findings and Recommendations of the Committee. In January 2005, the Committee issued its final report, finding Mexico in violation of articles 1–3, 5, 6, and 15 of the Convention for its failure to protect women against violence.[188] The Committee also found that Mexico had offended the Declaration on the Elimination of Violence against Women[189] as well as General Recommendation No. 19.[190] The Committee characterized the violence as violations of "women's basic human rights and as the most 'radical' expressions of gender-based discrimination."[191] It emphasized that these acts were "not isolated, sporadic or episodic cases of violence."[192] Rather, it said, "they represent a structural situation and a social and cultural phenomenon deeply rooted in customs and mindsets . . . ;"[193] they were "founded in a culture of violence and discrimination that is based on women's alleged inferiority, a situation that has resulted in impunity."[194]

The Committee identified serious lapses and violations in Mexico's fulfillment of article 2 obligations to eliminate discrimination against women. It explained that "While there is now a greater political will . . . to deal with discrimination and violence . . . the policies adopted and the measures taken . . . have been ineffective and have fostered a climate of impunity and lack of confidence in the justice system. . . ."[195] It explained that Mexico had not fulfilled its article 5(a) obligations: "even the campaigns aimed at preventing violence . . . have focused not on promoting social responsibility, change in social and cultural patterns of conduct of men and women and women's dignity, but on making potential victims responsible for their own protection by maintaining traditional cultural stereotypes."[196] Thus, not only had Mexico failed to adopt positive measures to end stereotyping, but also its agents and officials had entrenched stereotypes. The Committee made a number of recommendations on how Mexico might address the situation of violence against women,[197] including the implementation of "a global and integrated response, a strategy aimed at transforming existing sociocultural patterns, especially with regard to eradicating the notion that gender violence is inevitable."[198]

* * *

The Ciudad Juárez inquiry is a significant development in international women's rights law. Yet, an opportunity was missed to fully elaborate the wrong of gender stereotyping and its linkages to violence. This section considers how the Women's Committee might have developed its reasoning around the stereotyping issue, and what recommendations it might have issued to address this wrong. This section builds on an amicus brief submitted by the authors and the Center for Justice and International Law (CEJIL) in *Campo Algodonero: Claudia Ivette González, Esmeralda Herrera Monreal, and Laura Berenice Ramos Monárrez v. Mexico*,[199] arguing for the naming of the operative gender stereotypes, the exposure of their harm, and a finding that they constitute a form of discrimination.[200]

The Women's Committee named gender stereotyping as a wrong when it noted that: the Ciudad Juárez situation was "founded in a culture of violence and discrimination that is based on women's alleged inferiority;"[201] Mexico had made "potential victims responsible for their own protection by maintaining cultural stereotypes;"[202] and, Mexico had perpetuated a "stereotyped view of men's and women's social roles."[203] However, the Committee did not identify the operative gender stereotypes that facilitated gender-based violence against women in Ciudad Juárez, in the state of Chihuahua.

In order to expose those stereotypes, the Women's Committee might have asked: what are the attributes, characteristics and roles ascribed to the women of Ciudad Juárez? In this connection, it could have linked women's alleged "inferiority" to the sex stereotype that *women are subordinate beings*, which suggests that men can treat women as they see fit, including subjecting them to violence. The Committee could have linked Mexico's practice of blaming victims[204] to the sexual stereotype that *women should dress modestly*, which implies that an "immodestly" dressed woman is responsible for her own violent encounter. It could have linked stereotypical views of sex roles to the stereotype that *women should be wives, mothers, and homemakers* and, therefore, they ought not to be working outside the home or, for example, frequenting bars.

Perhaps, most significantly, the Women's Committee could have named the compounded stereotype that *poor, young, migrant women are inferior to men and other subgroups of women* and, therefore, once their value has been used up, they can be discarded like waste.[205] State authorities in Mexico, specifically in Ciudad Juarez, have perpetuated the compounded stereotype that poor, young, migrant women are inferior and subordinate to men. In this instance, it is not just attributes, characteristics or roles associated with a woman's sex or gender that make a poor, young, migrant woman inferior (a gender stereotype); it is also the attributes, characteristics and roles associated with her age, race, socioeconomic status, type of employment and, for example, her status as a migrant (a compounded stereotype). Usage of this stereotype implies that state authorities do not have to treat the subgroup of poor, young, migrant women as having intrinsic and equal worth; this subgroup is subordinate and inferior to men and other subgroups of women. The connotation of inferiority further indicates that state authorities do not consider women belonging to this subgroup to be important and valuable members of society. For example, it has been explained that Mexico's inadequate response to gender-based violence against women in Ciudad Juárez has been fuelled by stereotypical beliefs that devalue women: "The arrogant behaviour and obvious indifference shown by some state officials in regard to these cases leave the impression that many of the crimes were deliberately never investigated for the sole reason that *the victims were 'only' young girls with no particular social status and who therefore were regarded as expendable.*"[206]

In order to foster understanding of how victims were wronged by these gender stereotypes, the Women's Committee could have analyzed the contexts within which they operated and the means by which they have been perpetuated and how they might be eliminated. Taking as an example the compounded stereotype that poor, young, migrant women are inferior, the Committee could have determined whether this stereotype is socially pervasive or persistent in Ciudad Juárez and explained how it facilitates the conditions for the social stratification and subordination of women. For example, the Committee could have paid more attention to the broader contextual factors, such as the fact that the operative stereotype is perpetuated through the laws and the legal culture in Chihuahua that enforces gender stereotypes and promotes a climate of impunity around women's subordinate status. The Civil Code of Chihuahua, for instance, provides that husbands should nourish and financially provide for their families and administer marital property,[207] with the implication that women are not worthy or capable of fulfilling, and should therefore not be allowed to perform, such roles. Such laws establish a situation of de jure dependency for women,[208] foster women's inferiority and economic subordination, and promote unequal power relations between women and men. The perpetuation of this stereotype must also be considered in the broader context of a socially pervasive culture of misogyny and discrimination in the state of Chihuahua that has condoned gender-based violence against women, including systemic abduction, rape, and murder, for more than a decade. The physical and mental suffering of the victims of Ciudad Juárez is indicative of a type of violence based on their domination and humiliation as young women.

Evidence of the perpetuation of the sex stereotype that women are inferior and subordinate to men can also be found in the conduct and inaction of state authorities. The State's grossly inadequate response to gender-based violence in Ciudad Juárez, and the resulting climate of impunity, has reflected and perpetuated the view that such violence is not a serious crime because, according to the stereotype, poor, young, migrant women are inferior and less valuable than men (and other subgroups of women), and therefore crimes against them are lesser crimes that do not warrant the State's attention. For example, it has been explained that only 20 percent of the murder cases have gone to trial and resulted in convictions, leaving the overwhelming majority of cases unresolved and unpunished.[209] In addition, one report has indicated that local authorities in Ciudad Juárez have treated violent crimes against women as private and common violence, not recognizing the existence of a persistent pattern of violence against women that has deeper roots based on discrimination and gender stereotyping.[210] Significantly, there has been no real attempt to collect and systematize information and data concerning gender violence.

Ciudad Juárez's rapidly changing socioeconomic landscape and the vulnerability of victims have further perpetuated the stereotype that poor, young, migrant women are inferior and subordinate to men. Following explosive growth of the *maquiladora* industry, Ciudad Juárez has developed into an unstable, exploitative environment with a high rate of migration and illicit/criminal activity, including trafficking in drugs and women. Many of the victims of gender-based violence have migrated to Ciudad Juárez in search of employment. In contrast to the majority of women in the state of Chihuahua, who have traditionally conformed to prescriptive sex role stereotypes, victims of violence have tended to occupy a significant space in the labor market. Owing to their sex, age, socioeconomic status, ethnicity, and migrant status, most, if not all, victims have been marginalized members of the Ciudad Juárez community. However, all women—young and old, migrant, local or otherwise—share a subordinate position in society.

The contextual factors described above have enabled women—specifically, the subgroup of women with the lowest socioeconomic and cultural standing in Ciudad Juárez—to be targeted as victims of gender-based violence. Perpetuation of the compounded stereotype of young, poor, migrant women as inferior has resulted in discrimination and violence against them. It has meant that crimes against this particular subgroup have not elicited a significant response from state authorities, which, in turn, has fed the spiral of violence and impunity in Ciudad Juárez.

In its report, the Women's Committee might have described how the application, enforcement, or perpetuation of the operative gender stereotypes harmed the victims of Ciudad Juárez, including how it enabled and/or justified violence against them. Again, taking the example of the operative compounded stereotype, the Committee could have described how this stereotype diminished the dignity of poor women by constructing them as a subgroup of women that lacks intrinsic worth. The Committee could have explained how this stereotype burdened poor women with violence, by suggesting that, once their value had been used up, they could be discarded—specifically, abducted, raped, and/or murdered—and that, because these women were no longer valuable, it was not considered incumbent upon the state to investigate, punish, or remedy the crimes against them. The Committee could have also described how this stereotype enabled the marginalization of an already vulnerable group: it entrenched the subordination of poor, young, migrant women in all sectors of the Ciudad Juárez community; enabled pervasive and persistent discrimination against them; and, for example, denied them legal recourse for the injustices they suffered.

The Women's Committee missed an important opportunity to articulate Mexico's obligations to address gender stereotyping by its three branches of government. In its findings, the Committee could have been more explicit that the three branches of government are obligated, under articles 2(f), 5(a), and 15(1) of the Women's Convention, to eliminate gender stereotyping that wrongs women, and that impedes women's equality of and before the law. In this connection, the Committee could have stressed that Mexico's agents and officials must not perpetuate gender stereotypes by neglecting their state duties toward women. As an example of what state agents and officials should not do, the Committee could have emphasized the stereotypical statements of Mr. González Rascón, former Attorney General for the state of Chihuahua, and Mr. Parra Molina, a criminologist contracted by the Mexican government, which attributed the violence to women's lifestyles. Parra Molina stated that for women to be out at night is "'like putting a caramel in the door of an elementary school.' When somebody gobbles them up, like children with candy, at least the source of the tawdry temptation is destroyed."[211] Consistent with this comment, the former Attorney General observed: "it's very hard to go out on the street when it's raining and not get wet."[212]

Regarding the Convention's article 2(e) obligations, the Committee could have explained that Mexico is required to eliminate gender stereotyping by non-state actors, such as the *maquiladoras*, that facilitates violence against women. For example, the Committee could have explained that the Convention obligates Mexico to address socially pervasive *maquiladora* practices that increase women's vulnerability to gender-based violence through the perpetuation of stereotypes of women as docile and submissive[213] and as sexual objects of men.[214]

In finding a violation of article 2 of the Women's Convention,[215] the Committee could have highlighted Mexico's violation of paragraph (f) of that provision. More specifically, it might have explained that Chihuahua's laws, policies, and practices made a difference in treatment on the basis of the stereotype, among others, that poor, young, migrant women are inferior. For example, the Committee could have described how use of this stereotype sends a disturbing message that young, poor, migrant women lack intrinsic and equal worth. In so doing, it suggests that the state does not consider women belonging to this subgroup to be important or valued members of the community. In contrast, however, Chihuahua's laws, policies, and practices do not stereotype poor, young, migrant men in the same way. While men in this particular subgroup may be considered inferior to other subgroups of men in the community, they are still treated as superior to this particular subgroup of women.

The Women's Committee might have further explained that the differential treatment resulting from the enforcement of this stereotype had the purpose or effect of impairing or nullifying the equal recognition, enjoyment, or exercise by women of the rights to nondiscrimination and equality, and the right to be free of gender-based violence. The Committee could have further noted that the construction of this subgroup of women as inferior led to the denial of women's other human rights and fundamental freedoms, including women's right to be free of gender-based violence. It might have also stated explicitly that gender stereotyping that facilitates gender-based violence against women, especially egregious forms of violence, is never justified under the Women's Convention.

In its report, the Committee could have made specific recommendations on how Mexico could tackle the structural nature of the problem of gender stereotyping in Ciudad Juárez, and Mexico generally. In this connection, the Committee could have urged Mexico, among other things, to

- issue a public statement acknowledging and apologizing for its stereotyping of young, poor, migrant victims as inferior and the role this stereotyping played in facilitating gender-based violence against them;
- review its laws, policies, and practices and their application by the criminal justice system with a view to eradicating the operative gender stereotypes that have facilitated the murder, rape, and the disappearance of women in Ciudad Juárez; and,
- sensitize its agents and officials through, for example, training programs to the dangers and wrongs of gender stereotyping, emphasizing the importance of transforming the climate of gender

stereotyping in its legal system, which impedes women from realizing equality of and before the law.

As this discussion of the Ciudad Juárez inquiry shows, naming the operative gender stereotypes; identifying their forms, their contexts, their
means of perpetuation, and means of elimination; describing the ways
in which they harmed the women of Ciudad Juárez; articulating Mexico's obligations to eliminate wrongful gender stereotypes; and identifying such gender stereotyping as a form of discrimination against women
and as a violation of their other human rights and fundamental freedoms, would have enabled the Committee to significantly strengthen its
approach to this egregious problem.

Chapter 6
Moving Forward with the Elimination of Gender Stereotyping

Our working hypothesis is that abolishing wrongful forms of gender stereotyping is essential to the elimination of all forms of discrimination against women, their realization of substantive equality, and their exercise of their other human rights and fundamental freedoms. If this hypothesis is correct, then state and non-state actors need to give greater priority to overcoming the obstacles that impede the elimination of wrongful gender stereotyping. As the transnational legal perspectives offered in this book demonstrate, treating women according to their individual needs, abilities, priorities, and circumstances, and not according to stereotypical generalizations of what it means to be a woman, has contributed to their emancipation and their exercise of their human rights and fundamental freedoms.

This book is only a beginning of a transnational conversation on how to eliminate wrongful gender stereotyping. It is by no means comprehensive. Its aim is to be suggestive of the kinds of debates among nations, among disciplines, and across sectors that are needed to address the pernicious effects of wrongful gender stereotyping. An agenda for future research might include greater understanding of how societies stereotype different subgroups of women, how women stereotype each other, how stereotypes of men harm women, and vice versa, and how the price of prejudice against women harms societies. More needs to be understood about how seemingly innocuous stereotyping enables more egregious violations of women's rights such as sexual torture and disappearance. More needs to be done to implement programs to eliminate stereotyping, such as those of the Irish Equality Authority,[1] and to assess their effectiveness.

As state and non-state actors move forward with the elimination of gender stereotyping, it is important to take stock of what has been learned about the role of transnational law in addressing the challenge of wrongful gender stereotyping, and what might be helpful to know in setting the agenda for its elimination. Important progress has been

made toward the goal of eliminating wrongful forms of gender stereotyping. Stereotyping is now prohibited through a range of human rights
treaties.[2] Courts and international human rights treaty bodies are beginning to identify wrongful gender stereotyping,[3] and in some cases
have explicitly held that it violates constitutional and human rights.[4]
Moreover, an international consensus is emerging on the importance of
combating wrongful gender stereotyping in order to achieve the elimination of all forms of discrimination against women, and ensure substantive equality and the exercise of women's other human rights and
fundamental freedoms.[5]

Understanding of unjust gender stereotyping and of the multifaceted
ways in which it wrongs women and men has improved, particularly in
some sectors.[6] The parallel growth in understanding gender and gender
identities has also been significant.[7] There is now greater recognition of
how gender operates as a social stratifier,[8] and how it interacts with other
traits to subordinate different subgroups of women.[9] The combination
of the two bodies of knowledge about stereotypes and gender identities has produced greater appreciation of the various forms of gender
stereotypes, including sex, sexual, sex role or compounded stereotypes,
and how their application, enforcement, and perpetuation can subordinate women.

In addition to identifying the various forms of gender stereotyping,
it is also helpful to examine the contexts in which they take place. An
examination of the contexts helps us to understand the reasons for the
pervasiveness of gender stereotyping across sectors and its persistence
over time, and to find clues of appropriate measures to eliminate its
practice. An approach to analyzing context is to understand the individual factors, such as cognitive and behavioral factors, situational factors such as predisposing conditions that operate in different sectors of
social activity, and broader factors such as cultural, religious, economic,
and legal factors.

Understanding the individual, situational, or broader social factors
that enable the perpetuation of gender stereotypes also helps in determining how they can be dismantled. The stereotyping from which
women seek to escape might be due to prescriptive expectations of them
as homemakers that their teachers had of them early in their lives. If this
is the case, teachers need to be trained to expect more of women, for
example to encourage them to take leadership positions in school and
wider society. It might be necessary for a critical mass of women to exist
in some sectors before stereotypes can be dismantled in those sectors.
Temporary special measures (affirmative action) might be appropriate
to bring together a critical number of women needed to achieve this
goal.[10]

Significant research on stereotypes has been applied to determine how gender stereotypes wrong women in different sectors, such as employment.[11] The lessons learned from the application of the psychological research to understand how stereotypes operate, for instance, to deny promotion in employment,[12] might well be applicable to other sectors, such as removing stereotypes that inhibit women's access to health services. There are also lessons learned from legal research on how stereotypes of women deny them equal protection of the law in certain situations, such as in divorce,[13] which might be applicable to other situations, such as equal inheritance rights.

Broader cultural, religious, economic, or legal factors help to entrench gender stereotypes, in part due to how they reflect patriarchal values. Where prevailing stereotypes are challenged, they can reemerge in the biased application of a new law because judges are often influenced by the same stereotypical thinking as members of the dominant society in which they enjoy their status and authority. It has been seen that this problem can be addressed where there is the ability to appeal decisions to an enlightened superior court[14] or a regional human rights treaty body.[15]

In order to tackle the pervasiveness across sectors and persistence over time of gender stereotypes, more than the ability to appeal decisions is needed. Naming the stereotype, identifying its form, exposing its harm, and developing appropriate remedies for its elimination are all necessary to move toward the eradication of a gender stereotype. Naming a gender stereotype, identifying its form, and exposing its harm are critical to making it recognizable, and therefore legally cognizable, that is, able to be judicially examined. Naming a stereotype is necessary in much the same way that a medical diagnosis is required before treatment can be applied.

The cases and reports examined in this book demonstrate that certain forms of gender stereotyping can have egregious effects on women, as well as on men, children, and society more generally. The application, enforcement, or perpetuation of gender stereotypes in laws, policies, or practices can harm women in profound ways, including through the denial of benefits, the imposition of burdens, or degrading them, diminishing their dignity, or otherwise marginalizing them. The application, enforcement, or perpetuation of gender stereotypes can also constitute a form of discrimination against women, impairing or nullifying the recognition, enjoyment or exercise by women, on a basis of equality of men and women, of human rights, and fundamental freedoms.[16]

Research has shown that, while some stereotypes have disappeared, gender stereotypes have remained extremely resistant to change.[17] Gender stereotypes have proven resistant to change, not just in some, but in all regions of the world. Gender stereotyping is a complex social and psychological phenomenon, involving a diverse range of state and non-state actors with varied reasons for stereotyping, and with different levels of awareness that they are applying, enforcing, or perpetuating stereotypes. Moreover, reasons for the resilience of gender stereotyping may vary in different regions, countries, and communities. There are numerous explanations of why wrongful gender stereotyping remains a steadfast obstacle to the elimination of all forms of discrimination against women, their realization of substantive equality, and their exercise of other human rights and fundamental freedoms.

Explanations include that gender stereotypes can help us to understand and process sex and gender-based differences between men and women. For example, girls wear feminine pink, whereas boys wear masculine blue. Stereotypes can provide stability, predictability, and certainty in gender roles and relations. Explanations include the persistent stereotype of women as "the weaker sex," or, as has been explained, "one more 'scientific' story of female fragility."[18] This explanation of women's fragility has been applied in the health sector as a reason to deny women the ability to make decisions about whether to consent to certain medical treatments.[19] Uncovering and understanding explanations of wrongful gender stereotypes enable identification of obstacles that impede their elimination. Once obstacles are identified, it is possible to work toward overcoming them and, through that process, eliminate gender stereotypes and other forms of discrimination against women.

Another explanation for the continued resilience of wrongful gender stereotyping is that, even when societies have identified harmful or discriminatory treatment of women based on gender stereotypes, they have been reluctant to eliminate them in part due to the existence of gender hierarchies. Those occupying positions of social, religious, economic, and other power (typically men), and those who have been largely responsible for the application, enforcement, and perpetuation of gender stereotypes (typically men), demonstrate unwillingness to eliminate gender stereotypes when it is not in their best interest to change the status quo. They may prefer perpetuation of their own privilege and authority, which often necessitates the use of hostile stereotyping of women. This may be the case even when they know that women can contribute in significant ways, and that denial of these contributions can be detrimental to the wider interests and justice of their societies.

Often hostile stereotyping is used to "keep women in their place" when they seek emancipation, when they move outside the stereotypical perceptions of their traditional roles, for example when they run for public office. It is also appreciated that hostile stereotyping is used when certain subgroups of women, such as immigrant women or women from ethnic minority groups, move into occupations and vocations that were formerly filled by women of a dominant group.

Yet, despite the progress made in finding that the application of gender stereotypes violates women's and men's rights,[20] courts and human rights treaty bodies are still generally reluctant to find that resort to gender stereotypes constitutes discrimination[21] or violates other human rights.[22] It would help if advocates before courts and human rights treaty bodies make the harms of gender stereotyping in their cases more explicit. This book suggests that the use of a more coherent methodology to address gender stereotyping would be helpful in presenting arguments, and in proposing and drafting remedial judgments. This book has sought to explain how state and non-state actors might take steps to

- name operative gender stereotypes, identify their forms, contexts, and means of perpetuation, and describe the ways in which they harm women;
- articulate States Parties' normative obligations to eliminate gender stereotypes, and determine whether gender stereotyping violates women's rights, such as their privacy rights or their rights to be free from degrading treatment, or whether it constitutes a form of discrimination; and, if so,
- devise remedies for the individual whose rights were violated, and to address the structural nature of the stereotype, perhaps through the use of temporary special measures or programs of affirmative action.

The role of the Women's Committee in articulating and applying a coherent methodology is key to dismantling wrongful gender stereotyping. The Committee can articulate the nature and scope of States Parties' normative obligations to eliminate gender stereotyping through its mandates to issue Concluding Observations based on its examination of States Parties' periodic progress reports; develop General Recommendations that elaborate the content and meaning of the *Convention on the Elimination of All Forms of Discrimination against Women* ("Women's Convention" or "Convention"; see Appendix A); consider communications from those individuals in countries that have ratified the Optional Protocol to the Convention on the Elimination of All Forms of Discrimination against Women ("Optional Protocol"; see Appendix B); and, undertake inquiries into grave or systematic violations. Through its Concluding Observations, the Committee can clarify and provide an authoritative interpretation of the obligations that States Parties have to eliminate wrongful gender stereotyping in a particular situation. Under the communication and inquiry procedures of the Optional Protocol, the Committee can apply the Convention to determine whether gender stereotyping has constituted a form of discrimination against women, contrary to article 2(f), and whether it otherwise violates women's rights under article 5(a) to be free from prejudices and practices that are based on the inferiority of women or on their stereotyped roles.

These procedures can be used to name gender stereotypes, elaborate consequent wrongs, give concrete meaning to States Parties' obligations, determine the existence of discrimination and/or other violations based on gender stereotyping, and remedy the individual and structural wrongs of offensive stereotyping. Significantly, these procedures that allow the Women's Committee to apply the Convention to specific instances of gender stereotyping can also highlight facts and contextual information that States Parties can apply to dismantle gender stereotypes.

In order for all the players attempting to apply the Women's Convention to eliminate all forms of discrimination against women, and to ensure their exercise of their human rights and fundamental freedoms, clearer guidance on the obligations to eliminate wrongful gender stereotyping would helpful. A useful way to achieve this goal would be for the Women's Committee to craft a General Recommendation on the nature and scope of obligations under articles 2(f) and 5(a) of the Convention, and to elaborate how these articles interact with other Convention obligations. Guidance through a General Recommendation would enhance understanding and application of these provisions domestically and internationally. Where the nature and scope of the treaty obligation are more fully understood, courts and treaty bodies might be more likely to rule that gender stereotyping is a form of discrimination. A General Recommendation might make clear that where stereotype-disconfirming information is provided, the dismantling of stereotypes is generally accelerated.[23] As a result, there might be a more concerted effort by all players to identify the harms of gender-based judgments, and to provide information that disconfirms wrongful stereotypes.

The Committee has an opportunity to leverage its position as the international human rights treaty body responsible for monitoring compliance with the Women's Convention, to raise awareness of transnational approaches to eliminating wrongful gender stereotyping. Of particular importance is the need to foster understanding of how different States Parties have dismantled gender stereotypes, overcoming challenges of gender stereotypes that are socially pervasive and persistent. One approach is to examine how domestic courts have found that gender stereotyping is unlawful discrimination or otherwise violates legal protections of women's constitutional and human rights. In this connection, one former Committee member, Savitri Goonesekere, has suggested that the Committee, in preparing its Concluding Observations, "seek more information on . . . national case law, and reflect further on the potential for both women victims of discrimination and their lawyers and judges to use the Convention and the Committee's general recommendations in the domestic Courts."[24] She further explained: "Specific reference to case law in [Concluding Observations] can help to expand the scope for integrating CEDAW standards in domestic courts, as well as legislation and policy, and stimulate a 'traveling jurisprudence' on women's rights that can fertilize domestic law in other jurisdictions of States Parties to the Convention."[25]

The Women's Committee's composition of experts in the field of women's rights, drawn from diverse regional and disciplinary backgrounds and experiences, allows it to act as a mirror. The Committee can reflect gender stereotyping practices in ways that allow States Parties to see the wrongful nature of the practice. In addition, in entering into dialogue with States Parties on their periodic progress reports, individual Committee members can explore how the experiences of eliminating wrongful gender stereotyping in one country or sector might be applied to another country or sector. The Committee members can thereby provide insights into the gender stereotyping phenomenon.

Responding to the challenge of dismantling wrongful gender stereotyping is not limited to the Women's Committee. The specialized agencies and offices of the United Nations, such as the World Health Organization, International Labour Organization, and UN High Commissioner for Refugees, can play significant roles in reporting to the Committee how gender stereotypes operate to deny women their rights in their areas of responsibility.[26] States Parties implementing the Convention and reporting on the progress they have made domestically are also key players.[27] Nongovernmental organizations monitoring observance of the Women's Convention domestically and internationally, including their submission of shadow reports to the Committee, and their use of the communication and inquiry procedures under the Optional Protocol, are also essential. These organizations can be significant in naming gender stereotypes, identifying their harms, and explaining both how the stereotypes violate women's rights and what might be effective remedies for these violations.

Understanding different experiences of gender stereotyping is important, because it can help us break free of our own social and cultural conditioning, to identify and move beyond our stereotypical understanding of different people of the world.[28] It has been explained that "What makes it possible for us to genuinely judge, to move beyond our private idiosyncrasies and preferences, is our capacity to achieve an 'enlargement of mind.' We do this by taking different perspectives into account. This is the path out of the blindness of our subjective private conditions. The more views we are able to take into account, the less likely we are to be locked into one perspective. . . . It is the capacity for 'enlargement of mind' that makes autonomous, impartial judgment possible."[29]

In this sense, state and non-state actors can help to enlarge the global consciousness of the wrongs of gender stereotyping and appropriate measures for their elimination. This can assist in challenging dominant, stereotypical versions of social reality by illuminating the sheer diversity of women's actual needs, abilities, interests and priorities.[30] This, in turn, can motivate and inspire state and non-state actors to reject measures that perpetuate gender stereotypes in favor of those that accommodate the actual realities of women's diverse characteristics shaped by their various experiences.

Appendix A. The Convention on the Elimination of All Forms of Discrimination against Women

The States Parties to the Present Convention,

Noting that the Charter of the United Nations reaffirms faith in fundamental human rights, in the dignity and worth of the human person and in the equal rights of men and women,

Noting that the Universal Declaration of Human Rights affirms the principle of the inadmissibility of discrimination and proclaims that all human beings are born free and equal in dignity and rights and that everyone is entitled to all the rights and freedoms set forth therein, without distinction of any kind, including distinction based on sex,

Noting that the States Parties to the International Covenants on Human Rights have the obligation to ensure the equal rights of men and women to enjoy all economic, social, cultural, civil and political rights,

Considering the international conventions concluded under the auspices of the United Nations and the specialized agencies promoting equality of rights of men and women,

Noting also the resolutions, declarations and recommendations adopted by the United Nations and the specialized agencies promoting equality of rights of men and women,

Concerned, however, that despite these various instruments extensive discrimination against women continues to exist,

Recalling that discrimination against women violates the principles of equality of rights and respect for human dignity, is an obstacle to the participation of women, on equal terms with men, in the political, social, economic and cultural life of their countries, hampers the growth of the prosperity of society and the family and makes more difficult the full development of the potentialities of women in the service of their countries and of humanity,

Concerned that in situations of poverty women have the least access to food, health, education, training and opportunities for employment and other needs,

Convinced that the establishment of the new international economic order based on equity and justice will contribute significantly towards the promotion of equality between men and women,

Emphasizing that the eradication of apartheid, all forms of racism, racial discrimination, colonialism, neo-colonialism, aggression, foreign occupation and domination and interference in the internal affairs of States is essential to the full enjoyment of the rights of men and women,

Affirming that the strengthening of international peace and security, the relaxation of international tension, mutual co-operation among all States irrespective of their social and economic systems, general and complete disarmament, in particular nuclear disarmament under strict and effective international control, the affirmation of the principles of justice, equality and mutual benefit in relations among countries and the realization of the right of peoples under alien and colonial domination and foreign occupation to self-determination and independence, as well as respect for national sovereignty and territorial integrity, will promote social progress and development and as a consequence will contribute to the attainment of full equality between men and women,

Convinced that the full and complete development of a country, the welfare of the world and the cause of peace require the maximum participation of women on equal terms with men in all fields,

Bearing in mind the great contribution of women to the welfare of the family and to the development of society, so far not fully recognized, the social significance of maternity and the role of both parents in the family and in the upbringing of children, and aware that the role of women in procreation should not be a basis for discrimination but that the upbringing of children requires a sharing of responsibility between men and women and society as a whole,

Aware that a change in the traditional role of men as well as the role of women in society and in the family is needed to achieve full equality between men and women,

Determined to implement the principles set forth in the Declaration on the Elimination of Discrimination against Women and, for that purpose, to adopt the measures required for the elimination of such discrimination in all its forms and manifestations,

Have agreed on the following:

PART I

ARTICLE I

For the purposes of the present Convention, the term "discrimination against women" shall mean any distinction, exclusion or restriction made on the basis of sex which has the effect or purpose of impairing or nullifying the recognition, enjoyment or exercise by women, irrespective of their marital status, on a basis of equality of men and women, of human rights and fundamental freedoms in the political, economic, social, cultural, civil or any other field.

ARTICLE 2

States Parties condemn discrimination against women in all its forms, agree to pursue by all appropriate means and without delay a policy of eliminating discrimination against women and, to this end, undertake:

(a) To embody the principle of the equality of men and women in their national constitutions or other appropriate legislation if not yet incorporated therein and to ensure, through law and other appropriate means, the practical realization of this principle;

(b) To adopt appropriate legislative and other measures, including sanctions where appropriate, prohibiting all discrimination against women;

(c) To establish legal protection of the rights of women on an equal basis with men and to ensure through competent national tribunals and other public institutions the effective protection of women against any act of discrimination;

(d) To refrain from engaging in any act or practice of discrimination against women and to ensure that public authorities and institutions shall act in conformity with this obligation;

(e) To take all appropriate measures to eliminate discrimination against women by any person, organization or enterprise;

(f) To take all appropriate measures, including legislation, to modify or abolish existing laws, regulations, customs and practices which constitute discrimination against women;

(g) To repeal all national penal provisions which constitute discrimination against women.

ARTICLE 3

States Parties shall take in all fields, in particular in the political, social, economic and cultural fields, all appropriate measures, including legislation, to ensure the full development and advancement of women, for the purpose of guaranteeing them the exercise and enjoyment of human rights and fundamental freedoms on a basis of equality with men.

ARTICLE 4

(1) Adoption by States Parties of temporary special measures aimed at accelerating de facto equality between men and women shall not be considered discrimination as defined in the present Convention, but shall in no way entail as a consequence the maintenance of unequal or separate standards; these measures shall be discontinued when the objectives of equality of opportunity and treatment have been achieved.

(2) Adoption by States Parties of special measures, including those measures contained in the present Convention, aimed at protecting maternity shall not be considered discriminatory.

ARTICLE 5

States Parties shall take all appropriate measures:

(a) To modify the social and cultural patterns of conduct of men and women, with a view to achieving the elimination of prejudices and customary and all other practices which are based on the idea of the inferiority or the superiority of either of the sexes or on stereotyped roles for men and women;

(b) To ensure that family education includes a proper understanding of maternity as a social function and the recognition of the common responsibility of men and women in the upbringing and development of their children, it being understood that the interest of the children is the primordial consideration in all cases.

ARTICLE 6

States Parties shall take all appropriate measures, including legislation, to suppress all forms of traffic in women and exploitation of prostitution of women.

PART II

ARTICLE 7

States Parties shall take all appropriate measures to eliminate discrimination against women in the political and public life of the country and, in particular, shall ensure to women, on equal terms with men, the right:

(a) To vote in all elections and public referenda and to be eligible for election to all publicly elected bodies;

(b) To participate in the formulation of government policy and the implementation thereof and to hold public office and perform all public functions at all levels of government;

(c) To participate in non-governmental organizations and associations concerned with the public and political life of the country.

ARTICLE 8
States Parties shall take all appropriate measures to ensure to women, on equal terms with men and without any discrimination, the opportunity to represent their Governments at the international level and to participate in the work of international organizations.

ARTICLE 9
(1) States Parties shall grant women equal rights with men to acquire, change or retain their nationality. They shall ensure in particular that neither marriage to an alien nor change of nationality by the husband during marriage shall automatically change the nationality of the wife, render her stateless or force upon her the nationality of the husband.

(2) States Parties shall grant women equal rights with men with respect to the nationality of their children.

PART III

ARTICLE 10
States Parties shall take all appropriate measures to eliminate discrimination against women in order to ensure to them equal rights with men in the field of education and in particular to ensure, on a basis of equality of men and women:

(a) The same conditions for career and vocational guidance, for access to studies and for the achievement of diplomas in educational establishments of all categories in rural as well as in urban areas; this equality shall be ensured in pre-school, general, technical, professional and higher technical education, as well as in all types of vocational training;

(b) Access to the same curricula, the same examinations, teaching staff with qualifications of the same standard and school premises and equipment of the same quality;

(c) The elimination of any stereotyped concept of the roles of men and women at all levels and in all forms of education by encouraging coeducation and other types of education which will help to achieve this aim and, in particular, by the revision of textbooks and school programmes and the adaptation of teaching methods;

(d) The same opportunities to benefit from scholarships and other study grants;

(e) The same opportunities for access to programmes of continuing education, including adult and functional literacy programmes, particularly those aimed at reducing, at the earliest possible time, any gap in education existing between men and women;

(f) The reduction of female student drop-out rates and the organization of programmes for girls and women who have left school prematurely;

(g) The same opportunities to participate actively in sports and physical education;

(h) Access to specific educational information to help to ensure the health and well-being of families, including information and advice on family planning.

ARTICLE 11

(1) States Parties shall take all appropriate measures to eliminate discrimination against women in the field of employment in order to ensure, on a basis of equality of men and women, the same rights, in particular:

(a) The right to work as an inalienable right of all human beings;

(b) The right to the same employment opportunities, including the application of the same criteria for selection in matters of employment;

(c) The right to free choice of profession and employment, the right to promotion, job security and all benefits and conditions of service and the right to receive vocational training and retraining, including apprenticeships, advanced vocational training and recurrent training;

(d) The right to equal remuneration, including benefits, and to equal treatment in respect of work of equal value, as well as equality of treatment in the evaluation of the quality of work;

(e) The right to social security, particularly in cases of retirement, unemployment, sickness, invalidity and old age and other incapacity to work, as well as the right to paid leave;

(f) The right to protection of health and to safety in working conditions, including the safeguarding of the function of reproduction.

(2) In order to prevent discrimination against women on the grounds of marriage or maternity and to ensure their effective right to work, States Parties shall take appropriate measures:

(a) To prohibit, subject to the imposition of sanctions, dismissal on the grounds of pregnancy or of maternity leave and discrimination in dismissals on the basis of marital status;

(b) To introduce maternity leave with pay or with comparable social benefits without loss of former employment, seniority or social allowances;

(c) To encourage the provision of the necessary supporting social services to enable parents to combine family obligations with work responsibilities and participation in public life, in particular through promoting the establishment and development of a network of child-care facilities;

(d) To provide special protection to women during pregnancy in types of work proved to be harmful to them.

(3) Protective legislation relating to matters covered in this article shall be reviewed periodically in the light of scientific and technological knowledge and shall be revised, repealed or extended as necessary.

ARTICLE 12

(1) States Parties shall take all appropriate measures to eliminate discrimination against women in the field of health care in order to ensure, on a basis of equality of men and women, access to health care services, including those related to family planning.

(2) Notwithstanding the provisions of paragraph I of this article, States Parties shall ensure to women appropriate services in connection with pregnancy, confinement and the post-natal period, granting free services where necessary, as well as adequate nutrition during pregnancy and lactation.

ARTICLE 13

States Parties shall take all appropriate measures to eliminate discrimination against women in other areas of economic and social life in order to ensure, on a basis of equality of men and women, the same rights, in particular:

(a) The right to family benefits;

(b) The right to bank loans, mortgages and other forms of financial credit;

(c) The right to participate in recreational activities, sports and all aspects of cultural life.

ARTICLE 14

(1) States Parties shall take into account the particular problems faced by rural women and the significant roles which rural women play in the economic survival of their families, including their work in the non-monetized sectors of the economy, and shall take all appropriate

measures to ensure the application of the provisions of the present Convention to women in rural areas.

(2) States Parties shall take all appropriate measures to eliminate discrimination against women in rural areas in order to ensure, on a basis of equality of men and women, that they participate in and benefit from rural development and, in particular, shall ensure to such women the right:

(a) To participate in the elaboration and implementation of development planning at all levels;

(b) To have access to adequate health care facilities, including information, counselling and services in family planning;

(c) To benefit directly from social security programmes;

(d) To obtain all types of training and education, formal and non-formal, including that relating to functional literacy, as well as, inter alia, the benefit of all community and extension services, in order to increase their technical proficiency;

(e) To organize self-help groups and co-operatives in order to obtain equal access to economic opportunities through employment or self employment;

(f) To participate in all community activities;

(g) To have access to agricultural credit and loans, marketing facilities, appropriate technology and equal treatment in land and agrarian reform as well as in land resettlement schemes;

(h) To enjoy adequate living conditions, particularly in relation to housing, sanitation, electricity and water supply, transport and communications.

PART IV

ARTICLE 15

(1) States Parties shall accord to women equality with men before the law.

(2) States Parties shall accord to women, in civil matters, a legal capacity identical to that of men and the same opportunities to exercise that capacity. In particular, they shall give women equal rights to conclude contracts and to administer property and shall treat them equally in all stages of procedure in courts and tribunals.

(3) States Parties agree that all contracts and all other private instruments of any kind with a legal effect which is directed at restricting the legal capacity of women shall be deemed null and void.

(4) States Parties shall accord to men and women the same rights with

regard to the law relating to the movement of persons and the freedom to choose their residence and domicile.

ARTICLE 16

(1) States Parties shall take all appropriate measures to eliminate discrimination against women in all matters relating to marriage and family relations and in particular shall ensure, on a basis of equality of men and women:

(a) The same right to enter into marriage;

(b) The same right freely to choose a spouse and to enter into marriage only with their free and full consent;

(c) The same rights and responsibilities during marriage and at its dissolution;

(d) The same rights and responsibilities as parents, irrespective of their marital status, in matters relating to their children; in all cases the interests of the children shall be paramount;

(e) The same rights to decide freely and responsibly on the number and spacing of their children and to have access to the information, education and means to enable them to exercise these rights;

(f) The same rights and responsibilities with regard to guardianship, wardship, trusteeship and adoption of children, or similar institutions where these concepts exist in national legislation; in all cases the interests of the children shall be paramount;

(g) The same personal rights as husband and wife, including the right to choose a family name, a profession and an occupation;

(h) The same rights for both spouses in respect of the ownership, acquisition, management, administration, enjoyment and disposition of property, whether free of charge or for a valuable consideration.

(2) The betrothal and the marriage of a child shall have no legal effect, and all necessary action, including legislation, shall be taken to specify a minimum age for marriage and to make the registration of marriages in an official registry compulsory.

PART V

ARTICLE 17

(1) For the purpose of considering the progress made in the implementation of the present Convention, there shall be established a Committee on the Elimination of Discrimination against Women (hereinafter referred to as the Committee) consisting, at the time of entry

into force of the Convention, of eighteen and, after ratification of or accession to the Convention by the thirty-fifth State Party, of twenty-three experts of high moral standing and competence in the field covered by the Convention. The experts shall be elected by States Parties from among their nationals and shall serve in their personal capacity, consideration being given to equitable geographical distribution and to the representation of the different forms of civilization as well as the principal legal systems.

(2) The members of the Committee shall be elected by secret ballot from a list of persons nominated by States Parties. Each State Party may nominate one person from among its own nationals.

(3) The initial election shall be held six months after the date of the entry into force of the present Convention. At least three months before the date of each election the Secretary-General of the United Nations shall address a letter to the States Parties inviting them to submit their nominations within two months. The Secretary-General shall prepare a list in alphabetical order of all persons thus nominated, indicating the States Parties which have nominated them, and shall submit it to the States Parties.

(4) Elections of the members of the Committee shall be held at a meeting of States Parties convened by the Secretary-General at United Nations Headquarters. At that meeting, for which two thirds of the States Parties shall constitute a quorum, the persons elected to the Committee shall be those nominees who obtain the largest number of votes and an absolute majority of the votes of the representatives of States Parties present and voting.

(5) The members of the Committee shall be elected for a term of four years. However, the terms of nine of the members elected at the first election shall expire at the end of two years; immediately after the first election the names of these nine members shall be chosen by lot by the Chairman of the Committee.

(6) The election of the five additional members of the Committee shall be held in accordance with the provisions of paragraphs 2, 3 and 4 of this article, following the thirty-fifth ratification or accession. The terms of two of the additional members elected on this occasion shall expire at the end of two years, the names of these two members having been chosen by lot by the Chairman of the Committee.

(7) For the filling of casual vacancies, the State Party whose expert has ceased to function as a member of the Committee shall appoint another expert from among its nationals, subject to the approval of the Committee.

(8) The members of the Committee shall, with the approval of the General Assembly, receive emoluments from United Nations resources

on such terms and conditions as the Assembly may decide, having regard to the importance of the Committee's responsibilities.

(9) The Secretary-General of the United Nations shall provide the
necessary staff and facilities for the effective performance of the functions of the Committee under the present Convention.

ARTICLE 18

(1) States Parties undertake to submit to the Secretary-General of the
United Nations, for consideration by the Committee, a report on the
legislative, judicial, administrative or other measures which they have
adopted to give effect to the provisions of the present Convention and
on the progress made in this respect:

(a) Within one year after the entry into force for the State concerned;
(b) Thereafter at least every four years and further whenever the
Committee so requests.

(2) Reports may indicate factors and difficulties affecting the degree
of fulfilment of obligations under the present Convention.

ARTICLE 19

(1) The Committee shall adopt its own rules of procedure.
(2) The Committee shall elect its officers for a term of two years.

ARTICLE 20

(1) The Committee shall normally meet for a period of not more than
two weeks annually in order to consider the reports submitted in accordance with article 18 of the present Convention.

(2) The meetings of the Committee shall normally be held at United
Nations Headquarters or at any other convenient place as determined
by the Committee.

ARTICLE 21

(1) The Committee shall, through the Economic and Social Council, report annually to the General Assembly of the United Nations on
its activities and may make suggestions and general recommendations
based on the examination of reports and information received from
the States Parties. Such suggestions and general recommendations shall
be included in the report of the Committee together with comments, if
any, from States Parties.

(2) The Secretary-General of the United Nations shall transmit the

reports of the Committee to the Commission on the Status of Women
for its information.

ARTICLE 22

The specialized agencies shall be entitled to be represented at the consideration of the implementation of such provisions of the present Convention as fall within the scope of their activities. The Committee may invite the specialized agencies to submit reports on the implementation of the Convention in areas falling within the scope of their activities.

PART VI

ARTICLE 23

Nothing in the present Convention shall affect any provisions that are more conducive to the achievement of equality between men and women which may be contained:

(a) In the legislation of a State Party; or

(b) In any other international convention, treaty or agreement in force for that State.

ARTICLE 24

States Parties undertake to adopt all necessary measures at the national level aimed at achieving the full realization of the rights recognized in the present Convention.

ARTICLE 25

(1) The present Convention shall be open for signature by all States.

(2) The Secretary-General of the United Nations is designated as the depositary of the present Convention.

(3) The present Convention is subject to ratification. Instruments of ratification shall be deposited with the Secretary-General of the United Nations.

(4) The present Convention shall be open to accession by all States. Accession shall be effected by the deposit of an instrument of accession with the Secretary-General of the United Nations.

ARTICLE 26

(1) A request for the revision of the present Convention may be made at any time by any State Party by means of a notification in writing addressed to the Secretary-General of the United Nations.

(2) The General Assembly of the United Nations shall decide upon the steps, if any, to be taken in respect of such a request.

ARTICLE 27

(1) The present Convention shall enter into force on the thirtieth day after the date of deposit with the Secretary-General of the United Nations of the twentieth instrument of ratification or accession.

(2) For each State ratifying the present Convention or acceding to it after the deposit of the twentieth instrument of ratification or accession, the Convention shall enter into force on the thirtieth day after the date of the deposit of its own instrument of ratification or accession.

ARTICLE 28

(1) The Secretary-General of the United Nations shall receive and circulate to all States the text of reservations made by States at the time of ratification or accession.

(2) A reservation incompatible with the object and purpose of the present Convention shall not be permitted.

(3) Reservations may be withdrawn at any time by notification to this effect addressed to the Secretary-General of the United Nations, who shall then inform all States thereof. Such notification shall take effect on the date on which it is received.

ARTICLE 29

(1) Any dispute between two or more States Parties concerning the interpretation or application of the present Convention which is not settled by negotiation shall, at the request of one of them, be submitted to arbitration. If within six months from the date of the request for arbitration the parties are unable to agree on the organization of the arbitration, any one of those parties may refer the dispute to the International Court of Justice by request in conformity with the Statute of the Court.

(2) Each State Party may at the time of signature or ratification of the present Convention or accession thereto declare that it does not consider itself bound by paragraph I of this article. The other States Parties shall not be bound by that paragraph with respect to any State Party which has made such a reservation.

(3) Any State Party which has made a reservation in accordance with paragraph 2 of this article may at any time withdraw that reservation by notification to the Secretary-General of the United Nations.

ARTICLE 30

The present Convention, the Arabic, Chinese, English, French, Russian and Spanish texts of which are equally authentic, shall be deposited with the Secretary-General of the United Nations.

IN WITNESS WHEREOF the undersigned, duly authorized, have signed the present Convention.

Appendix B. The Optional Protocol to the Convention on the Elimination of All Forms of Discrimination against Women

The States Parties to the Present Protocol,

Noting that the Charter of the United Nations reaffirms faith in fundamental human rights, in the dignity and worth of the human person and in the equal rights of men and women,

Also noting that the Universal Declaration of Human Rights proclaims that all human beings are born free and equal in dignity and rights and that everyone is entitled to all the rights and freedoms set forth therein, without distinction of any kind, including distinction based on sex,

Recalling that the International Covenants on Human Rights Resolution and other international human rights instruments prohibit discrimination on the basis of sex,

Also recalling the Convention on the Elimination of All Forms of Discrimination against Women ("the Convention"), in which the States Parties thereto condemn discrimination against women in all its forms and agree to pursue by all appropriate means and without delay a policy of eliminating discrimination against women,

Reaffirming their determination to ensure the full and equal enjoyment by women of all human rights and fundamental freedoms and to take effective action to prevent violations of these rights and freedoms,

Have agreed as follows:

ARTICLE 1

A State Party to the present Protocol ("State Party") recognizes the competence of the Committee on the Elimination of Discrimination against Women ("the Committee") to receive and consider communications submitted in accordance with article 2.

ARTICLE 2

Communications may be submitted by or on behalf of individuals or groups of individuals, under the jurisdiction of a State Party, claiming to be victims of a violation of any of the rights set forth in the Convention by that State Party. Where a communication is submitted on behalf of individuals or groups of individuals, this shall be with their consent unless the author can justify acting on their behalf without such consent.

ARTICLE 3
Communications shall be in writing and shall not be anonymous. No communication shall be received by the Committee if it concerns a State Party to the Convention that is not a party to the present Protocol.

ARTICLE 4
(1) The Committee shall not consider a communication unless it has ascertained that all available domestic remedies have been exhausted unless the application of such remedies is unreasonably prolonged or unlikely to bring effective relief.

(2) The Committee shall declare a communication inadmissible where:

(a) The same matter has already been examined by the Committee or has been or is being examined under another procedure of international investigation or settlement;

(b) It is incompatible with the provisions of the Convention;

(c) It is manifestly ill-founded or not sufficiently substantiated;

(d) It is an abuse of the right to submit a communication;

(e) The facts that are the subject of the communication occurred prior to the entry into force of the present Protocol for the State Party concerned unless those facts continued after that date.

ARTICLE 5
(1) At any time after the receipt of a communication and before a determination on the merits has been reached, the Committee may transmit to the State Party concerned for its urgent consideration a request that the State Party take such interim measures as may be necessary to avoid possible irreparable damage to the victim or victims of the alleged violation.

(2) Where the Committee exercises its discretion under paragraph 1 of the present article, this does not imply a determination on admissibility or on the merits of the communication.

ARTICLE 6
(1) Unless the Committee considers a communication inadmissible without reference to the State Party concerned, and provided that the

individual or individuals consent to the disclosure of their identity to that State Party, the Committee shall bring any communication submitted to it under the present Protocol confidentially to the attention of the State Party concerned.

(2) Within six months, the receiving State Party shall submit to the Committee written explanations or statements clarifying the matter and the remedy, if any, that may have been provided by that State Party.

ARTICLE 7

(1) The Committee shall consider communications received under the present Protocol in the light of all information made available to it by or on behalf of individuals or groups of individuals and by the State Party concerned, provided that this information is transmitted to the parties concerned.

(2) The Committee shall hold closed meetings when examining communications under the present Protocol.

(3) After examining a communication, the Committee shall transmit its views on the communication, together with its recommendations, if any, to the parties concerned.

(4) The State Party shall give due consideration to the views of the Committee, together with its recommendations, if any, and shall submit to the Committee, within six months, a written response, including information on any action taken in the light of the views and recommendations of the Committee.

(5) The Committee may invite the State Party to submit further information about any measures the State Party has taken in response to its views or recommendations, if any, including as deemed appropriate by the Committee, in the State Party's subsequent reports under article 18 of the Convention.

ARTICLE 8

(1) If the Committee receives reliable information indicating grave or systematic violations by a State Party of rights set forth in the Convention, the Committee shall invite that State Party to cooperate in the examination of the information and to this end to submit observations with regard to the information concerned.

(2) Taking into account any observations that may have been submitted by the State Party concerned as well as any other reliable information available to it, the Committee may designate one or more of its members to conduct an inquiry and to report urgently to the Committee. Where warranted and with the consent of the State Party, the inquiry may include a visit to its territory.

(3) After examining the findings of such an inquiry, the Committee shall transmit these findings to the State Party concerned together with any comments and recommendations.

(4) The State Party concerned shall, within six months of receiving the findings, comments and recommendations transmitted by the Committee, submit its observations to the Committee.

(5) Such an inquiry shall be conducted confidentially and the cooperation of the State Party shall be sought at all stages of the proceedings.

ARTICLE 9

(1) The Committee may invite the State Party concerned to include in its report under article 18 of the Convention details of any measures taken in response to an inquiry conducted under article 8 of the present Protocol.

(2) The Committee may, if necessary, after the end of the period of six months referred to in article 8.4, invite the State Party concerned to inform it of the measures taken in response to such an inquiry.

ARTICLE 10

(1) Each State Party may, at the time of signature or ratification of the present Protocol or accession thereto, declare that it does not recognize the competence of the Committee provided for in articles 8 and 9.

(2) Any State Party having made a declaration in accordance with paragraph 1 of the present article may, at any time, withdraw this declaration by notification to the Secretary-General.

ARTICLE 11

A State Party shall take all appropriate steps to ensure that individuals under its jurisdiction are not subjected to ill treatment or intimidation as a consequence of communicating with the Committee pursuant to the present Protocol.

ARTICLE 12

The Committee shall include in its annual report under article 21 of the Convention a summary of its activities under the present Protocol.

ARTICLE 13

Each State Party undertakes to make widely known and to give publicity to the Convention and the present Protocol and to facilitate access to information about the views and recommendations of the Committee, in particular, on matters involving that State Party.

ARTICLE 14

The Committee shall develop its own rules of procedure to be followed when exercising the functions conferred on it by the present Protocol.

ARTICLE 15

(1) The present Protocol shall be open for signature by any State that has signed, ratified or acceded to the Convention.

(2) The present Protocol shall be subject to ratification by any State that has ratified or acceded to the Convention. Instruments of ratification shall be deposited with the Secretary-General of the United Nations.

(3) The present Protocol shall be open to accession by any State that has ratified or acceded to the Convention.

(4) Accession shall be effected by the deposit of an instrument of accession with the Secretary-General of the United Nations.

ARTICLE 16

(1) The present Protocol shall enter into force three months after the date of the deposit with the Secretary-General of the United Nations of the tenth instrument of ratification or accession.

(2) For each State ratifying the present Protocol or acceding to it after its entry into force, the present Protocol shall enter into force three months after the date of the deposit of its own instrument of ratification or accession.

ARTICLE 17

No reservations to the present Protocol shall be permitted.

ARTICLE 18

(1) Any State Party may propose an amendment to the present Protocol and file it with the Secretary-General of the United Nations. The Secretary-General shall thereupon communicate any proposed amendments to the States Parties with a request that they notify her or him whether they favour a conference of States Parties for the purpose of considering and voting on the proposal. In the event that at least one third of the States Parties favour such a conference, the Secretary-General shall convene the conference under the auspices of the United

Nations. Any amendment adopted by a majority of the States Parties present and voting at the conference shall be submitted to the General Assembly of the United Nations for approval.

(2) Amendments shall come into force when they have been approved by the General Assembly of the United Nations and accepted by a two-thirds majority of the States Parties to the present Protocol in accordance with their respective constitutional processes.

(3) When amendments come into force, they shall be binding on those States Parties that have accepted them, other States Parties still being bound by the provisions of the present Protocol and any earlier amendments that they have accepted.

ARTICLE 19

(1) Any State Party may denounce the present Protocol at any time by written notification addressed to the Secretary-General of the United Nations. Denunciation shall take effect six months after the date of receipt of the notification by the Secretary-General.

(2) Denunciation shall be without prejudice to the continued application of the provisions of the present Protocol to any communication submitted under article 2 or any inquiry initiated under article 8 before the effective date of denunciation.

ARTICLE 20

The Secretary-General of the United Nations shall inform all States of:

(a) Signatures, ratifications and accessions under the present Protocol;

(b) The date of entry into force of the present Protocol and of any amendment under article 18;

(c) Any denunciation under article 19.

ARTICLE 21

(1) The present Protocol, of which the Arabic, Chinese, English, French, Russian and Spanish texts are equally authentic, shall be deposited in the archives of the United Nations.

(2) The Secretary-General of the United Nations shall transmit certified copies of the present Protocol to all States referred to in article 25 of the Convention.

Notes

Introduction

1. Sandra Fredman, *Women and the Law* (Oxford: Clarendon, 1997), 3.
2. Rikki Holtmaat, *Towards* Different *Law and Public Policy: The Significance of Article 5a CEDAW for the Elimination of Structural Gender Discrimination* (The Hague: Reed Business Information, 2004), xii.
3. Ibid.
4. See generally Reva B. Siegel, "Discrimination in the Eyes of the Law: How 'Color Blindness' Discourse Disrupts and Rationalizes Social Stratification," *California Law Review* 88 (2000): 77–118
5. See The Honourable Madame Justice Claire L'Heureux-Dubé, "Beyond the Myths: Equality, Impartiality, and Justice," *Journal of Social Distress and the Homeless* 10 (2001): 87–104, at 101.
6. See William L. F. Felstiner, Richard L. Abel and Austin Sarat, "The Emergence and Transformation of Disputes: Naming, Blaming, Claiming . . . ," *Law & Society Review* 15 (1980–1981): 631–54, at 633, 635–36.
7. See, e.g., *Bend It like Beckham* (about a woman who defied a stereotype of women as feminine, to become a first rate soccer player), directed by Gurinder Chadha (2002; Beverly Hills, Calif.: 20th Century Fox Home Entertainment, 2003); *A League of Their Own* (about a group of women who starred in a baseball league and became the first to join a women's baseball hall of fame), directed by Penny Marshall (1992; Culver City, Calif.: Sony Pictures Home Entertainment, 1997). See also Richard Goldstein, "Dottie Collins, 84, Star Pitcher of Women's Baseball League, Dies," *New York Times*, August 17, 2008, at 20.
8. See Robert Post, "Prejudicial Appearances: The Logic of American Antidiscrimination Law," *California Law Review* 88 (2000): 1–40, at 26.
9. Ibid., at 26–27.
10. See, e.g., Ida Raming, *The Exclusion of Women from the Priesthood: Divine Law or Sex Discrimination*, trans. Norman R. Adams (Metuchen, N.J.: Scarecrow Press, 1976), 5–7, 28–33; Uta Ranke-Heinemann, *Eunuchs for the Kingdom of Heaven: Women, Sexuality and the Catholic Church*, trans. Peter Heinegg (New York: Penguin, 1990), 125–36; Simone M. St. Pierre, *The Struggle to Serve: The Ordination of Women in the Roman Catholic Church* (Jefferson, N.C.: McFarland, 1994), 8–20.
11. See Katharine T. Bartlett, "Only Girls Wear Barrettes: Dress and Appearance Standards, Community Norms, and Workplace Equality," *Michigan Law Review* 92 (1993–1994): 2541–82.
12. Convention on the Elimination of All Forms of Discrimination against Women, Dec. 18, 1979 (entered into force Sept. 3, 1981), 1249 U.N.T.S. 13, reprinted in 19 *I.L.M.* 33 (1980) ("Women's Convention").

13. The term "States Parties" refers to states that have ratified, and acceded or succeeded to, the Women's Convention.

14. Women's Convention, art. 1.

15. Ibid., art. 17.

16. Women's Committee, General Recommendation No. 25: Article 4, Paragraph 1, of the Convention on the Elimination of All Forms of Discrimination against Women, on Temporary Special Measures, UN Doc. A/59/38 (2004), at para. 4 ("General Recommendation No. 25").

17. Ibid., at para. 7.

18. Women's Convention, prmbl. para. 14.

19. Women's Committee, General Recommendation No. 25, para. 10 (emphasis added).

20. Optional Protocol to the Convention on the Elimination of All Forms of Discrimination against Women, Oct. 19, 1999 (entered into force Dec. 22, 2000), G.A. Res. 54/4, UN G.A.O.R., 54th Sess., Supp. No. 49, at 4, UN Doc. A/54/4 (1999), reprinted in *I.L.M.* 281 (2000).

21. See generally Beverly Baines and Ruth Rubio-Marín, eds., *The Gender of Constitutional Jurisprudence* (Cambridge: Cambridge University Press, 2005); Sujit Choudhry, ed., *The Migration of Constitutional Ideas* (Cambridge: Cambridge University Press, 2006); Susan Williams, ed., *Constituting Equality: Gender Equality and Comparative Constitutional Rights* (Cambridge: Cambridge University Press, 2009).

22. Harold Hongju Koh, "Transnational Legal Process," *Nebraska Law Review* 75 (1996): 181–207, at 184; reprinted in Oona A. Hathaway and Harold Hongju Koh, *Foundations of International Law and Politics* (New York: Foundation Press, 2005), 202.

Chapter 1. Understanding Gender Stereotyping

1. See generally Sophia R. Moreau, "The Wrongs of Unequal Treatment," *University of Toronto Law Journal* 54 (2004): 291–326.

2. See generally Michelle O'Sullivan, "Stereotyping and Male Identification: 'Keeping Women in Their Place,'" in Christina Murray, ed., *Gender and the New South African Legal Order* (Kenwyn, South Africa: Juta, 1994), 185–201, at 187.

3. See Richard D. Ashmore and Frances K. Del Boca, "Conceptual Approaches to Stereotypes and Stereotyping," in David L. Hamilton, ed., *Cognitive Processes in Stereotyping and Intergroup Behaviour* (Hillsdale, N.J.: Erlbaum, 1981), 1–35, at 1–2; Arthur G. Miller, "Historical and Contemporary Perspectives on Stereotyping," in Arthur G. Miller, ed., *In the Eye of the Beholder: Contemporary Issues in Stereotyping* (New York: Praeger, 1982), 1–40, at 4; Penelope J. Oakes, S. Alexander Haslam, and John C. Turner, *Stereotyping and Social Reality* (Oxford: Blackwell, 1994), 15; Gordon W. Allport, *The Nature of Prejudice* (Cambridge, Mass.: Addison-Wesley, 1954), 191–92.

4. See Miller, *In the Eye of the Beholder*, note 3; Oakes, Haslam, and Turner, *Stereotyping and Social Reality*, note 3.

5. See Walter Lippmann, *Public Opinion* (1922; repr. New York: Macmillan, 1957), 79–94.

6. Ibid.

7. Ibid., at 90.

8. Ibid., at 3–32.

9. See, e.g., *President of the Republic of South Africa v. Hugo* 1997 (4) SA 1 (CC), at paras. 93 (Mokgoro J., concurring), 80 (Kriegler J., dissenting) (S. Afr., Constitutional Court). See also Moreau, note 1, at 299.

10. *President of the Republic of South Africa v. Hugo*, note 9, at para. 93 (Mokgoro J., concurring).

11. Ibid., at para. 80 (Kriegler J., dissenting).

12. See Moreau, note 1, at 300.

13. For an analysis of statistical stereotypes, see notes 26–35 and accompanying text. See also Kwame Anthony Appiah, "Stereotypes and the Shaping of Identity," *California Law Review* 88 (2000): 41–54, at 47.

14. See e.g., *Paton v. United Kingdom*, App. No. 8416/78, 3 Eur. H.R. Rep. 408 (1980) (European Commission of Human Rights); *R.H. v. Norway*, App. No. 17004/90, 73 Eur. Comm'n H.R. Dec. & Rep. 155 (1992) (European Commission of Human Rights); *Boso v. Italy*, App. No. 50490/99, 2002–VII Eur. Ct. H.R. 451 (European Court of Human Rights).

15. See Rebecca J. Cook and Susannah Howard, "Accommodating Women's Differences under the Women's Anti-Discrimination Convention," *Emory Law Journal* 56 (2007): 1039–91, at 1083–84.

16. See Oakes, Haslam and Turner, note 3, at 1.

17. *Public Prosecutor v. Kota*, [1993] VUSC 8; [1980–1994] Van LR 661 (Vanuatu, Supreme Court), http://www.worldlii.org/vu/cases/VUSC/1993/8.html (accessed Dec. 31, 2008).

18. Ibid. (Downing J.).

19. See generally Kwame Anthony Appiah, "Identity, Authenticity, Survival: Multicultural Societies and Social Reproduction," in Amy Gutmann, ed., *Multiculturalism: Examining the Politics of Recognition* (Princeton, N.J.: Princeton University Press, 1994), 149–64.

20. See Martha Minow, *Making All the Difference: Inclusion, Exclusion, and American Law* (Ithaca, N.Y.: Cornell University Press, 1990), 229–39.

21. Robert Post, "Response to Commentators," *California Law Review* 88 (2000): 119–26, at 120.

22. Ibid.

23. See Jocelynne A. Scutt, *Women and the Law: Commentary and Materials* (Sydney: Law Book, 1990), 60.

24. See, e.g., Appiah, note 13, at 47–52; Joan C. Williams, "*Hibbs* as a Federalism Case; *Hibbs* as a Maternal Wall Case," *University of Cincinnati Law Review* 73 (2004–2005): 365–98, at 387–95; Madeline E. Heilman, "Description and Prescription: How Gender Stereotypes Prevent Women's Ascent up the Organizational Ladder," *Journal of Social Issues* 57 (2001): 657–74; Linda Hamilton Krieger, "The Content of Our Categories: A Cognitive Bias Approach to Discrimination and Equal Employment Opportunity," *Stanford Law Review* 47 (1995): 1161–248; Diana Burgess and Eugene Borgida, "Who Women Are, Who Women Should Be: Descriptive and Prescriptive Gender Stereotyping in Sex Discrimination," *Psychology, Public Policy, and Law* 5 (1999): 665–92.

25. See Appiah, note 13, at 49.

26. Lippmann, note 5, at 16.

27. Ibid., at 88.

28. Ibid., at 95.

29. Ibid.

30. Ibid.

31. Burgess and Borgida, note 24, at 666.

32. See Joan Williams and Nancy Segal, "Beyond the Maternal Wall: Relief for Family Caregivers Who Are Discriminated Against on the Job," *Harvard Women's Law Journal* 26 (2003): 77–162, at 96.

33. See Appiah, note 13, at 47.

34. Ibid.

35. Ibid., at 49.

36. Ibid., at 48.

37. *Yilmaz-Dogan v. The Netherlands*, CERD, Communication No. 1/1984, UN Doc. CERD/C/36/D/1/1984 (1988) (Race Committee).

38. See, e.g., *Din v. Public Prosecutor*, [1964] MLJ 300, 301 (Malay., Federal Court) (Thomson L.P.); *Public Prosecutor v. Emran bin Nasir*, [1987] 1 MLJ 166, 171 (Malay., High Court, Brunei) (Roberts C.J.). See also Women's Center for Change Penang, *Seeking a Better Judicial Process for Sexual Crimes: Background Paper for Dialogue with Penang Judiciary* (Penang: Women's Center for Change Penang, 2007), 18, http://www.wccpenang.org/files/docs/Judiciary_Background_Paper.pdf (accessed Dec. 31, 2008).

39. *R. v. Henry and Manning*, (1968) 53 Cr. App. R. 150 (Austl., Privy Council).

40. Ibid., at 153 (Salmon L.J.).

41. See Taha J. Al'Alwani, "The Testimony of Women in Islamic Law," *American Journal of Islamic Social Sciences* 13 (1996): 173–96.

42. See, e.g., Ida Raming, *The Exclusion of Women from the Priesthood: Divine Law or Sex Discrimination*, trans. Norman R. Adams (Metuchen, N.J.: Scarecrow Press, 1976), 5–7, 28–33; Uta Renke-Heinemann, *Eunuchs for the Kingdom of Heaven: Women, Sexuality and the Catholic Church*, trans. Peter Heinegg (New York: Penguin, 1990), at 125–36; Simone M. St. Pierre, *The Struggle to Serve: The Ordination of Women in the Roman Catholic Church* (Jefferson, N.C.: McFarland, 1994), 8–20.

43. See Scutt, note 23, at 60.

44. Ibid.

45. Williams and Segal, note 32, at 95 (citation omitted). See generally Peter Glick and Susan T. Fiske, "An Ambivalent Alliance: Hostile and Benevolent Sexism as Complementary Justifications of Gender Inequality," *American Psychologist* 56 (2001): 109–18.

46. Williams and Segal, note 32, at 95–96 (citation omitted).

47. See Appiah, note 13, at 51–52.

48. See Burgess and Borgida, note 24, at 666.

49. Appiah, note 13, at 48.

50. See generally Naomi Wolf, *The Beauty Myth* (Toronto: Vintage Canada, 1994).

51. See, e.g., *Jespersen v. Harrah's Operating Co.*, 444 F.3d 1104 (9th Cir. 2006) (U.S., Court of Appeals, Ninth Circuit).

52. See, e.g., *EEOC v. Sage Realty Corp.*, 507 F. Supp. 599 (S.D.N.Y. 1981) (U.S., District Court-Southern District of New York).

53. See Aysan Sev'er, "Patriarchal Pressures on Women's Freedom, Sexuality, Reproductive Health & Women's Co-Optation into Their Own Subjugation," *Women's Health and Urban Life* 4, 1 (May 2005): 27–44, at 31–32.

54. *Price Waterhouse v. Hopkins*, 490 U.S. 228 (1989) (U.S., Supreme Court).

55. Ibid., at 235 (Brennan J.).

56. Ibid.

57. Ibid.

58. Ibid., at 256–58.

59. Ibid., at 250 (emphasis added).

60. Ibid., at 251.

61. Robert Post, "Prejudicial Appearances: The Logic of American Antidiscrimination Law," *California Law Review* 88 (2000): 1–40, at 18.

62. Richard D. Ashmore and Frances K. Del Boca, "Sex Stereotypes and Implicit Personality Theory: Toward a Cognitive-Social Psychological Conceptualization," *Sex Roles* 5 (1979): 219–48, at 222.

63. See Monica Biernat and Diane Kobrynowicz, "A Shifting Standards Perspective on the Complexity of Gender Stereotypes and Gender Stereotyping," in William B. Swann, Jr., Judith H. Langlois, and Lucia Albino Gilbert, eds., *Sexism and Stereotypes in Modern Society: The Gender Science of Janet Taylor Spence* (Washington, D.C.: American Psychological Association, 1999), 75–106, at 76–77.

64. See Diane N. Ruble and Thomas L. Ruble, "Sex Stereotypes," in Miller, *In the Eye of the Beholder*, note 3, 188–252, at 196.

65. Marilynn B. Brewer, "When Stereotypes Lead to Stereotyping: The Use of Stereotypes in Person Perception," in C. Neil Macrae, Charles Stangor, and Miles Hewstone, eds., *Stereotypes and Stereotyping* (New York: Guilford Press, 1996), 254–75, at 254.

66. See Robert Sharpe and Patricia I. McMahon, *The Persons Case: The Origins and Legacy of the Fight for Legal Personhood* (Toronto: Osgoode Society for Canadian Legal History, 2007).

67. See Albie Sachs and Joan Hoff Wilson, *Sexism and the Law: A Study of Male Beliefs and Legal Bias in Britain and the United States* (New York: Free Press, 1979), 1–66, 170–97.

68. See, e.g., *Beatriz Fernandez v. Malaysian Airlines*, [2005] MYFC 12 (Malay., Federal Court).

69. See Minority Staff of H. Comm. on Gov't Reform, 108th Cong., *The Content of Federally Funded Abstinence-Only Education Programs* (Comm. Print 2004), 17; Julie F. Kay and Ashley Jackson, *Sex, Lies, and Stereotypes: How Abstinence-Only Programs Harm Women and Girls* (New York: Legal Momentum, 2008), 20–22.

70. Carole R. McCann and Seung-Kyung Kim, "Introduction," in Carole R. McCann and Seung-Kyung Kim, eds., *Feminist Theory Reader: Local and Global Perspectives* (New York: Routledge, 2003), 12–23, at 14, citing Gayle Rubin, "The Traffic in Women: Notes on the 'Political Economy' of Sex," in Rayna R. Reitner, ed., *Toward an Anthropology of Women* (New York: Monthly Review Press, 1975), 157–210.

71. Dianne Otto, "Lost in Translation: Re-Scripting the Sexed Subjects of International Human Rights Law," in Anne Orford, ed., *International Law and Its Others* (Cambridge: Cambridge University Press, 2006), 318–56, at 319.

72. McCann and Kim, note 70, at 14.

73. Kay Deaux, "An Overview of Research on Gender: Four Themes from 3 Decades," in Swann, Langlois, and Gilbert, eds., note 63, 11–33, at 22.

74. See Rikki Holtmaat, *Towards Different Law and Public Policy: The Significance of Article 5a CEDAW for the Elimination of Structural Gender Discrimination* (The Hague: Reed Business Information, 2004), 85–86.

75. Deaux, note 73, at 21.

76. Women's Convention, art. 17.

77. Women's Committee, General Recommendation No. 25: Article 4, Paragraph 1, of the Convention on the Elimination of All Forms of Discrimination against Women, on Temporary Special Measures, UN Doc. A/59/38 (2004), at para. 8 ("General Recommendation No. 25").

78. *1999 World Survey on the Role of Women in Development* (New York: United Nations, 1999), ix, quoted in Women's Committee, General Recommendation No. 25, at para. 7, note 2.

79. Women's Committee, General Recommendation No. 25, at para. 7, note 2.

80. See Reva B. Siegel, "Discrimination in the Eyes of the Law: How 'Color Blindness' Discourse Disrupts and Rationalizes Social Stratification," *California Law Review* 88 (2000): 77–118, at 82. See generally David B. Brusky, ed., *Social Stratification: Class, Race, and Gender in Sociological Perspective*, 3rd ed. (Boulder, Colo: Westview Press, 2008).

81. See Siegel, note 80.

82. Frances Raday, "Culture, Religion, and CEDAW's Article 5(a)," in Hanna Beate Schöpp-Schilling and Cees Flinterman, eds., *The Circle of Empowerment: Twenty-Five Years of the UN Committee on the Elimination of Discrimination Against Women* (New York: Feminist Press, 2007), 68–85, at 71.

83. Ibid., at 74.

84. See generally Women's Committee, General Recommendation No. 23: Political and Public Life, UN Doc. A/52/38 Rev. 1 at 61 (1997).

85. See *Hoyt v. Florida*, 368 U.S. 57, 62 (1961) (Harlan J.) (U.S., Supreme Court).

86. Constitution of Ireland, 1937.

87. Women's Committee, Concluding Observations: Ireland, CEDAW, UN GAOR, 60th sess., supp. no. 38 (A/60/38) part II (2005) 151, at para. 382.

88. Ibid., at para. 383.

89. See Williams and Segal, note 32.

90. Deborah L. Rhode and Joan C. Williams, "Legal Perspectives on Employment Discrimination" in Faye J. Crosby, Margaret S. Stockdale, and S. Ann Ropp, eds., *Sex Discrimination in the Workplace: Multidisciplinary Perspectives* (Malden, Mass.: Blackwell, 2007), 235–70, at 248 (citation omitted).

91. Yakin Ertürk, "Considering the Role of Men in Agenda Setting: Conceptual and Policy Issues," *Feminist Review* 78 (2004): 3–21, at 7.

92. Sally Engle Merry, *Human Rights and Gender Violence: Translating International Law into Local Justice* (Chicago: University of Chicago Press, 2006), 75.

93. Peter Glick and Susan T. Fiske, "Sexism and other 'Isms': Interdependence, Status, and the Ambivalent Content of Stereotypes," in Swann, Gilbert, and Langlois, note 63, 193–217, at 195 (citations omitted). See also Ruble and Ruble, note 64, at 189, 228 (citations omitted); Minow, note 20, at 228–38.

94. Nancy Fraser, *Justice Interruptus: Critical Reflections on the "Postsocialist" Condition* (New York: Routledge, 1997), 19–21.

95. Ibid., at 19–20.

96. Ibid., at 20.

97. Ibid.

98. See Zanita E. Fenton, "Domestic Violence in Black and White: Racialized Gender Stereotypes in Gender Violence," *Columbia Journal of Gender and Law* 8 (1998–1999): 1–66, at 10–25.

99. Ibid.

100. See notes 68–69 and accompanying text.

101. See David H. Gans, "Stereotyping and Difference: *Planned Parenthood v. Casey* and the Future of Sex Discrimination Law," *Yale Law Journal* 104 (1994–1995): 1875–1906, at 1877; Esther D. Rothblum and Violet Franks, "Introduc-

tion: Warning! Sex Role Stereotypes May Be Hazardous to Your Health," in Violet Franks and Esther D. Rothblum, eds., *The Stereotyping of Women: Its Effects on Mental Health* (New York: Springer, 1983), 3–10 at 4; Anita Cava, "Taking Judicial Notice of Sexual Stereotyping," *Arkansas Law Review* 43 (1990): 27–56, at 34; Ruble and Ruble, note 64, at 194.

102. See Otto, note 71, at 321–29.

103. *Advisory Opinion on the Interpretation of the Convention of 1919 Concerning Employment of Women during the Night*, PCIJ, Ser. A/B, No. 50, at 365 (1932) (Permanent Court of International Justice). Compare *Vasantha R. v. Union of India*, [2001] II L.L.J. 843 (India, High Court of Madras).

104. See Sandra Fredman, *Women and the Law* (Oxford: Clarendon Press, 1997), 304–8 (discussing the effects of protective labor standards of ILO Conventions and the European Community Directives).

105. Otto, note 71, 324.

106. *Muller v. Oregon*, 208 U.S. 412, 422–23 (1908) (Brewer J.) (U.S., Supreme Court). See also Katharine T. Bartlett and Deborah Rhode, *Gender and the Law: Theory, Doctrine and Commentary*, 4th ed. (New York: Aspen Law & Business, 2006), at 42–136 (discussing formal equality in employment); Fredman, note 104, at 67–74 (discussing the evolution of protective labor legislation in Britain); Otto, note 71, at 321–29 (explaining how international law developed international protectionist standards of women in the areas of war, employment, and trafficking).

107. Case C-285/98, *Tanja Kreil v. Federal Republic of Germany*, [2000] E.C.R. I-69; ECJ Jan. 11, 2000, 57 (European Court of Justice), reprinted in Robyn Emerton et al., eds., *International Women's Rights Cases* (London: Cavendish, 2005), 413–19. See generally Marius Pieterse, "Stereotypes, Sameness, Difference and Human Rights: Catch 22?" *South African Public Law* 15 (2001): 93–121, at 109.

108. Case C-285/98, *Tanja Kreil v. Federal Republic of Germany*, note 107, at para. 30. See also *UAW v. Johnson Controls, Inc.*, 499 U.S. 187 (1991) (U.S., Supreme Court).

109. *Anuj Garg and Others v. Hotel Association of India and Others*, (2008) 3 SCC 1 (India, Supreme Court).

110. HCJ 4541/94, *Alice Miller v. Ministry of Defense*, [1995] IsrSC 49(4) 94, [1995–6] IsrLR 178 (Isr., Supreme Court). See also Daphne Barak-Erez, "The Feminist Battle for Citizenship: Between Combat Duties and Conscientious Objection," *Cardozo Journal of Law and Gender* 13 (2006–2007): 531–60.

111. Elsje Bonthuys, "Women's Sexuality in the South African Constitution," *Feminist Legal Studies* 14 (2006): 391–406, at 400, referring to *Jordan v. S.* 2002 (6) SA 642 (CC), at para. 83 (O'Regan and Sachs JJ., dissenting) (S. Afr., Constitutional Court).

112. See Veena Das, "Sexual Violation and Making of the Gendered Subject in Discrimination and Toleration," in George Ulrich and Kirsten Hastrup, eds., *Discrimination and Toleration: New Perspectives* (The Hague: Nijhoff, 2002), 257–74, at 273.

113. *Law & Advocacy for Women in Uganda v. Attorney General of Uganda*, Constitutional Petition Nos. 13/05 and 05/06, [2007] UGCC 1 (Apr. 5, 2007) (Uganda, Constitutional Court).

114. See, e.g., Women's Committee, General Recommendation No. 19: Violence against Women, UN Doc. A/47/38 (1992), at para. 11.

115. See, e.g., Rubin, note 70.

116. *Case Stated by the Director of Public Prosecution (No. 1 of 1993)*, (1993) A. Crim. R. 259 (Austl., Supreme Court of South Australia), summarized in Kathy Mack, "*B v. R.*: Negative Stereotypes and Women's Credibility," *Feminist Legal Studies* 2 (1994): 183–94, at 184–85.

117. *R. v. R.* [1991] 2 All ER 257 at 266, [1991] 2 WLR 1065 at 1074 [English Court of Appeal (Criminal Division)] (1992), 1 AC 599 (1992) appeal denied by the House of Lords (U.K., House of Lords) (Lord Keith of Kinkel citing Lord Lane), reprinted in Emerton et al., note 107, 691–700. See also *C.R. v. United Kingdom*, App. No. 20190/92, Eur. Ct. H.R. (ser. A), No. 335–c; 21 Eur. H.R. Rep. 363 (1995) (European Court of Human Rights) (finding that the decision in *R. v. R.* did not violate the European Convention on Human Rights).

118. *State v. Filipe Bechu*, [1999] FJMC 3, Criminal Case No 79/94 (1999) (Fiji, First Class Magistrate's Court, Levuka), http://www.worldlii.org/fj/cases/FJMC/1999/3.html (accessed Dec. 31, 2008).

119. Ibid.

120. See Gans, note 101, at 1877; Ruble and Ruble, note 64, at 194; Ashmore and Del Boca, note 62, at 21.

121. See Gans, note 101, at 1880.

122. Peter Glick and Susan T. Fiske, "Sex Discrimination: The Psychological Approach," in Crosby, Stockdale, and Ropp, eds., note 90, 155–88, at 161 (citations omitted).

123. *Haines v. Leves*, (1987) 8 N.S.W.L.R. 442, at 458 (Street C.J.), 472–74 (Kirby P.), 477 (Samuels J.A.) (Austl., Court of Appeal of New South Wales).

124. *Leves v. Haines*, (1986) E.O.C. 92–167 (Austl., Equal Opportunity Tribunal of New South Wales), excerpted in Scutt, *Women and the Law*, 63–71, at 70.

125. *Haines v. Leves*, note 123, at 473 (Kirby P.).

126. *Leves v. Haines*, note 124, at 70.

127. *Haines v. Leves*, note 123, at 473 (Kirby P.).

128. *Leves v. Haines*, note 124, at 70.

129. See Fenton, note 98.

130. *Yilmaz-Dogan v. The Netherlands*, note 37.

131. Ibid., at para. 2.2.

132. International Convention on the Elimination of All Forms of Racial Discrimination, Dec. 21, 1965 (entered into force Jan. 4, 1969), 660 U.N.T.S. 195.

133. *Yilmaz-Dogan v. The Netherlands*, note 37, at para. 2.4.

134. Ibid., at para. 9.3.

135. Ibid., at para. 10.

136. Convention on the Rights of Persons with Disabilities, Dec. 13, 2006 (entered into force May 3, 2008), G.A. Res. 61/106, UN Doc. A/61/611 (2006). See also Inter-American Convention on the Elimination of All Forms of Discrimination Against Persons with Disabilities, Jun. 7, 1999 (entered into force Sept. 21, 2001), AG/RES. 1608 (XXIX-O/99) (requiring States Parties to increase "public awareness through educational campaigns aimed at eliminating prejudices, stereotypes, and other attitudes that jeopardize the right of persons to live as equals, thus promoting respect for and coexistence with persons with disabilities:" art. 3(2)(c)).

137. Convention on the Rights of Persons with Disabilities, note 136, art. 8(1)(b).

138. *E.B. v. France,* Appl. No. 43546/02, Jan. 22, 2008, at paras. 96–98 (European Court of Human Rights).

139. See generally Deborah A. Widiss, Elizabeth L. Rosenblatt, and Douglas NeJaime, "Exposing Sex Stereotypes in Recent Same-Sex Marriage Jurisprudence," *Harvard Journal of Law & Gender* 30 (2007): 461–505.

140. Glick and Fiske, note 122, at 159.

141. See The Honourable Madame Justice Claire L'Heureux-Dubé, "Beyond the Myths: Equality, Impartiality, and Justice," *Journal of Social Distress and the Homeless* 10 (2001): 87–104 at 89 (citations omitted).

142. Ibid., at 89.

143. Rhode and Williams, note 90, at 245; Glick and Fiske, note 122, at 157–58.

144. See Ruble and Ruble, note 64, at 218–26 (citations omitted).

145. See ibid., at 215–17 (citations omitted).

146. Ibid., at 228–32 (citations omitted).

147. Glick and Fiske, note 122, at 156.

148. Ibid., at 165–75.

149. See Susan T. Fiske et al., "Social Science Research on Trial: Use of Sex Stereotyping Research in *Price Waterhouse v. Hopkins,*" *American Psychologist* 46 (1991): 1049–60, at 1050 (citations omitted); Biernat and Kobrynowicz, note 63, at 96 (citations omitted); American Psychological Association, "In the Supreme Court of the United States: *Price Waterhouse v. Ann B. Hopkins*; Amicus Curiae Brief for the American Psychological Association," *American Psychologist* 46 (1991): 1061–70, at 1067–68.

150. See Fiske et al., note 149, at 1050 (citations omitted).

151. See Rhode and Williams, note 90, at 246–47.

152. Ibid.

153. See Siegel, note 80, at 82.

154. Katharine T. Bartlett, "Tradition, Change, and the Idea of Progress in Feminist Legal Thought," *Wisconsin Law Review* 2 (1995): 303–44, at 305, 313–25. See also Saba Mahmood, *Politics of Piety: The Islamic Revival and the Feminist Subject* (Princeton, N.J.: Princeton University Press, 2005); Madhavi Sunder, "Piercing the Veil," *Yale Law Journal* 112 (2003): 1399–1427; Celestine I. Nyamu, "How Should Human Rights and Development Respond to Cultural Legitimization of Gender Hierarchy in Developing Countries?" *Harvard International Law Journal* 41 (2000): 381–418.

155. Bartlett, note 154, at 305 (emphasis in original).

156. See Siegel, note 80, at 88.

157. See Constance Backhouse, *Petticoats and Prejudice: Women and Law in Nineteenth-Century Canada* (Toronto: Women's Press, 1991); Gerda Lerner, *The Creation of Patriarchy* (Oxford: Oxford University Press, 1986); Farida Shaheed, "The Cultural Articulation of Patriarchy: Legal Systems, Islam and Women," *South Asian Bulletin* 6 (1) (1986): 38–44.

158. See, e.g., *Edwards v. Canada (Attorney General),* [1930] A.C. 124 (Can., Privy Council). See also Sharpe and McMahon, note 66; Sachs and Wilson, note 67, at 38–40.

159. See, e.g., *Breedlove v. Suttles,* 302 U.S. 277 (1937) (U.S., Supreme Court).

160. See, e.g., *Imelda Romualdez-Marcos v. Commission on Elections,* G.R. No. 119976 (Sept. 18, 1995) (Phil., Supreme Court), summarized in Amparita Sta. Maria, *CEDAW Benchbook* (Makati City, Philippines: Ateneo Human Rights Center, 2008), 39–41, www.cedawbenchbook.org/ (accessed Dec. 31, 2008).

161. See, e.g., *Ato del Avellanal v. Peru*, HRC, Communication No. 202/1986, UN Doc. CCPR/C/34/D/202/1986 (1988) (Human Rights Committee); *Morales de Sierra v. Guatemala*, Case 11.625, Inter-Am. C.H.R., Report No. 4/01, OEA/Ser.L/V/II.111, doc. 20 rev. (2001) (Inter-American Commission on Human Rights).

162. See, e.g., *Jex-Blake v. Senatus of the University of Edinburgh*, (1873) 11 M. 784 (U.K., Court of Session), summarized in Sachs and Wilson, note 67, at 14–17.

163. See, e.g., *Bradwell v. Illinois*, 83 U.S. (16 Wall.) 130 (1872) (U.S., Supreme Court); *In re French*, [1905] 37 N.B.R. 359 (Can., New Brunswick Supreme Court).

164. See Uche Ewelukwe, "Post-Colonialism, Gender, Customary Injustice: Widows in African Societies," in Bert Lockwood, ed., *Women's Rights: A Human Rights Quarterly Reader* (Baltimore: Johns Hopkins University Press, 2006), 152–213; Uma Narayan, *Dislocating Cultures: Identities, Traditions, and Third World Feminism* (New York: Routledge, 1997); Celestine Nyamu-Musembi, "Are Local Norms and Practices Fences or Pathways?: The Example of Women's Property Rights," in Abdullahi A. An-Na'im, ed., *Cultural Transformation and Human Rights in Africa* (London: Zed Books, 2002), 126–50.

165. See Courtney W. Howland, "The Challenge of Religious Fundamentalism to the Liberty and Equality Rights of Women: An Analysis Under the United Nations Charter," *Columbia Journal of Transnational Law* 35 (1997): 271–378; Courtney W. Howland, "Safeguarding Women's Political Freedoms Under the ICCPR in the Face of Religious Fundamentalism," in Courtney W. Howland, ed., *Religious Fundamentalisms and the Human Rights of Women* (New York: St. Martin's, 1999), 93–104.

166. See Indira Jaising, ed., *Men's Laws, Women's Lives: Constitutional Perspectives on Religion, Common Law and Culture in South Asia* (New Delhi: Women Unlimited, 2005); Farida Shaheed et al., eds., *Shaping Women's Lives: Law, Practices and Strategies in Pakistan* (Lahore/Karachi: Shirkat Gah, 1998); Lynn Welchman and Sara Hossain, eds., *"Honour": Crimes, Paradigms and Violence against Women* (London: Zed Books, 2005), 1–21; Rebecca J. Cook and Lisa M. Kelly, *Polygyny and Canada's Obligations Under International Human Rights Law* (Ottawa: Department of Justice, Canada, 2006), http://www.justice.gc.ca/eng/dept-min/pub/poly/poly.pdf (accessed Dec. 31, 2008).

167. See Merry, note 92, at 10–16.

168. See Narayan, note 164, at 34, 43–80.

169. See Raday, note 82, at 75.

170. *Lovelace v. Canada*, HRC, Communication No. R.24/1977, UN Doc. CCPR/C/13/D/24/1977 (1981) (Human Rights Committee).

171. See *Lavell v. Canada (Attorney General)*, [1974] S.C.R. 1349 (Can., Supreme Court).

172. International Covenant on Civil and Political Rights, Dec. 16, 1966 (entered into force Mar. 23, 1976), 999 U.N.T.S. 171.

173. See Siegel, note 80, at 88.

174. See Bartlett, note 154, at 305, 313–325.

175. See Erin Cho, "Caught in Confucius' Shadow: The Struggle for Women's Legal Equality in South Korea," *Columbia Journal of Asian Law* 12 (1998): 125–90 (explaining the origins of South Korea's gender role ideology).

176. Howland, "Safeguarding Women's Political Freedoms," note 165, at 97–98. See also Howland, "The Challenge of Religious Fundamentalism," note 165, at 282–324.

177. Gamal I. Serour and Bernard M. Dickens, "Assisted Reproduction Devel-

opments in the Islamic World," *International Journal of Gynecology & Obstetrics* 74 (2001): 187–93, at 188.

178. See Lynn Welchman and Sara Hossain, "Introduction: 'Honour' Rights and Wrong," in Welchman and Hossain, note 166, 1–21, at 6.

179. See Sohail Akbar Warraich, "'Honour Killings' and the Law in Pakistan," in Welchman and Hossain, note 166, 78–110, at 79; Centre for Egyptian Women's Legal Assistance, "'Crimes of Honour' as Violence Against Women in Egypt," in ibid., 137–59, at 140; Aida Touma-Sliman, "Culture, National Minority and the State: Working Against the 'Crime of Family Honour' Within the Palestinian Community in Israel," in ibid., 181–98, at 186.

180. See Welchman and Hossain, note 166, at 4–6; Lama Abu Odeh, "Crimes of Honour and the Construct of Gender in Arab Societies," in Mai Yamani, ed., *Feminism and Islam: Legal and Literary Perspectives* (Ithaca, N.Y.: Ithaca Press, 1996), 141–94, at 141.

181. Welchman and Hossain, note 166, at 4.

182. Zoya Hassan, "Governance and Reform of Personal Laws in India," in Jaising, ed., note 166, 353–73; Asma Jahangir, "The Origins of the MFLO: Reflections for Activism," in Shaheed et al., note 166, 93–103.

183. Raday, note 82, at 71.

184. Ibid.

185. See, e.g., *Bruker v. Marcovitz*, [2007] 3 S.C.R. 607 (Can., Supreme Court). See also Dahlia Eissa, "Constructing the Notion of Male Superiority over Women in Islam: The Influence of Sex and Gender Stereotyping in the Interpretation of the Qur'an and the Implications for a Modernist Exegesis of Rights," WLUML Occasional Paper No. 11 (London: Women Living Under Muslim Laws, 1999), http://www.wluml.org/english/pubs/rtf/occpaper/OCP-11.rtf (accessed Dec. 31, 2008).

186. See Sunder, note 154, at 1425–27.

187. See Cho, note 175; Howland, "Safeguarding Women's Political Freedoms," note 165.

188. See Joan. C. Williams, "Deconstructing Gender," *Michigan Law Review* 87 (1988–1989): 797–845, at 837–43.

189. See Stuart Ewan and Elizabeth Ewan, *Typecasting: On the Arts and Sciences of Human Inequality: A History of Dominant Ideas* (New York: Steven Stories Press, 2006), 1–10; Katharine T. Bartlett, "Only Girls Wear Barrettes: Dress and Appearance Standards, Community Norms, and Workplace Equality," *Michigan Law Review* 92 (1993–1994): 2541–82, at 2551–53.

190. See Mary Joe Frug, "A Postmodern Feminist Legal Manifesto (An Unfinished Draft)," *Harvard Law Review* 105 (1991–1992): 1045–75, at 1051.

Chapter 2. Naming Gender Stereotyping

1. See William L. F. Felstiner, Richard L. Abel, and Austin Sarat, "The Emergence and Transformation of Disputes: Naming, Blaming, Claiming . . . ," *Law & Society Review* 15 (1980–1981): 631–54.

2. Ruth Halperin-Kaddari, *Women in Israel: A State of Their Own* (Philadelphia: University of Pennsylvania Press, 2004), 7.

3. Pierre Bourdieu, "The Force of Law: Toward a Sociology of the Juridical Field," trans. Richard Terdiman, *Hastings Law Journal* 38 (1986–1987): 814–54, at 838.

4. Ibid.

5. Women's Committee, General Recommendation No. 19: Violence against Women, UN Doc. A/47/38 (1992), at para. 6 ("General Recommendation No. 19").

6. Convention on the Elimination of All Forms of Discrimination against Women, Dec. 18, 1979 (entered into force Sept. 3, 1981), 1249 U.N.T.S. 13, reprinted in 19 *I.L.M.* 33 (1980) ("Women's Convention"), prmbl. para. 14.

7. See Women's Committee, General Recommendation No. 19, at para. 6.

8. See Savitri Goonesekere, "Overview: Reflections on Violence against Women and the Legal Systems of Some South Asian Countries," in Savitri Goonesekere, ed., *Violence, Law, and Women's Rights in South Asia* (New Delhi: Sage, 2004), 13–76, at 13.

9. See, e.g., Women's Committee, General Recommendation No. 19; Declaration on the Elimination of Violence against Women, Feb. 23, 1994, G.A. Res. 48/104, UN G.A.O.R., 11th Sess., Supp. No. 49 at 217, UN Doc. A/48/49 (1993); Inter-American Convention on the Prevention, Punishment and Eradication of Violence against Women, Jun. 9, 1994 (entered into force Mar. 5, 1995), OAS/Ser.L/V/I.4 Rev (Jan 2000), reprinted in 33 *I.L.M.* 1534 (1994); Protocol to the African Charter on Human and Peoples' Rights on the Rights of Women in Africa, Sept. 13, 2000 (entered into force Nov. 25, 2005), O.A.U. Doc. CAB/LEG/66.6, reprinted in 1 *Afr. Hum. Rts. L.J.* 40.

10. See, e.g., *A.T. v. Hungary*, CEDAW, Communication No. 2/2003, UN Doc. CEDAW/C/32/D/2/2003 (2005); *Şahide Goekce v. Austria*, CEDAW, Communication No. 5/2005, UN Doc. CEDAW/C/39/D/5/2005 (2007); *Fatma Yildirim v. Austria*, CEDAW, Communication No. 6/2005, UN Doc. CEDAW/C/39/D/6/2005 (2007) (Women's Committee).

11. See, e.g., *Airey v. Ireland*, 32 Eur. Ct. H.R. (ser. A); 2 Eur. H.R. Rep. 305 (1979) (European Court of Human Rights); *M.C. v. Bulgaria*, 646 Eur. Ct. H.R. 150 (2003) (European Court of Human Rights); *Maria Da Penha Maia Fernandes v. Brazil*, Case 12.051, Inter-Am. C.H.R., Report No. 54/01, OEA/Ser.L/V/II.111, doc.20 rev. 704 (2000) (Inter-American Commission on Human Rights); *Raquel Martí de Mejía v. Peru*, Case 10.970, Inter-Am. C.H.R., Report No. 5/96, OEA/Ser.L/V/II.91, doc.7 rev. 157 (1996) (Inter-American Commission on Human Rights).

12. See, e.g., *Vishaka & Others v. State of Rajasthan & Others*, (1997) A.I.R. 3011; (1997) 6 S.C.C. 241 (India, Supreme Court); *State v. Felipe Bechu*, [1999] FJMC 3, Criminal Case No. 79/94 (1999) (Fiji, First Class Magistrate's Court, Levuka), http://www.worldlii.org/fj/cases/FJMC/1999/3.html (accessed Dec. 31, 2008).

13. UN Secretary General, In-Depth Study on All Forms of Violence against Women, UN Doc. A/61/122/Add.1 (2006), at para. 23 (emphasis added), http://www.un.org/womenwatch/daw/vaw/SGstudyvaw.htm#more (accessed Dec. 31, 2008). See also Charlotte Bunch and Niamh Reilly, *Demanding Accountability: The Global Campaign and Vienna Tribunal for Women's Human Rights* (New Brunswick, N.J.: Center for Women's Global Leadership, Rutgers University; New York: United Nations Development Fund for Women, 1994).

14. See Deborah A. Widiss, Elizabeth L. Rosenblatt, and Douglas NeJaime, "Exposing Sex Stereotypes in Recent Same-Sex Marriage Jurisprudence," *Harvard Journal of Law & Gender* 30 (2007): 461–505, at 487.

15. Ibid., at 463.

16. See Katharine T. Bartlett, "Feminist Legal Methods," *Harvard Law Review*

103 (1989–1990): 829–88, at 863–64; Gerda Lerner, *The Creation of Feminist Consciousness: From the Middle Ages to Eighteen-Seventy* (New York: Oxford University Press, 1993).

17. Leslie Bender, "A Lawyer's Primer on Feminist Theory and Tort," *Journal of Legal Education* 38 (1988): 3–38, at 9, quoted in Bartlett, note 16, at 864.

18. See Reva B. Siegel, "Discrimination in the Eyes of the Law: How 'Color Blindness' Discourse Disrupts and Rationalizes Social Stratification," *California Law Review* 88 (2000): 77–118, at 82.

19. See Bender, note 17, at 9.

20. See The Honourable Madame Justice Claire L'Heureux-Dubé, "Beyond the Myths: Equality, Impartiality, and Justice," *Journal of Social Distress and the Homeless* 10 (2001): 87–104, at 89.

21. *To Eradicate Discrimination in Mexico: A Deceit.* Shadow Report to Convention for the Elimination of All Forms of Discrimination against Women in Mexico (CEDAW) 2002–2005: (2006), 22, http://www.iwraw-ap.org/resources/pdf/Mexico_SR.pdf (accessed Dec. 31, 2008).

22. Mary Joe Frug, "A Postmodern Feminist Legal Manifesto (An Unfinished Draft)," *Harvard Law Review* 105 (1991–1992): 1045–75, at 1051.

23. See, e.g., *A.T. v. Hungary*; *Şahide Goekce v. Austria*; *Fatma Yildirim v. Austria*, all note 10.

24. See generally Rikki Holtmaat, "Preventing Violence against Women: The Due Diligence Standard with Respect to the Obligation to Banish Gender Stereotypes on the Grounds of Article 5(a) of the CEDAW Convention," in Carin Benninger-Budel, ed., *Due Diligence and Its Application to Protect Women from Violence* (Leiden: Nijhoff, 2008), 63–89.

25. See, e.g., *Public Prosecutor v. Kota*, [1993] VUSC 8; [1980–1994] Van LR 661 (Vanuatu, Supreme Court), http://www.worldlii.org/vu/cases/VUSC/1993/8.html (accessed Dec. 31, 2008).

26. See, e.g., *R. v. Ewanchuk*, [1999] 1 S.C.R. 330 (Can., Supreme Court).

27. See, e.g., *Gonzales v. Carhart*, 550 U.S. 124 (2007); 127 S. Ct. 1610 (2007) (Ginsburg, J., dissenting) (U.S., Supreme Court).

28. See, e.g., *Petrovic v. Austria*, 33 Eur. H.R. Rep. 307 (1998) (Bernhardt and Spielmann JJ., dissenting) (European Court of Human Rights).

29. See, e.g., Rikki Holtmaat, *Towards Different Law and Public Policy: The Significance of Article 5a CEDAW for the Elimination of Structural Gender Discrimination* (The Hague: Reed Business Information, 2004); Michelle O'Sullivan, "Stereotyping and Male Identification: 'Keeping Women in Their Place,'" in Christina Murray, ed., *Gender and the New South African Legal Order* (Kenwyn, South Africa: Juta, 1994), 185–201; David H. Gans, "Stereotyping and Difference: *Planned Parenthood v. Casey* and the Future of Sex Discrimination Law," *Yale Law Journal* 104 (1994–1995): 1875–1906; Joan. C. Williams and Elizabeth S. Westfall, "Deconstructing the Maternal Wall: Strategies for Vindicating the Civil Rights of 'Carers' in the Workplace," *Duke Journal of Gender Law & Policy* 13 (2006): 31–53; Reva B. Siegel, "The New Politics of Abortion: An Equality Analysis of Woman-Protective Abortion Restrictions," *University of Illinois Law Review* (2007): 991–1054.

30. *Morales de Sierra v. Guatemala*, Case 11.625, Inter-Am. C.H.R., Report No. 4/01, OEA/Ser.L/V/II.111, doc. 20 rev (2001) (Inter-American Commission on Human Rights).

31. Ibid., at para. 44.

32. Ibid., at para. 45.

33. Ibid., at para. 38.

34. Ibid., at para. 44.

35. Ibid., at paras. 39, 45, 48–50, 54.

36. *R. v. Ewanchuk*, note 26.

37. Ibid., at paras. 31, 67 (Major J., majority), 87, 102 (L'Heureux-Dubé J., concurring), 103–4 (McLachlin J., concurring).

38. *President of the Republic of South Africa v. Hugo* 1997 (4) SA 1 (CC) (S. Afr., Constitutional Court).

39. Ibid., at paras. 36–37 (Goldstone J., majority).

40. Ibid., at para. 36.

41. Ibid., at para. 52.

42. Ibid., at paras. 108, 115 (O'Regan J., concurring).

43. Ibid., at para. 106 (Mokgoro J., concurring).

44. Ibid., at paras. 64, 66 (Kriegler J., dissenting).

45. See, e.g., *Paulina Ramírez v. Mexico*, Case 161–02, Inter-Am. C.H.R., Report No. 21/07, OEA/Ser.l/V/II.130, doc. 22, rev. 1 (2007) (Inter-American Commission on Human Rights); *Tysiąc v. Poland*, 2007 Eur. Ct. H.R. 219 (European Court of Human Rights). See also Rebecca J. Cook and Susannah Howard, "Accommodating Women's Differences Under the Women's Anti-Discrimination Convention," *Emory Law Journal* 56 (2007): 1039–91, at 1044.

46. See generally Sumi K. Cho, "Converging Stereotypes in Racialized Sexual Harassment: Where the Model Minority Meets Suzie Wong," *Journal of Gender, Race & Justice* 1 (1997): 177–212; Catherine So-Kum Tang, Day Wong, Fanny Mui-Ching Cheung, "Social Construction of Women as Legitimate Victims of Violence in Chinese Societies," *Violence Against Women* 8 (2002): 968–96.

47. *Morales de Sierra v. Guatemala*, note 30.

48. *R. v. Ewanchuk*, note 26.

49. *President of the Republic of South Africa v. Hugo*, note 38.

50. See generally Bourdieu, note 3.

51. See Susan T. Fiske et al., "Social Science Research on Trial: Use of Sex Stereotyping Research in *Price Waterhouse v. Hopkins*," *American Psychologist* 46 (1991): 1049–60, at 1050–51.

52. See Bartlett, note 16, at 837.

53. See *Reed v. Reed*, 404 U.S. 71 (1971) (U.S., Supreme Court).

54. *Morales de Sierra v. Guatemala*, note 30, at para. 44.

55. *R. v. Ewanchuk*, note 26, at para. 82 (L'Heureux-Dubé J., concurring).

56. Ibid., at para. 83.

57. Ibid., at paras. 83–84.

58. Ibid., at para. 87.

59. Ibid.

60. Ibid.

61. *President of the Republic of South Africa v. Hugo*, note 38, at para. 36 (Goldstone J., majority), quoting affidavit of President Mandela, at para. 6.

62. Ibid., quoting affidavit of President Mandela, at para. 7.

63. Ibid., quoting affidavit of Starke, at paras. 4, 6.

64. Ibid., quoting affidavit of Starke, at para. 6.

65. *President of the Republic of South Africa v. Hugo*, ibid., at para. 37.

66. *Schuler-Zgraggen v. Switzerland*, 16 Eur. H.R. Rep. 405 (1993) (European Court of Human Rights); *Broeks v. The Netherlands*, HRC, Communication No. 172/1984, UN Doc. CCPR/C/OP/2 at 196 (1990) (Human Rights Committee); *Zwaan-de Vries v. The Netherlands*, HRC, Communication No. 182/1984, UN Doc.

CCPR/C/OP/2 at 209 (1990) (Human Rights Committee); *Vos v. The Netherlands*, HRC, Communication No. 218/1986, UN Doc. CCPR/C/35/D/218/1986 (1989) (Human Rights Committee).

67. *Morales de Sierra v. Guatemala*, note 30, at paras. 2, 35, 37.

68. Ibid., at paras. 2, 35, 44.

69. Ibid.

70. Ibid., at para. 37.

71. Ibid., at para. 44.

72. *R. v. Ewanchuk*, note 26, at para. 82 (L'Heureux-Dubé J., concurring), quoting David Archard, *Sexual Consent* (Boulder, Colo.: Westview Press, 1998), 131.

73. Ibid.

74. Ibid.

75. *R. v. Ewanchuk*, ibid., at para. 87.

76. Ibid., at para. 92.

77. *President of the Republic of South Africa v. Hugo*, note 38, at paras. 36–37 (Goldstone J., majority), 70, 79–80, 83 (Kriegler J., dissenting), 105 (Mokgoro J., concurring), 109, 110 (O'Regan J., concurring).

78. Ibid., at para. 92 (Mokgoro J., concurring).

79. Ibid., at paras. 39 (Goldstone J., majority), 83 (Kriegler J., dissenting), 93 (Mokgoro J., concurring).

80. See, e.g., Zanita E. Fenton, "Domestic Violence in Black and White: Racialized Gender Stereotypes in Gender Violence," *Columbia Journal of Gender and Law* 8 (1998–1999): 2–66, at 39–55.

81. See Likhaan, ReproCen and Center for Reproductive Rights, *Imposing Misery: The Impact of Manila's Contraception Ban on Women and Families* (New York: Center for Reproductive Rights, 2007).

82. Ibid., at 12.

83. See ibid., at 14–15.

84. Family Code of the Philippines, Executive Order No. 209 (1987), http://www.chanrobles.com/executiveorderno209.htm (accessed Dec. 31, 2008).

85. Likhaan, ReproCen and Center for Reproductive Rights, note 81, at 37.

86. Ibid., at 23.

87. Interview with City Councilor Cita Astals, Manila, Phil. (Jan. 24, 2007), quoted in ibid., at 27.

88. See Likhaan, ReproCen and Center for Reproductive Rights, note 81, at 27–31.

89. *President of the Republic of South Africa v. Hugo*, note 38, at para. 80 (Kriegler J., dissenting) (emphasis added).

90. Ibid.

91. *R. v. Ewanchuk*, note 26, at paras. 79–80 (L'Heureux-Dubé J., concurring).

92. Ibid., at para. 80.

93. *Morales de Sierra v. Guatemala*, note 30, at para. 34.

94. *R v. Ewanchuk*, note 26, at para. 94 (L'Heureux-Dubé J., concurring).

95. *President of the Republic of South Africa v. Hugo*, note 38, at paras. 37–38 (Goldstone J., majority).

96. Ibid., at para. 85 (Kriegler J., dissenting).

97. *R v. Ewanchuk*, note 26, at para. 95 (L'Heureux-Dubé J., concurring).

98. Ibid.

99. Crimes Act 1958 (Vic), s 37AAA(e)(i).

100. Diane N. Ruble and Thomas L. Ruble, "Sex Stereotypes," in Arthur G. Miller, ed., *In the Eye of the Beholder: Contemporary Issues in Stereotyping* (New York: Praeger, 1982), 188–252, at 201.

101. See generally Kay Deaux, "An Overview of Research on Gender: Four Themes from 3 Decades," in William B. Swann, Jr., Judith H. Langlois, and Lucia Albino Gilbert, eds., *Sexism and Stereotypes in Modern Society: The Gender Science of Janet Taylor Spence* (Washington, D.C.: American Psychological Association, 1999), 11–33, at 16.

102. See *Hoyt v. Florida*, 368 U.S. 57 (1961) (U.S., Supreme Court).

103. See Sophia R. Moreau, "The Wrongs of Unequal Treatment," *University of Toronto Law Journal* 54 (2004): 291–326, at 301–2.

104. See generally Nancy Fraser, *Justice Interruptus: Critical Reflections on the "Postsocialist" Condition* (New York: Routledge, 1997), 11–39.

105. Cook and Howard, note 45.

106. See Robert Worth, "Tiny Voices Defy the Fate of Girls in Yemen: Child Brides Escape Forced Marriages," *New York Times*, June 29, 2008, at A8.

107. See Nadine Dostrovsky, Rebecca J. Cook, and Michaël Gagnon, *Annotated Bibliography on Comparative and International Law Relating to Forced Marriage* (Ottawa: Department of Justice, Canada, 2007).

108. See Asma Jahangir, "Mukhtar Mai: Challenging a Tribal Code of 'Honor,'" *Time Asia*, Oct. 11, 2004, http://www.time.com/time/asia/2004/heroes/hmukhtar_mai.html (accessed Dec. 31, 2008).

109. See Moreau, note 103, at 298.

110. See K. Anthony Appiah, "Stereotypes and the Shaping of Identity," *California Law Review* 88 (2000): 41–54, at 47.

111. *President of the Republic of South Africa v. Hugo*, note 38, at para. 47 (Goldstone J., majority).

112. See Moreau, note 103, at 298.

113. See generally Joan C. Williams and Stephanie Bornstein, "The Evolution of 'FRED': Family Responsibilities Discrimination and Developments in the Law of Stereotyping and Implicit Bias," *Hastings Law Journal* 59 (2008): 1311–58.

114. See generally Holtmaat, note 24.

115. *R. v. Ewanchuk*, note 26, at para. 87 (L'Heureux-Dubé J., concurring).

116. Ibid.

117. Ibid., at para. 93.

118. Ibid.

119. Ibid., at para. 80.

120. See, e.g., Eugene Borgida, Corrie Hunt, and Anita Kim, "On the Use of Gender Stereotyping Research in Sex Discrimination Litigation," *Journal of Law and Policy* 13 (2005): 613–28; Susan A. Basow, *Gender Stereotypes and Roles*, 3rd ed. (Pacific Grove, Calif.: Brooks/Cole, 1992), 12; Norma Costrich et al., "When Stereotypes Hurt: Three Studies of Penalties for Sex Role Reversals," *Journal of Experimental Social Psychology* 11 (1975): 520–30.

121. See *Price Waterhouse v. Hopkins*, 490 U.S. 228, 256 (1989) (U.S., Supreme Court).

122. See Moreau, note 103, at 298.

123. See *Morales de Sierra v. Guatemala*, note 30.

124. See Deborah L. Rhode, "Association and Assimilation," *Northwestern University Law Review* 81 (1986–1987): 106–45, at 130.

125. Basow, note 120, at 11, quoting Mark Snyder, E. Decker Tanke, and Ellen Berscheid, "Social Perception and Interpersonal Behavior: On the Self-

Fulfilling Nature of Social Stereotypes," *Journal of Personality and Social Psychology* 35 (1977): 656–66.

126. See *Jordan v. S.* 2002 (6) SA 642 (CC) (S. Afr., Constitutional Court).

127. See INTERIGHTS, *Prohibition of Torture and Inhuman or Degrading Treatment or Punishment Under the European Convention on Human Rights (Article 3): INTERIGHTS Manual for Lawyers* (London: INTERIGHTS, 2007), 33, http://www.interights.org/documentbank/index.htm?id=242 (accessed Dec. 31, 2008).

128. See Rebecca J. Cook, Simone Cusack, and Joanna N. Erdman, Written Comments to the European Court of Human Rights Regarding Application No. 27617/04, *RR v. Poland*, (Sept. 2007), at para. 31, http://www.law.utoronto.ca/documents/reprohealth/BriefPoland2007.pdf (accessed Dec. 31, 2008).

129. See, e.g., *A.S. v. Hungary*, CEDAW, Communication No. 4/2004, UN Doc. CEDAW/C/36/D/4/2004 (2006) (Women's Committee). See also *María Mamérita Mestanza Chávez v. Peru*, Petition 12.191, Inter-Am. C.H.R. Report No. 71/03, OEA/Ser.L/V/II.118, doc. 5 rev. 2 (2003) (Inter-American Commission on Human Rights).

130. See Moreau, note 103, at 299.

131. *President of the Republic of South Africa v. Hugo*, note 38, at para. 80 (Kriegler J., dissenting).

132. Ibid., at para. 93 (Mokgoro J., concurring).

133. *Morales de Sierra v. Guatemala*, note 30, at paras. 39, 44, 50.

134. See, e.g., *Law v. Canada (Minister of Employment and Immigration)*, [1999] 1 S.C.R. 497, at para. 53 (Iacobucci J.) (Can., Supreme Court); *Egan v. Canada*, [1995] 2 S.C.R. 513, at para. 36 (L'Heureux-Dubé J., dissenting) (Can., Supreme Court). See also Moreau, note 103, at 300–301.

135. Joan Williams and Nancy Segal, "Beyond the Maternal Wall: Relief for Family Caregivers Who Are Discriminated Against on the Job," *Harvard Women's Law Journal* 26 (2003): 77–162, at 95–96.

136. *President of the Republic of South Africa v. Hugo*, note 38, at para. 92 (Mokgoro J., concurring).

137. Ibid.

138. Ibid., at para. 47 (Goldstone J., majority).

139. *Morales De Sierra v. Guatemala*, note 30, at para. 46.

140. Ibid., at para. 50.

141. Ibid.

142. *R. v. Ewanchuk*, note 26, at para. 88 (L'Heureux-Dubé J., concurring).

143. Ibid., at para. 82.

144. *Morales de Sierra v. Guatemala*, note 30, at paras. 38, 44.

145. Ibid., at para. 39.

146. Ibid.

147. *President of the Republic of South Africa v. Hugo*, note 38, at para. 38 (Goldstone J., majority).

148. Ibid., at para. 93 (Mokgoro J., majority).

149. Ibid.

150. Ibid., at para. 113 (O'Regan J., concurring).

151. Ibid., at paras. 33, 40, 70 (Goldstone J., majority).

152. See, e.g., *Volks NO v. Robinson and Others* 2005 (5) BCLR 446 (CC), at para. 154 (Sachs J., dissenting) (S. Afr., Constitutional Court). See also Holtmaat, note 29, at xii.

153. Women's Convention, at para. 14.

154. *Mississippi University for Women v. Hogan*, 458 U.S. 718 (1982) (U.S., Supreme Court).
155. Ibid., at 733 (O'Connor J.).
156. Ibid., at 724–25.
157. Ibid., at 729–30.
158. *Petrovic v. Austria*, note 28.
159. Ibid., at paras. 38–40 (majority).
160. European Convention on Human Rights and Fundamental Freedoms, Nov. 4, 1950 (entered into force Sept. 3, 1953), 213 U.N.T.S. 221, E.T.S. 5.
161. *Petrovic v. Austria*, note 28 (Bernhardt and Spielmann JJ., dissenting).
162. Ibid.
163. Ibid.

Chapter 3. State Obligations to Eliminate Gender Stereotyping

1. Convention on the Elimination of All Forms of Discrimination against Women, Dec. 18, 1979 (entered into force Sept. 3, 1981), 1249 U.N.T.S. 13, reprinted in 19 *I.L.M.* 33 (1980), arts. 2(f), 5(a) ("Women's Convention").
2. Women's Committee, General Recommendation No. 25: Article 4, Paragraph 1, of the Convention on the Elimination of All Forms of Discrimination against Women, on Temporary Special Measures, UN Doc. A/59/38(Part I) (2004), at Annex I, at para. 3 ("General Recommendation No. 25").
3. See ibid., at paras. 6–7.
4. See Vienna Convention on the Law of Treaties, May 23, 1969 (entered into force Jan. 27, 1980), 1155 U.N.T.S. 331, reprinted in 8 *I.L.M.* 679 (1969), art. 31.
5. Declaration on the Elimination of Discrimination against Women, Nov. 7, 1967, G.A. Res. 2263 (XXII). See generally Lars Adam Rehof, *Guide to the Travaux Préparatoires of the United Nations Convention on the Elimination of All Forms of Discrimination Against Women* (Dordrecht: Nijhoff, 1993), 77–81; Rikki Holtmaat, *Towards Different Law and Public Policy: The Significance of Article 5a CEDAW for the Elimination of Structural Gender Discrimination* (The Hague: Reed Business Information, 2004), 27–28; Kinjo Kiyoko, "Article 5: Elimination of the Discriminatory Customs and Practices, Stereotyped Notions of the Attributes and Roles of Women and Men or the Superiority of Either Sex," in Japanese Association of International Women's Rights, ed., *Convention on the Elimination of All Forms of Discrimination Against Women: A Commentary* (Tokyo: Shogakusya, 1995), 114–27.
6. See Dianne Otto, "Lost in Translation: Re-Scripting the Sexed Subjects of International Human Rights Law," in Anne Orford, ed., *International Law and Its Others* (Cambridge: Cambridge University Press, 2006), 318–56, at 343.
7. *President of the Republic of South Africa v. Hugo* 1997 (4) SA 1 (CC) (S. Afr., Constitutional Court).
8. Ibid., at para. 106 (Mokgoro J., concurring).
9. Ibid., at paras. 64, 66 (Kriegler J., dissenting).
10. See generally INTERIGHTS, *Prohibition of Torture and Inhuman or Degrading Treatment or Punishment Under the European Convention on Human Rights (Article 3): INTERIGHTS Manual for Lawyers* (London: INTERIGHTS, 2007), 21–35, http://www.interights.org/documentbank/index.htm?id=242 (accessed Dec. 31, 2008).

11. See Holtmaat, note 5, at 74–75.

12. Women's Convention, art. 10(c).

13. Women's Committee, General Recommendation No. 19: Violence against Women, UN Doc. A/47/38 (1992), at para. 11 (General Recommendation No. 19).

14. See Holtmaat, note 5, at 75.

15. See Andrew Byrnes, María Herminia Graterol and Renée Chartres, *State Obligation and the Convention on the Elimination of All Forms of Discrimination against Women*, IWRAW Asia Pacific Expert Group Meeting on CEDAW Article 2: National and International Dimensions of State Obligation. Background Discussion Paper (May 2007), at para. 53, http://www.iwraw-ap.org/aboutus/pdf/Background%20paper.pdf (accessed Dec. 31, 2008).

16. See Committee on Economic, Social and Cultural Rights, General Comment No. 16: The Equal Rights of Men and Women to the Enjoyment of All Economic, Social and Cultural Rights, UN Doc. E/C.12/2005/4 (2005), at paras. 17–21 ("General Comment No. 16").

17. See Women's Convention, art. 15; Committee on Economic, Social and Cultural Rights, General Comment No. 16, at para. 18.

18. Women's Convention, art. 5(a).

19. *President of the Republic of South Africa v. Hugo*, note 7, at para. 85 (Kriegler J., dissenting).

20. See, e.g., *Abdulaziz, Cabales and Balkandali v. United Kingdom*, App. Nos. 9214/80, 9473/81, 9474/81, 7 Eur. H.R. Rep. 471 (1985) (European Court of Human Rights).

21. The Honourable Madame Justice Claire L'Heureux-Dubé, "Beyond the Myths: Equality, Impartiality, and Justice," *Journal of Social Distress and the Homeless* 10 (2001): 87–104, at 99.

22. *Attorney General of Botswana v. Unity Dow*, (1992) LRC (Const.) 623, (1994) 6 BCLR 1 (Botswana, Court of Appeal), reprinted in Robyn Emerton, Kristine Adams, Andrew Byrnes, and Jane Connors, eds., *International Women's Rights Cases* (London: Cavendish, 2005), 572–607. See Unity Dow, *The Citizenship Case: The Attorney General of the Republic of Botswana v. Unity Dow* (Gaborone: Lentswe La Lesedi, 1995). See also *Meera Gurung v. Her Majesty's Government, Department of Central Immigration, Ministry of Home Affairs*, Decision No. 4858 of 1994 (Nepal, Supreme Court, Full Bench), summarized in Christine Forster, Vedna Jivan, Imrana Jalal, and Madhu Mehra, eds., *A Digest of Case Law on the Human Rights of Women (Asia Pacific)* (Chiangmai, Thailand: Asia Pacific Forum on Women Law and Development, 2003), 62–63.

23. Citizenship (Amendment) Act of 1995 (Botswana).

24. *Attorney General of Botswana v. Unity Dow*, note 22, at 586 (Amissah J.P.).

25. *Morales de Sierra v. Guatemala*, Case 11.625, Inter-Am. C.H.R., Report No. 4/01, OEA/Ser./L/V/II.111, doc. 20 rev. (2001) (Inter-American Commission on Human Rights).

26. Annual Report of the Inter-American Commission on Human Rights: 2007, OEA/Ser.L/V/II.130 doc. 22 rev. 1 at Ch.III, Section D, at paras. 356–58, http://www.cidh.org/annualrep/2007eng/Chap.3n.htm#11.625 (accessed Dec. 31, 2008).

27. Ibid., at para. 356.

28. Ibid., at paras. 357–58.

29. See *Bradwell v. Illinois*, 83 U.S. (16 Wall.) 130 (1872) (U.S., Supreme Court); *Muojekwu v. Ejikeme*, [2000] 5 N.W.L.R. 402 (Nig., Court of Appeal, Enugu Division); *Jordan v. S.* 2002 (6) SA 642; 2002 (11) BCLR 1117 (Ngcobo J., Majority)

(S. Afr., Constitutional Court); *Gonzales v. Carhart*, 550 U.S. 124 (2007); 127 S. Ct. 1610 (2007) (Kennedy J., majority) (U.S., Supreme Court).

30. L'Heureux-Dubé, note 21, at 92 (citations omitted).

31. See *R. v. Ewanchuk*, [1999] 1 S.C.R. 330, at para. 95 (L'Heureux-Dubé J., concurring) (Can., Supreme Court).

32. Ibid.

33. *Miller v. Albright*, 118 S. Ct 1428 (1998) (U.S., Supreme Court); 523 U.S. 420 (1998). See also Roger Craig Green, "Equal Protection and the Status of Stereotypes," *Yale Law Journal* 108 (1998–1999): 1885–92.

34. Immigration and Nationality Act, 8 U.S.C. Sec 1409 (1994), s 309.

35. *Miller v. Albright*, note 33, at 1463 (citations omitted).

36. See Green, note 33, at 1888.

37. Ibid., at 1892.

38. *Muojekwu v. Ejikeme*, note 29.

39. Ibid., at 418, paras. F–G (Fabiyi, J.C.A.).

40. Ibid., at 436, paras. E–F (Tobi, J.C.A.).

41. Ibid., at 432, paras. G–H (Tobi, J.C.A.).

42. See Onyema Oluebube Afulukwe, "Protecting the Human Rights of Women by Re-Conceiving the Repugnancy Doctrine in Nigeria: The Case of *Muojekwu v. Ejikeme*" (Aug. 31, 2007) (unpublished LL.M. thesis, University of Toronto) (on file with Bora Laskin Law Library, University of Toronto), 49–52.

43. *Frontiero v. Richardson*, 411 U.S. 677 (1973) (U.S., Supreme Court).

44. Ibid., at 684.

45. Ibid., at 685.

46. *W. v. New Zealand [A.G.]*, [1999] 2 N.Z.L.R. 709 (Thomas J.) (N.Z., Court of Appeal).

47. Ibid., at para. 93.

48. Ibid., at para. 95.

49. See Byrnes, Graterol, and Chartres, note 15, at para. 59; Rebecca J. Cook, "State Responsibility for Violations of Women's Human Rights," *Harvard Human Rights Journal* 7 (1994): 125–76, at 150–52; Rebecca J. Cook, "State Accountability Under the Convention on the Elimination of All Forms of Discrimination Against Women," in Rebecca J. Cook, ed., *Human Rights of Women: National and International Perspectives* (Philadelphia: University of Pennsylvania Press, 1994), 228–56, at 236–39.

50. See Naila Kabeer, "From Feminist Insights to an Analytical Framework: An Institutional Perspective on Gender Inequality," in Naila Kabeer and Ramya Subrahmanian, eds., *Institutions, Relations and Outcomes: A Framework and Case Studies for Gender-Aware Planning* (London: Zed Books, 1999), 3–48, at 13.

51. Committee on Economic, Social and Cultural Rights, General Comment No. 16, at para. 19.

52. Ibid., at para. 20.

53. See *Forum for Fact Finding Documentation and Advocacy v. Union of India & Others*, filed April 2003 (India, Supreme Court), summarized in Christine M. Forster and Vedna Jivan, "Public Interest Litigation and Human Rights Implementation: The Indian and Australian Experience," *Asian Journal of Comparative Law* 3, Article 6 (2008): 1–32, at 24–25.

54. Women's Convention, art. 2(f).

55. Ibid., art. 5(a).

56. *X and Y v. The Netherlands*, App. No. 8978/80, 91 Eur. Ct. H.R. (ser. A); 8 Eur. H.R. Rep. 235 (1985) (European Court of Human Rights).

57. See *Final Report of the Michigan Supreme Court Task Force on Gender Issues in the Courts* (Lansing, Mich.: Task Force on Gender Issues in the Courts, 1989), at 69.

58. See Amparita Sta. Maria, *CEDAW Benchbook* (Makati City, Phil.: Ateneo Human Rights Center, 2008), http://www.cedawbenchbook.org/ (accessed Dec. 31, 2008).

59. Inter-American Commission on Human Rights, *Access to Justice for Women Victims of Violence in the Americas*, OEA/Ser.L/V/II. Doc. 68 (2007), at para. 249.

60. See, e.g., Sheilah L. Martin and Kathleen E. Mahoney, eds., *Equality and Judicial Neutrality* (Toronto: Carswell, 1987); Kathleen Mahoney, "Canadian Approaches to Equality Rights and Gender Equity in the Courts," in Cook, ed., note 49, 436–61, at 449–56.

61. See Michelle O'Sullivan, "Stereotyping and Male Identification: 'Keeping Women in their Place,'" in Christina Murray, ed., *Gender and the New South African Legal Order* (Kenwyn, South Africa: Juta, 1994), 185–201.

62. See Zanita E. Fenton, "Domestic Violence in Black and White: Racialized Gender Stereotypes in Gender Violence," *Columbia Journal of Gender & Law* 8 (1998–1999): 1–66, at 56–64.

63. *Jordan v. S.*, note 29, at paras. 64–73 (O'Regan and Sachs JJ., dissenting).

64. Ibid., at paras. 8–20 (Ngcobo J., majority).

65. See, e.g., *Bhe and Others v. The Magistrate, Khayelitsha and Others*, [2005] 1 BCLR 1 (S. Afr., Constitutional Court). See Fareda Banda, *Women, Law and Human Rights: An African Perspective* (Oxford: Hart, 2005), 38–39.

66. See Women's Committee, General Recommendation No. 21: Equality in Marriage and Family Relations, UN Doc. A/49/38(Supp) (1994), at para. 14 ("General Recommendation No. 21"); Rebecca J. Cook and Lisa M. Kelly, *Polygyny and Canada's Obligations Under International Human Rights Law* (Ottawa: Department of Justice, Canada, 2006), http://www.justice.gc.ca/eng/dept-min/pub/poly/poly.pdf (accessed Dec. 31, 2008); Susan Deller Ross, "Gender and Polygyny: Religion, Culture, and Equality in Marriage," in Susan Deller Ross, *Women's Human Rights: The International and Comparative Law Casebook* (Philadelphia: University of Pennsylvania Press, 2008), 512–70; Women Living Under Muslim Laws, *Knowing Our Rights: Women, Family, Laws and Customs in the Muslim World*, 3rd ed. (London: Women Living Under Muslim Laws, 2006), 107–212.

67. See Women's Convention, art. 2(e).

68. See, e.g., *Open Door Counselling v. Ireland*, (1992), App. No. 14234/88; 14235/88, Eur. Ct. H.R. Ser. A, No. 246, 15 E.H.R.R. 244 (European Court of Human Rights).

69. See, e.g., *Tysiąc v. Poland*, App. No. 5410/03, 2007 Eur. Ct. H.R. 219 (European Court of Human Rights).

70. See Claire A. Smearman, "Drawing the Line: The Legal, Ethical and Public Policy Implications of Refusal Clauses for Pharmacists," *Arizona Law Review* 48 (2006): 469–540.

71. See Cynthia Steele and Susana Chiarotti, "With Everything Exposed: Cruelty in Post-Abortion Care in Rosario, Argentina," *Reproductive Health Matters* 12, 24 (Supp. 2004): 39–46, at 40.

72. See Northwest Territories, Department of Health, Abortion Services Review Committee, *Report of the Abortion Services Review Committee* (Yellowknife NWT, 1992); Childbirth by Choice Trust, ed., *No Choice: Canadian Women Tell Their Stories of Illegal Abortion* (Toronto: Childbirth by Choice Trust, 1998), 154.

73. See, e.g., *K.L. v. Peru*, HRC, Communication No. 1153/2003, UN Doc. CCPR/C/85/D/1153/2003 (2005) (Human Rights Committee); *Paulina Ramírez v. Mexico*, Case 161–02, Inter-Am. C.H.R., Report No. 21/07, OEA/Ser.L/V/II.130, doc. 22, rev. 1 (2007) (Inter-American Commission on Human Rights).
74. See, e.g., *A.S. v. Hungary*, CEDAW, Communication No. 4/2004, UN Doc. CEDAW/C/36/D/4/2004 (2006) (Women's Committee); *Maria Mamérita Mestanza Chávez v. Peru*, Petition 12.191, Inter-Am. C.H.R. Report No. 71/03, OEA/Ser.L/V/II.118, doc. 5 rev. 2 (2003) (Inter-American Commission on Human Rights).
75. See, e.g. *Paton v. United Kingdom*, App. No. 8416/78, 3 Eur. H.R. Rep. 408 (1980) (European Commission on Human Rights); *R.H. v. Norway*, App. No. 17004/90, 73 Eur. Comm'n H.R. Dec. & Rep. 155 (1992) (European Commission on Human Rights); *Boso v. Italy*, App. No. 50490/99, 2002–VII Eur. Ct. H.R. 451 (European Court of Human Rights); *Tremblay v. Daigle*, [1989] 2 S.C.R. 530 (Can., Supreme Court). See also Women's Committee, General Recommendation No. 24: Women and Health, UN Doc. A/54/38 Rev. 1 (1999), at para. 14 ["General Recommendation No. 24]; Rebecca J. Cook and Susannah Howard, "Accommodating Women's Differences under the Women's Anti-Discrimination Convention" *Emory Law Journal* 56, 4 (2007): 1039–92, at 1083–84.
76. See, e.g., *Gonzales v. Carhart*, note 29, at 1634.
77. Reva B. Siegel, "The Right's Reasons: Constitutional Conflict and the Spread of Woman-Protective Antiabortion Argument" *Duke Law Journal* 57 (2008): 1641–92, at 1641–51.
78. Ibid., at 1651–56.
79. See, e.g., *Pichon and Sajous v. France*, App. No. 49853/99 2001–X Eur. Ct. H.R. 3 (European Court of Human Rights); Decision T-209 of 2008 (Colomb., Constitutional Court). See also Adriana Lamackova, "Conscientious Objection in Reproductive Health Care: Analysis of *Pichon and Sajous v. France*," *European Journal of Health Law* 15 (2008): 7–43; Rebecca J. Cook, Mónica Arango Olaya and Bernard M. Dickens, "Healthcare Responsibilities and Conscientious Objection," *International Journal of Gynecology and Obstetrics* 104 (2009) 249–52; Cook and Howard, note 75, at 1085–87.
80. See, e.g., *Paulina Ramírez v. Mexico*, note 73.
81. See, e.g., *K.L. v. Peru*, note 73. See also Human Rights Watch, *My Rights, and My Right to Know: Lack of Access to Therapeutic Abortion in Peru* (New York: Human Rights Watch, 2008).
82. See note 75.
83. See, e.g., *Pichon and Sajous v. France*, note 79; Decision T-209 of 2008, note 79.
84. *Gonzales v. Carhart*, note 29.
85. See Committee on the Rights of the Child, Concluding Observations: Mexico, UN Doc. CRC/C/15/Add.112 (1999), at para. 16.
86. Rebecca J. Cook, Bernard M. Dickens and Mahmoud F. Fathalla, *Reproductive Health and Human Rights: Integrating Medicine, Ethics and Law* (Oxford: Clarendon, 2003), 200.
87. See *Gonzales v. Carhart*, note 29, at 1634–35 (Kennedy J., majority) (U.S., Supreme Court).
88. Ibid., at 1634 (citations omitted).
89. Ibid., at 1648–49 (Ginsburg, J., dissenting) (citations omitted).

90. Ibid., at 1649.
91. See *Muller v. Oregon*, 208 U.S. 412, 422–23 (1908) (U.S., Supreme Court).
92. See *Bradwell v. Illinois*, note 29.
93. See *United States v. Virginia*, 518 U.S. 515, 533, 542, (1996) (U.S., Supreme Court).
94. *Califano v. Goldfarb*, 430 U.S. 199, 207 (1977) (U.S., Supreme Court).
95. *In re Abortion Law Challenge, No. C-355/06*, 2006 (Colomb., Constitutional Court), excerpted in English, at para. 8.1, http://www.womenslinkworldwide.org/pdf_pubs/pub_c3552006.pdf (accessed Dec. 31, 2008).
96. Ibid., at para. 8.1.
97. Women's Committee, General Recommendation No. 19, at para. 9.
98. Kabeer, note 50, at 13.
99. See *Fatma Yildirim v. Austria*, CEDAW, Communication No. 6/2005, UN Doc. CEDAW/C/39/D/6/2005 (2007); *Şahide Goekce v. Austria*, CEDAW, Communication No. 5/2005, UN Doc. CEDAW/C/39/D/5/2005 (2007); Report on Mexico Produced By the Committee on the Elimination of Discrimination against Women Under Article 8 of the Optional Protocol to the Convention, and Reply from the Government of Mexico, CEDAW, UN Doc. CEDAW/C/2005/OP.8/MEXICO (2005) ("Ciudad Juárez inquiry"); *A.T. v. Hungary*, CEDAW, Communication No. 2/2003, UN Doc. CEDAW/C/32/D/2/2003 (2005) (Women's Committee). See also Savitri Gooneseker, "Universalizing Women's Human Rights Through CEDAW," in Hanna Beate Schöpp-Schilling and Cees Flinterman, eds., *The Circle of Empowerment: Twenty-Five Years of the UN Committee on the Elimination of Discrimination Against Women* (New York: Feminist Press, 2007), 52–67, at 61–62.
100. See, e.g., *Osman v. United Kingdom*, App. No. 23452/94, 1998–VIII Eur. Ct. H.R. 3169 (European Court of Human Rights).
101. See Lynn Welchman and Sara Hossain, eds., *"Honour": Crimes, Paradigms, and Violence against Women* (London: Zed Books, 2005).
102. See Nadine Dostrovsky, Rebecca J. Cook and Michaël Gagnon, *Annotated Bibliography on Comparative and International Law Relating to Forced Marriage* (Ottawa: Department of Justice, Canada, 2007), http://www.justice.gc.ca/eng/pi/pad-rpad/rep-rap/mar/co.html (accessed Dec. 31, 2008).
103. See Jaya Sagade, *Child Marriage in India: Socio-Legal and Human Rights Dimensions* (New Delhi: Oxford University Press, 2005); UNICEF Innocenti Research Centre, "Early Marriage: Child Spouses," *Innocenti Digest* 7 (2001).
104. See Kumar Regmi, "Nepalese Legislative and Judicial Responses to Women/Girls Trafficking into Prostitution" in Bhimarjun Acharya, ed., *Annual Survey of Nepalese Law 2002* (Kathmandu: Nepal Bar Council, 2003) 185–212.
105. See Courtney W. Howland, "Safeguarding Women's Political Freedoms Under the International Covenant on Civil and Political Rights in the Face of Religious Fundamentalism," in Courtney W. Howland, ed., *Religious Fundamentalisms and the Human Rights of Women* (New York: St. Martin's, 1999), 93–103. See generally Welchman and Hossain, note 101.
106. See Symposium, "Makeup, Identity Performance and Discrimination," *Duke Journal of Gender Law & Policy* 14 (2007).
107. See Asma Jahangir, "Mukhtar Mai: Challenging a Tribal Code of 'Honor,'" *Time Asia*, Oct. 4, 2004, http://www.time.com/time/asia/2004/heroes/hmukhtar_mai.html (accessed Dec. 31, 2008).
108. See Madhu Mehra and Deepika Udagama, "Evolving Understanding of Women's Human Rights and Emerging Human Rights Standards: Non-State

Actors," in IWRAW Asia Pacific and Australian Human Rights Centre, *Report of Expert Group Meeting on CEDAW Article 2: National and International Dimensions of State Obligation* (2007), 18–20, http://www.iwraw-ap.org/aboutus/pdf/ EGM%20Report.pdf (accessed Dec. 31, 2008).

109. See, e.g., *Ciudad Juárez inquiry*, note 99.

110. See Mary Romero, "Nanny Diaries and Other Stories: Imagining Immigrant Women's Labor in the Social Reproduction of American Families," *DePaul Law Review* 52 (2002–2003): 809–48, at 840, 822–32.

111. See Brad R. Roth, "The CEDAW as a Collective Approach to Women's Rights," *Michigan Journal of International Law* 24 (2002–2003): 187–226, at 211–14.

112. Byrnes, Graterol and Chartres, note 15, at para. 127.

113. See Amnesty International, *Making Rights a Reality: The Duty of States to Address Violence against Women* (London: Amnesty International, 2004), 21–23.

114. See Byrnes, Graterol and Chartres, note 15, at para. 130.

115. *Raquel Martí de Mejía v. Peru*, Case 10.970, Inter-Am. C.H.R., Report No. 5/96, OEA/Ser.L/V/II.91, doc.7 rev. 157 (1996), at paras. 35–36.

116. *E and Others v. United Kingdom*, App. No. 33218/96, Nov. 26, 2002, at para. 99 (European Court of Human Rights) (emphasis added).

117. Ibid.

118. See *Pichon and Sajous v. France*, note 79.

119. See *D. v. France*, App. No. 10180/82, 35 Eur. Comm'n H.R. Dec. & Rep. 199 (1983), at 201–2 (European Commission on Human Rights).

120. See *Bruker v. Marcovitz*, [2007] 3 S.C.R. 607, 2007 SCC 54, at paras. 134–56 (Can., Supreme Court) (reviewing similar rulings of courts of England, France, Israel and the U.S. (New York, New Jersey)). See also Ruth Halperin-Kaddari, "Women, Religion and Multiculturalism in Israel," *UCLA Journal of International Law & Foreign Affairs* 5 (2000): 339–66, at 349–52.

121. See HC 3358/95, *Hoffman v. Director General of Prime Minister's Office*, [2000] IsrSC 54(2) 345 (High Court) (Isr., Supreme Court). See also Halperin-Kaddari, note 120, at 358–61; Ran Hirschl, "Constitutional Courts vs. Religious Fundamentalism: Three Middle Eastern Tales," *Texas Law Review* 82 (2004): 1819–60, at 1843–44.

122. See HC 153/87, *Shakdiel v. Minister of Religious Affairs & Others*, [1988] IsrSC 42(2) 221 (Isr., Supreme Court), translated in Arnold N. Enker and Julius Kopelowitz, eds, *Selected Judgments of the Supreme Court of Israel: Constitutional Law Cases 1969–1988*, Vol. 3 (Jerusalem: Israel Bar Publishing House, 1992), 186.

123. Cass R. Sunstein, "Should Sex Equality Law Apply to Religious Institutions?" in Susan Moller Olkin, ed., *Is Multiculturalism Bad for Women?* (Princeton, N.J.: Princeton University Press, 1999), 85–94; Martha C. Nussbaum, "Religion, Culture and Sex Equality" in Indira Jaising, ed., *Men's Laws, Women's Lives: A Constitutional Perspective on Religion, Common Law and Culture in South Asia* (New Delhi: Women Unlimited, 2005), 109–37.

124. See note 116.

125. See *Airey v. Ireland*, App. No. 6289/73, 32 Eur. Ct. H.R. (ser. A); 2 Eur. H.R. Rep. 305 (1979) (European Court of Human Rights); *X and Y v. The Netherlands*, note 56.

126. Women's Committee, General Recommendation No. 25, at para. 7.

127. Kent Roach, "The Challenges of Crafting Remedies for Violations of Socio-Economic Rights," in Malcolm Langford, ed., *Social Rights Jurisprudence:*

Emerging Trends in International and Comparative Law (Cambridge: Cambridge University Press, forthcoming 2009), 46–58, at 46.

128. See notes and accompanying text. 40–42.

129. See Kwame Anthony Appiah, "Stereotypes and the Shaping of Identity," *California Law Review* 88 (2000): 41–54, at 49.

130. Ibid.

131. Ibid., at 52.

132. See Yakin Ertürk, "Considering the Role of Men in Gender Agenda Setting: Conceptual and Policy Issues," *Feminist Review* 78 (2004): 3–21, at 14–15.

133. Monica Biernat and Diane Kobrynowicz, "A Shifting Standards Perspective on the Complexity of Gender Stereotypes and Gender Stereotyping," in William B. Swann, Jr., Judith H. Langlois, and Lucia Albino Gilbert, eds., *Sexism and Stereotypes in Modern Society: The Gender Science of Janet Taylor Spence* (Washington, D.C.: American Psychological Association, 1999), 75–106, at 78.

134. *Yilmaz-Dogan v. The Netherlands*, CERD, Communication No. 1/1984, UN Doc. CERD/C/36/D/1/1984 (1988) (Committee on the Elimination of Racial Discrimination).

135. Ibid., at para. 2.2.

136. Ibid., at para. 10.

137. See Joan C. Williams, "Deconstructing Gender," *Michigan Law Review* 87 (1988–1989): 797–845, at 800; Holtmaat, note 5, at 11–13, 99–115.

138. See Williams, note 137, at 801–6.

139. *Morales de Sierra v. Guatemala*, note 25.

140. *Brown v. Board of Education*, 347 U.S. 483 (1954), 494 (Warren J.) (U.S., Supreme Court).

141. *Aloeboetoe et al. v. Suriname*, Judgment of September 10, 1993, Inter-Am. Ct. H.R. (Ser. C) No. 15 (1993) (Inter-American Court of Human Rights), at para. 20.

142. Rebecca J. Cook, "Obligations to Adopt Temporary Special Measures Under the Convention on the Elimination of All Forms of Discrimination Against Women," in Ineke Boerefijn et al., eds., *Temporary Special Measures: Accelerating de facto Equality of Women under Article 4(1) UN Convention on the Elimination of All Forms of Discrimination Against Women* (Antwerpen: Intersentia, 2003), 119–41, at 119.

143. Women's Committee, General Recommendation No. 25, at para. 18.

144. See Human Rights Committee, General Comment No. 18: Non-Discrimination, UN Doc. HRI/GEN/1/Rev.1 at 26 (1994), at para. 10.

145. Committee on Economic, Social and Cultural Rights, General Comment No. 16, at para. 15.

146. See Inter-American Commission on Human Rights, "Considerations regarding the Compatibility of Affirmative Action Measures Designed to Promote the Political Participation of Women with the Principles of Equality and Non-Discrimination," in Inter-American Commission on Human Rights, *Annual Report of the Inter-American Commission on Human Rights 1999*, OEA/Ser.L/V/II.106 doc. 6 rev. (1999).

147. Women's Convention, art. 16(h).

148. Ibid., art. 4(1).

149. *Yilmaz-Dogan v. The Netherlands*, note 134.

150. Women's Convention, art. 28(2). See also Vienna Convention on the Law of Treaties, art. 19(c).

151. Vienna Convention on the Law of Treaties, art. 2(1)(d).

152. Women's Convention, art. 28(2). See also *Reservations to the Convention on the Prevention and Punishment of the Crime of Genocide*, Advisory Opinion, 1951 I.C.J. 15 (May 28, 1951).

153. See Women's Committee, General Recommendation No. 25, at para. 4.

154. See ibid., at paras. 6–7.

155. Indira Jaising, *The Validity of Reservations and Declarations to CEDAW: The Indian Experience*, IWRAW Asia Pacific Occasional Paper Series No. 5 (Kuala Lumpur: IWRAW Asia Pacific, 2005), 3.

156. Women's Committee, Statement on Reservations to the Convention on the Elimination of All Forms of Discrimination against Women, CEDAW, UN GAOR, 53rd sess., supp. no. 38, UN Doc. A/53/38/Rev.1 (1998) at Part II, para.15.

157. See http://www2.ohchr.org/english/bodies/ratification/8.htm#declarations for reservations and objections of States Parties to the Women's Convention, and their dates of filing (accessed Dec. 31, 2008).

158. See Shaheen Sardar Ali, "Part I: Conceptual Framework," in Shaheen Sardar Ali, ed., *Conceptualising Islamic Law, CEDAW and Women's Human Rights in Plural Legal Settings: A Comparative Analysis of Application of CEDAW in Bangladesh, India and Pakistan* (New Delhi: UNIFEM South Asia Regional Office, 2006), 1–106, at 77–90, http://www.unifem.org.in/PDF/complete%20study.pdf (accessed Dec. 31, 2008).

159. See Halperin-Kaddari, note 120, at 352–58.

160. Objections made by France regarding to the reservations made by Niger to the CEDAW, reprinted by Netherlands Institute of Human Rights, Utrecht School of Law, 14 November 2000, http://sim.law.uu.nl/SIM/Library/RATIF.nsf/f4fa141b5305360f41256c160046577a/7b887b078ace43ce41256d82003886 6c?OpenDocument (accessed Dec. 31, 2008).

161. See Rebecca J. Cook, "Reservations to the Convention on the Elimination of All Forms of Discrimination against Women," *Virginia Journal of International Law* 30 (1990): 643–716, at 658.

162. See Women's Committee, General Comment No. 20: Reservations to the Convention, UN Doc. A/47/38 at 7 (1993); Women's Committee, General Recommendation No. 21, at paras. 41–48.

163. Women's Committee, General Recommendation No. 21, at para. 42.

164. See Women's Convention, art. 28.

165. See Women's Committee, Concluding Observations: Israel, CEDAW, UN GAOR, 52nd sess., supp. no.38, UN Doc. A/52/38/Rev.1 (1997) at Part II, para.157.

166. Women's Committee, Concluding Observations: Israel, CEDAW, UN GAOR, 60th sess., supp. no. 38, UN Doc. A/60/38, (2005) at Part II, para. 245.

167. See ibid., at para. 246.

168. See Women's Committee, Reporting Guidelines of the Committee on the Elimination of Discrimination against Women, UN Doc. CEDAW/SP/2008/INF/1 (2008), at para. C.3; United Nations, International Human Rights Instruments, Compilation of Guidelines on the Form and Content of Reports to be Submitted by States Parties to the International Human Rights Treaties, UN Doc. HRI/GEN/2/Rev.1/Add.2 (2003), at para. C.2. See also Hanna Beate Schöpp-Schilling, "Elements of Practice of Human Rights Monitoring Bodies, Reservations to the Convention on the Elimination of All Forms of Discrimination Against Women: An Unresolved Issue or (No) New Developments?," in Ineta Ziemele, ed., *Reservations to Human Rights Treaties*

and the *Vienna Convention Regime: Conflict, Harmony or Reconciliation* (Leiden: Nijhoff, 2004), 3–39, at 21.

169. Human Rights Committee, General Comment No. 24: Issues relating to Reservations made upon Ratification or Accession to the Covenant or the Optional Protocols thereto, or in relation to Declarations Under Article 41 of the Covenant, UN Doc. CCPR/C/21/Rev.1/Add.6 (1994), at para. 19.

170. Women's Committee, Working Paper on Reservations in the Context of Individual Communications, UN Doc. CEDAW/C/2008/II/WP.2, (2008), at para. 11.

171. *Constance Ragan Salgado v. United Kingdom of Great Britain and Northern Ireland,* CEDAW, Communication No. 11/2006, UN Doc. CEDAW/C/37/D/11/2006 (2007) (Women's Committee).

172. Ibid., at paras. 8.4–8.7.

173. See *Belilos v. Switzerland,* App. No. 10328/83,132 Eur. Ct. H.R. (ser. A) (1988), 10 E.H.RR. 466 (European Court of Human Rights); *Loizidou v. Turkey,* App. No. 15318/89, 310 Eur. Ct HR (Ser. A) 7; [1995] 20 EHRR 99 (European Court of Human Rights).

174. See *Kennedy v. Trinidad and Tobago,* HRC, Communication No. 845, UN Doc. CCPR/C/67/D/845/1999 (1999) (Human Rights Committee).

Chapter 4. Gender Stereotyping as a Form of Discrimination

1. Convention on the Elimination of All Forms of Discrimination against Women, Dec. 18, 1979 (entered into force Sept. 3, 1981), 1249 U.N.T.S. 13, reprinted in 19 *I.L.M.* 33 (1980) ("Women's Convention"). See also Women's Committee, General Recommendation No. 25: Article 4, Paragraph 1, of the Convention on the Elimination of All Forms of Discrimination Against Women, on Temporary Special Measures, UN Doc. A/59/38 (2004), at paras. 3–14 ("General Recommendation No. 25").

2. See Women's Committee, General Recommendation No. 25, at paras. 6–7.

3. Ibid., at para. 7 note 1.

4. Committee on Economic, Social and Cultural Rights, General Comment No. 16: The Equal Rights of Men and Women to the Enjoyment of All Economic, Social, and Cultural Rights, UN Doc. E/C.12/2005/4 (2005), at para. 11 (emphasis added) ("General Comment No. 16").

5. See Women's Convention, art. 1. See also General Comment No. 16, at para. 12.

6. See Women's Convention, art. 1. See also Women's Committee, General Recommendation No. 25, at para. 7 note 1; Committee on Economic, Social and Cultural Rights, General Comment No. 16, at para. 13.

7. See Women's Committee, General Recommendation No. 25, at paras. 8, 18.

8. Women's Convention, art. 5(a).

9. See, e.g., International Covenant on Civil and Political Rights, Dec. 16, 1966 (entered into force Mar. 23, 1976), 999 U.N.T.S. 171, art. 7.

10. *Morales de Sierra v. Guatemala,* Case 11.625, Inter-Am. C.H.R., Report No. 4/01, OEA/Ser.L/V/II.111, doc. 20 rev. (2001) (Inter-American Commission on Human Rights).

11. *President of the Republic of South Africa v. Hugo* 1997 (4) SA 1 (CC) (S. Afr., Constitutional Court).

12. *Nevada Department of Human Resources v. Hibbs*, 538 U.S. 721 (2003) (U.S., Supreme Court).

13. Ibid., at 725 (Rehnquist C.J.). See generally Joan C. Williams, "*Hibbs* as a Federalism Case; *Hibbs* as a Maternal Wall Case," *University of Cincinnati Law Review* 73 (2004–2005): 365–98; Reva B. Siegel, "You've Come a Long Way, Baby: Rehnquist's New Approach to Pregnancy Discrimination in *Hibbs*," *Stanford Law Review* 58 (2006): 1871–98.

14. *Nevada Department of Human Resources v. Hibbs*, note 12, at 730.

15. Ibid., at 731, 735.

16. Women's Committee, General Recommendation No. 24: Women and Health, UN Doc. A/54/38/Rev.1 (1999), at para. 30 ("General Recommendation No. 24").

17. See Women's Committee, General Recommendation No. 25, at para. 8. See generally *Thlimmenos v. Greece*, App. No. 34369/97, 31 Eur. H.R. Rep. 15 (2001), at para. 44 (European Court of Human Rights).

18. See *Philippine Telegraph and Telephone Company v. National Labor Relations Commission and Grace De Guzman*, G.R. No. 118978 (May 23, 1997), (1997) 272 Sup. Ct. Reports Annotated 596 (Phil., Supreme Court).

19. See *C. B. Muthamma v. Union of India and Others*, [1979] INSC 183; (1980) S.C.R. (1) 668; (1979) A.I.R. 1868; (1979) S.C.C. (4) 260 (Supreme Court) (India, Supreme Court).

20. See Women's Committee, General Recommendation No. 24.

21. See *Van Gorkom v. Attorney-General*, [1977] 1 N.Z.L.R. 535 (N.Z., Supreme Court); aff'd [1978] 2 N.Z.L.R. 387 (N.Z., Court of Appeal).

22. See *J.Y. Interpretation NO-365*, 1994 TWCC 32 (Taiwan, Constitutional Court), http://www.asianlii.org/tw/cases/TWCC/1994/32.html (accessed Dec. 31, 2008). But see Family Code of the Philippines, Executive Order No. 209 (1987), art. 211 (providing that "The father and the mother shall jointly exercise parental authority over the persons of their common children. In case of disagreement, the father's decision shall prevail, unless there is a judicial order to the contrary), http://www.chanrobles.com/executiveorderno209.htm (accessed Dec. 31, 2008).

23. *Nevada Department of Human Resources v. Hibbs*, note 12, at 731.

24. Women's Convention, art. 3.

25. See, e.g., *Anuj Garg and Others v. Hotel Association of India and Others*, (2008) 3 SCC 1 (India, Supreme Court).

26. See *Taylor v. Louisiana*, 419 U.S. 522, 530–31 (1975) (U.S., Supreme Court). But see *Hoyt v. Florida*, 368 U.S. 57 (1961) (U.S., Supreme Court).

27. See *J.Y. Interpretation NO-490*, [1999] TWCC 19 (Taiwan, Constitutional Court), http://www.asianlii.org/tw/cases/TWCC/1999/19.html (accessed Dec. 31, 2008).

28. See HCJ 4541/94, *Alice Miller v. Ministry of Defense*, [1995] IsrSC 49(4) 94, [1995–6] IsrLR 178 (Isr., Supreme Court); Case C-285/98, *Tanja Kreil v. Federal Republic of Germany*, [2000] E.C.R. I-69, ECJ Jan. 11, 2000, 57 (European Court of Justice), reprinted in Robyn Emerton, Kristine Adams, Andrew Byrnes, and Jane Connors, eds., *International Women's Rights Cases* (London: Cavendish, 2005), 413–19.

29. See *Vásquez v. Naval Academy of "Almirante Padilla,"* No. T-624, 1995 (Colom.,

Constitutional Court), cited in Center for Reproductive Rights and Universidad de los Andes School of Law, *Bodies on Trial: Reproductive Rights in Latin American Courts* (New York: Center for Reproductive Rights, 2003), 64; *United States v. Virginia*, 518 U.S. 515 (1996) (U.S., Supreme Court); *Faulkner v. Jones*, 66 F.3d 661 (4th Cir. 1995) (U.S., Court of Appeals, Fourth Circuit).

30. *Morales de Sierra v. Guatemala*, note 10, at para. 37.

31. Ibid, at para. 42.

32. See Women's Convention, art. 2(a).

33. See *Hariharan v. Reserve Bank of India*, (1999) 2 S.C.C. 228; [1999] 1 L.R.I. 35; [1999] INSC 37 (17 February 1999) (India, Supreme Court).

34. See, e.g., *Tysiąc v. Poland*, App. No. 5410/03, 2007 Eur. Ct. H.R. 219 (European Court of Human Rights); *Paulina Ramírez v. Mexico*, Case 161–02, Inter-Am. C.H.R., Report No. 21/07, OEA/Ser.l/V/II.130, doc. 22, rev. 1 (2007) (Inter-American Commission on Human Rights).

35. See, e.g., *Abdulaziz, Cabales and Balkandali v. United Kingdom*, App. Nos. 9214/80, 9473/81, 9474/81, 7 Eur. H.R. Rep. 471 (1985) (European Court of Human Rights).

36. See, e.g., Women's Committee, Report on Mexico Produced by the Committee on the Elimination of Discrimination against Women Under Article 8 of the Optional Protocol to the Convention, and Reply from the Government of Mexico, CEDAW, UN Doc. CEDAW/C/2005/OP.8/MEXICO (2005); *Maria Da Penha Maia Fernandes v. Brazil*, Case 12.051, Inter-Am. C.H.R., Report No. 54/01, OEA/Ser.L/V/II.111, doc. 20 rev. 704 (2000) (Inter-American Commission on Human Rights).

37. *Morales de Sierra v. Guatemala*, note 10, at paras. 2, 43.

38. Ibid., at para. 50.

39. Ibid.

40. See generally Mary Anne Case, "'The Very Stereotype the Law Condemns': Constitutional Sex Discrimination Law as a Quest for Perfect Proxies," *Cornell Law Review* 85 (1999–2000): 1447–91, at 1449.

41. See generally ibid.

42. See Deborah A. Widiss, Elizabeth L. Rosenblatt, and Douglas NeJaime, "Exposing Sex Stereotypes in Recent Same-Sex Marriage Jurisprudence," *Harvard Journal of Law & Gender* 30 (2007): 461–505, at 464, 469, 488; Reva B. Siegel, "The New Politics of Abortion: An Equality Analysis of Woman-Protective Abortion Restrictions," *University of Illinois Law Review* (2007): 991–1054, at 1048.

43. See, e.g., *Bradwell v. Illinois*, 83 U.S. (16 Wall.) 130 (1872) (U.S., Supreme Court); *In re French*, [1905] 37 N.B.R. 359 (Can., New Brunswick Supreme Court).

44. See Women's Convention, arts. 1, 2(f), 5(a); Women's Committee, General Recommendation No. 25. See also Widiss, note 42, at 464, 469, 488; Siegel, note 42, at 1042–43.

45. See *Orr v. Orr*, 440 U.S. 268, 279–80, 283 (1979) (U.S., Supreme Court).

46. See *Volks NO v. Robinson and Others* 2005 (5) BCLR 446 (S. Afr., Constitutional Court), at para. 154 (Sachs J., dissenting). See also Rikki Holtmaat, *Towards Different Law and Public Policy: The Significance of Article 5a CEDAW for the Elimination of Structural Gender Discrimination* (The Hague: Reed Business Information, 2004), xii.

47. *Morales de Sierra v. Guatemala*, note 10, at para. 44.

48. *Nevada Department of Human Resources v. Hibbs*, note 12, at 731.

49. Ibid., at 736.

50. *President of the Republic of South Africa v. Hugo*, note 11, at para. 37 (Goldstone J., majority).

51. Ibid., at para. 33.

52. See *Back v. Hastings-on-Hudson Union Free School District*, 365 F.3d 107, 113, 121 (2d Cir. 2004) (U.S., Court of Appeals, Second Circuit). See also Joan C. Williams and Elizabeth S. Westfall, "Deconstructing the Maternal Wall: Strategies for Vindicating the Civil Rights of 'Carers' in the Workplace," *Duke Journal of Gender Law & Policy* 13 (2006): 31–53, at 42; Sophia Reibetanz Moreau, "Equality Rights and the Relevance of Comparator Groups," *Journal of Law and Equality* 5 (2006): 81–96, at 90; Sophia R. Moreau, "The Wrongs of Unequal Treatment," *University of Toronto Law Journal* 54 (2004): 291–326, at 303. See generally David H. Gans, "Stereotyping and Difference: *Planned Parenthood v. Casey* and the Future of Sex Discrimination Law," *Yale Law Journal* 104 (1994–1995): 1875–1906.

53. *Back v. Hastings-on-Hudson Union Free School District*, note 52, at 122 (Calabresi J.).

54. Ibid., at 121.

55. Women's Convention, art. 3.

56. Ibid., arts. 1, 2(f).

57. See Committee on Economic, Social and Cultural Rights, General Comment No. 16, at para. 12.

58. *President of the Republic of South Africa v. Hugo*, note 11, at para. 83 (Kriegler J., dissenting).

59. *Nevada Department of Human Resources v. Hibbs*, note 12, at 731.

60. See Women's Convention, art. 1; Women's Committee, General Recommendation No. 25, at para. 7; Committee on Economic, Social and Cultural Rights, General Comment No. 16, at para. 13. See also *D.H. and Others v. The Czech Republic*, Appl. No. 57325/00, Nov. 13, 2007 (European Court of Human Rights).

61. See Women's Committee, General Recommendation No. 25.

62. See Claire A. Smearman, "Drawing the Line: The Legal, Ethical and Public Policy Implications of Refusal Clauses for Pharmacists," *Arizona Law Review* 48 (2006): 469–540.

63. Women's Committee, General Recommendation No. 25. See also Committee on Economic, Social and Cultural Rights, General Comment No. 16, at para. 13.

64. *Jordan v. S.* 2002 (6) SA 642 (CC) (S. Afr., Constitutional Court). See also Denise Meyerson, "Does the Constitutional Court of South Africa Take Rights Seriously? The Case of *S. v. Jordan*," *Acta Juridica* (2004): 138–54; Elsje Bonthuys, "Women's Sexuality in the South African Constitution," *Feminist Legal Studies* 14 (2006): 391–406.

65. Sexual Offences Act of 1957, s. 20(1)(aA) (S. Afr.).

66. *Jordan v. S.*, note 64, at para. 9

67. Ibid., at para. 10 (Ngcobo J., majority).

68. Ibid., at para. 11 (at common law, the customer is a *socius criminis* and also commits an offence under section 18 of the Riotous Assemblies Act of 1856).

69. Ibid., at para. 16.

70. Ibid., at para. 17.

71. Ibid., at para. 60 (O'Regan and Sachs JJ., dissenting).

72. Ibid., at para. 64.

73. Ibid., at para. 63.

74. Ibid., at para. 72.

75. Ibid., at para. 65.

76. Bonthuys, note 64, at 398.

77. The Honourable Madame Justice Claire L'Heureux-Dubé, "Beyond the Myths: Equality, Impartiality, and Justice," *Journal of Social Distress and the Homeless* 10 (2001): 87–104, at 89.

78. See Jocelynne A. Scutt, *Women and the Law: Commentary and Materials* (Sydney: Law Book, 1990), 60–61; Jody Amour, "Stereotypes and Prejudice: Helping Legal Decisionmakers Break the Prejudice Habit," *California Law Review* 83 (1995): 733–72, at 759–72; Charles Stangor, "Volume Overview," in Charles Stangor, ed., *Stereotypes and Prejudice: Essential Readings* (Philadelphia: Psychology Press, 2000), 1–16, at 12; Widiss, note 42, at 479.

79. L'Heureux-Dubé, note 77, at 92.

80. See Women's Committee, General Recommendation No. 25, at paras. 6–7.

81. *Cristina Muñoz-Vargas y Sainz de Vicuña v. Spain*, CEDAW, Communication No. 7/2005, UN Doc. CEDAW/C/39/D/7/2005 (2007) (Women's Committee), at para. 13.9 (Women's Committee member Shanthi Dairiam, dissenting).

82. See Women's Committee, General Recommendation No. 25, at para. 4.

83. *Cristina Muñoz-Vargas y Sainz de Vicuña v. Spain*, note 81, at para. 13.9 (Women's Committee member Shanthi Dairiam, dissenting).

84. See *Haines v. Leves*, (1987) 8 N.S.W.L.R. 442 (Austl., Court of Appeal of New South Wales).

85. See *Public Prosecutor v. Kota*, [1993] VUSC 8; [1980–1994] Van LR 661 (Vanuatu, Supreme Court), http://www.worldlii.org/vu/cases/VUSC/1993/8.html (accessed Dec. 31, 2008).

86. See *Jespersen v. Harrah's Operating Co.*, 444 F.3d 1104 (9th Cir. 2006) (U.S., Court of Appeals, Ninth Circuit). But see *EEOC v. Sage Realty Corp.*, 507 F. Supp. 599 (S.D.N.Y. 1981) (U.S., District Court–Southern District of New York) (finding a requirement to wear a sexually revealing work uniform to be discriminatory). See generally Katharine T. Bartlett, "Only Girls Wear Barrettes: Dress and Appearance Standards, Community Norms, and Workplace Equality," *Michigan Law Review* 92 (1993–1994): 2541–82; Symposium, "Makeup, Identity Performance and Discrimination," *Duke Journal of Gender Law & Policy* 14 (2007).

87. *Morales de Sierra v. Guatemala*, note 10, at para. 38.

88. Ibid., at paras. 38–39.

89. Ibid., at para. 44.

90. Ibid.

91. Ibid., at paras. 44–45.

92. Ibid., at paras. 51–54.

93. Ibid., at para. 52.

94. Ibid.

95. *Nevada Department of Human Resources v. Hibbs*, note 12, at 729–30 (Rehnquist, C.J.).

96. Ibid., at 730–32.

97. Ibid., at 731.

98. Ibid., at 732.

99. *President of the Republic of South Africa v. Hugo*, note 11, at para. 47 (Goldstone J., majority).

100. Ibid., at para. 38 (citations omitted).

101. Ibid., at paras. 39–40.

102. Cathi Albertyn and Beth Goldblatt, "Facing the Challenge of Transformation: Difficulties in the Development of an Indigenous Jurisprudence on Equality," *South African Journal on Human Rights* 14 (1998): 248–76, at 265.

103. Ibid.

104. Ibid.

105. Ibid., at 264–65.

106. *President of the Republic of South Africa v. Hugo*, note 11, at para. 80 (Kriegler J., dissenting).

107. Ibid., at para. 83.

108. Ibid.

109. See *Belgian Linguistics Case (No. 2)*, Eur. Ct. H.R. (ser. A), No. 6; 1 Eur. H.R. Rep. 252 (1968), at para. 41 (European Court of Human Rights).

110. *President of the Republic of South Africa v. Hugo*, note 11.

111. *Morales de Sierra v. Guatemala*, note 10.

112. *Nevada Department of Human Resources v. Hibbs*, note 12.

113. *President of the Republic of South Africa v. Hugo*, note 11, at para. 105 (Mokgoro J., concurring).

114. Ibid., at para. 106.

115. *Morales de Sierra v. Guatemala*, note 10, at para. 37.

116. *Nevada Department of Human Resources v. Hibbs*, note 12, at 734 (Rehnquist C.J.).

117. Ibid., at 729, citing *United States v. Virginia*, 518 U.S. 515, 533 (1996) (U.S., Supreme Court).

118. *Jordan v. S.*, note 64, at para. 15 (Ngcobo J., majority).

119. Ibid., at para. 10.

120. Ibid., at para. 96 (O'Regan and Sachs JJ., dissenting).

121. Ibid., at para. 98.

122. *Abdulaziz, Cabales and Balkandali v. United Kingdom*, note 35.

123. Ibid., at paras. 78–79.

124. Ibid., at para. 75.

125. Ibid.

126. Ibid., at para. 79.

127. Ibid., at para. 83.

128. HCJ 4541/94, *Alice Miller v. Ministry of Defense*, note 28.

129. Ibid., at 240 (Dorner J.).

130. *President of the Republic of South Africa v. Hugo*, note 11, at para. 106 (Mokgoro J., concurring).

131. Ibid.

132. Ibid., at para. 72 (Kriegler J., dissenting).

133. See, e.g., *J.Y. Interpretation NO-490*, note 27; *Bradwell v. Illinois*, note 43, at 141–42.

134. *Bradwell v. Illinois*, ibid.

135. Ibid., at 141 (Bradley, J. concurring).

136. See, e.g., *Mississippi University for Women v. Hogan*, 458 U.S. 718 (1982) (U.S., Supreme Court), at 724–25 (O'Connor J.); *Orr v. Orr*, note 45, at 279–80, 283 (Brennan J.) (citations omitted); *United States v. Virginia*, note 117, at 533–34 (Ginsburg J.) (citations omitted).

137. See Kwame Anthony Appiah, "Stereotypes and the Shaping of Identity," *California Law Review* 88 (2000): 41–54, at 43, 52–53.

138. *President of the Republic of South Africa v. Hugo*, note 11, at para. 47 (Goldstone J., majority).

139. Ibid.
140. Ibid., at para. 92 (Mokgoro J., concurring).
141. Ibid., at para. 93.
142. Ibid.

Chapter 5. The Role of the Women's Committee in Eliminating Gender Stereotyping

1. Convention on the Elimination of All Forms of Discrimination against Women, Dec. 18, 1979 (entered into force Sept. 3, 1981), 1249 U.N.T.S. 13, reprinted in 19 *I.L.M.* 33 (1980) ("Women's Convention"). See generally Simone Cusack and Rebecca J. Cook, "Combating Discrimination Based on Sex and Gender," in Catarina Krause and Martin Scheinin, eds., *International Protection of Human Rights: A Textbook* (Turku/Abo: Institute for Human Rights, Abo Akademi University, forthcoming 2009), 205–26.

2. See, e.g., Women's Committee, General Recommendation No. 25: Article 4, Paragraph 1, of the Convention on the Elimination of All Forms of Discrimination against Women, on Temporary Special Measures, UN Doc. A/59/38 (2004), at paras. 6–7 ("General Recommendation No. 25"); Committee on Economic, Social and Cultural Rights, General Comment No. 16: The Equal Rights of Men and Women to the Enjoyment of All Economic, Social and Cultural Rights, UN Doc. E/C.12/2005/4 (2005), at para. 19 ("General Comment No. 16").

3. Optional Protocol to the Convention on the Elimination of All Forms of Discrimination against Women, Oct. 19, 1999 (entered into force Dec. 22, 2000), G.A. Res. 54/4, UN G.A.O.R., 54th Sess., Supp. No. 49 at 4, UN Doc. A/54/4 (1999), reprinted in *I.L.M.* 281 (2000) ("Optional Protocol").

4. See Rikki Holtmaat, *Towards Different Law and Public Policy: The Significance of Article 5a CEDAW for the Elimination of Structural Gender Discrimination* (The Hague: Reed Business Information, 2004), 31–45; Frances Raday, "Culture, Religion, and CEDAW's Article 5(a)," in Hanna Beate Schöpp-Schilling and Cees Flinterman, eds., *Circle of Empowerment: Twenty-Five Years of the UN Committee on the Elimination of Discrimination Against Women* (New York: Feminist Press, 2007), 68–85.

5. Women's Convention, art. 17. See generally Schöpp-Schilling and Flinterman, eds., note 4; Hanna Beate Schöpp-Schilling, "Treaty Body Reform: The Case of the Committee on the Elimination of Discrimination Against Women," *Human Rights Law Review* 7 (2007): 201–24; Elizabeth Evatt, "Finding a Voice for Women's Rights: The Early Days of CEDAW," *George Washington International Law Review* 34 (2002–2003): 515–54; Andrew C. Byrnes, "The Convention on the Elimination of All Forms of Discrimination Against Women," in Wolfgang Benedek, Esther M. Kisaakye and Gerd Oberleitner, eds., *Human Rights of Women: International Instruments and African Experiences* (London: Zed Books, 2002), 119–72.

6. Women's Convention, art. 18(1).

7. Ibid., art. 18(2).

8. Ruth Halperin-Kaddari, *Women in Israel: A State of Their Own* (Philadelphia: University of Pennsylvania Press, 2004), 5–6. See generally Sally Engle Merry, *Human Rights and Gender Violence: Translating International Law into Local Justice* (Chicago: University of Chicago Press, 2006), 72–102.

9. See, e.g., L. S. Groenman et al., *Het Vrouwenverdrag in Nederland Anno 1997* (Den Haag: Ministerie van SZW, 1997), discussed in Holtmaat, note 4.

10. See Women's Committee, Consideration of Reports Submitted by States Parties Under Article 18 of the Convention on the Elimination of All Forms of Discrimination against Women; Second and Third Periodic Reports of States Parties: Thailand, UN Doc. CEDAW/C/THA/2–3 (1997), at para. 160.

11. Ibid., at para. 161.

12. See, e.g., Women's Committee, Concluding Observations: Jamaica, CEDAW, UN GAOR, 61st sess., supp. no. 38 (A/61/38) part III (2006) 228, at paras. 383–84, 401–2; Women's Committee, Concluding Observations: Ireland, CEDAW, UN GAOR, 60th sess., supp. no. (A/60/38) part II (2005) 151, at paras. 380, 382–83; Women's Committee, Concluding Observations: Norway, UN Doc. CEDAW/C/NOR/CO/7 (2007), at paras. 17–18; Women's Committee, Concluding Observations: Mozambique, UN Doc. CEDAW/C/MOZ/CO/2 (2007), at paras. 20–21; Women's Committee, Concluding Observations: Syrian Arab Republic, UN Doc. CEDAW/C/SYR/CO/1 (2007), at paras. 27–28.

13. Women's Committee, Concluding Observations: Democratic People's Republic of Korea, CEDAW, UN GAOR, 60th sess., supp. no. 38 (A/60/38) part II (2005) 101, at para. 35.

14. Ibid., at para. 36.

15. Women's Convention, art. 21. See Dianne Otto, "'Gender Comment': Why Does the UN Committee on Economic, Social and Cultural Rights Need a General Comment on Women?" *Canadian Journal of Women and the Law* 14 (2002): 1–52 (discussing General Recommendations and General Comments concerning women's rights).

16. Women's Committee, General Recommendation No. 19: Violence against Women, UN Doc. A/47/38 (1992) ("General Recommendation No. 19").

17. Women's Committee, General Recommendation No. 21: Equality in Marriage and Family Relations, UN Doc. A/49/38 (1994) ("General Recommendation No. 21").

18. Women's Committee, General Recommendation No. 23: Political and Public Life, UN Doc. A/52/38/Rev.1 at 61 (1997) ("General Recommendation No. 23").

19. Women's Committee, General Recommendation No. 24: Women and Health, UN Doc. A/54/38/Rev.1 (1999) ("General Recommendation No. 24").

20. Women's Committee, General Recommendation No. 25.

21. Women's Committee, General Recommendation No. 26: Women Migrant Workers, UN Doc. CEDAW/C/2009/WP.1/R (2008).

22. See Women's Committee, General Recommendation No. 3: Education and Public Information Campaigns—Education and Public Information Campaigns, UN Doc. A/42/38 at 78 (1987) ("General Recommendation No. 3"); Women's Committee, General Recommendation No. 19, at paras. 11–12, 21, 23, 24(e)–(f), (t)(ii); Women's Committee, General Recommendation No. 21, at paras. 3, 11–12, 14, 17, 41–44, 46–47, 48(b), 50; Women's Committee, General Recommendation No. 23, at paras. 8, 10–12, 20(c), 44; Women's Committee, General Recommendation No. 25, at paras. 6–7, 38. See also Holtmaat, note 4, 31–45.

23. Women's Committee, General Recommendation No. 3.

24. Women's Committee, General Recommendation No. 23, at para. 8.

25. Ibid., at para. 10.

26. Ibid., at para. 44.

27. Ibid.
28. Ibid., at para. 11.
29. See Women's Committee, General Recommendation No. 25, at paras. 6–7.
30. Optional Protocol. See generally Bal Sokhi-Bulley, "The Optional Protocol to CEDAW: First Steps," *Human Rights Law Review* 6 (2006): 143–59; Felipe Gómez Isa, "The Optional Protocol for the Convention on the Elimination of All Forms of Discrimination Against Women: Strengthening the Protection Mechanisms of Women's Human Rights," *Arizona Journal of International & Comparative Law* 20 (2003): 291–322; Heidi Gilchrist, "The Optional Protocol to the Women's Convention: An Argument for Ratification," *Columbia Journal of Transnational Law* 39 (2001): 763–83; Laboni Amena Hoq, "The Women's Convention and Its Optional Protocol: Empowering Women to Claim Their Internationally Protected Rights," *Columbia Human Rights Law Review* 32 (2001): 677–726; Mireille G. E. Bijnsdorp, "The Strength of the Optional Protocol to the United Nations Women's Convention," *Netherlands Quarterly of Human Rights* 18 (2000): 329–55; Lilly Sucharipa-Behrmann, "The Individual Complaints Procedure Provided for by the Optional Protocol to CEDAW: A First Evaluation," in Wolfgang Benedek et al., eds., *Development and Developing International and European Law: Essays in Honour of Konrad Ginther on the Occasion of His 65th Birthday* (Frankfurt am Main: Peter Lang, 1999) 653–70.
31. See, e.g., Andrew Byrnes and Jane Connors, "Enforcing the Human Rights of Women: A Complaints Procedure for the Women's Convention," *Brooklyn Journal of International Law* 21 (1996): 679–798, at 698–705.
32. See Optional Protocol, art. 2. For a list of current States Parties to the Optional Protocol, see http://www2.ohchr.org/english/bodies/ratification/8_b.htm (accessed Dec. 31, 2008).
33. See Optional Protocol, arts. 8–10.
34. *Cristina Muñoz-Vargas y Sainz de Vicuña v. Spain*, CEDAW, Communication No. 7/2005, UN Doc. CEDAW/C/39/D/7/2005 (2007) (Women's Committee).
35. See *A.T. v. Hungary*, CEDAW, Communication No. 2/2003, UN Doc. CEDAW/C/32/D/2/2003 (2005); *Fatma Yildirim v. Austria*, CEDAW, Communication No. 6/2005, UN Doc. CEDAW/C/39/D/6/2005 (2007); *Şahide Goekce v. Austria*, CEDAW, Communication No. 5/2005, UN Doc. CEDAW/C/39/D/5/2005 (2007); Report on Mexico Produced by the Committee on the Elimination of Discrimination Against Women Under Article 8 of the Optional Protocol to the Convention, and Reply from the Government of Mexico, CEDAW, UN Doc. CEDAW/C/2005/OP.8/MEXICO (2005) ("Ciudad Juárez Inquiry") (Women's Committee).
36. *Karen T. Vertido v. The Philippines*, communication filed with the Women's Committee on Nov. 29, 2007. See Clara Rita A. Padilla, "A Call for Philippine Implementation of Women's Rights Under CEDAW," *Ateneo Law Journal* 52 (2008): 765–803, at 773–74 (discussing the *Karen T. Vertido* communication).
37. *Cristina Muñoz-Vargas y Sainz de Vicuña v. Spain*, note 34, at paras. 11.3–11.5 (Women's Committee, majority).
38. Ibid., at paras. 12.1–12.2 (Women's Committee, concurring).
39. Ibid., at para. 13.7 (Women's Committee member Shanthi Dairiam, dissenting) (emphasis added).
40. See Merry, note 8, at 75.
41. See Raday, note 4, at 81.

42. See Julie F. Kay and Ashley Jackson, *Sex, Lies and Stereotypes: How Abstinence-Only Programs Harm Women and Girls* (New York: Legal Momentum, 2008). See also Minority Staff of H. Comm. on Gov't Reform, 108th Congr., The Content of Federally Funded Abstinence-Only Education Programs (Comm. Print 2004), 16–18.

43. Kwame Anthony Appiah, "Stereotypes and the Shaping of Identity," *California Law Review* 88 (2000): 41–54, at 49.

44. Women's Committee, General Recommendation No. 25, at paras. 6–7.

45. See Joan. C. Williams, "Deconstructing Gender," *Michigan Law Review* 87 (1988–1989): 797–845.

46. See, e.g., Crimes Act 1958 (Vic), s 37AAA.

47. Women's Convention, arts. 1, 2(f).

48. See Optional Protocol, art. 2.

49. See ibid., art. 3.

50. See ibid., art. 4(1).

51. See ibid., art. 4(2)(a).

52. See ibid., art. 4(2)(e).

53. See ibid., art. 4(2)(b).

54. See ibid., art. 4(2)(c).

55. See ibid., art. 4(2)(d).

56. See ibid., art. 7.

57. See ibid., art. 7(3).

58. See ibid., art. 7(5).

59. See ibid., art. 4(1).

60. See *Şahide Goekce v. Austria*, note 35, at para. 7.2; *Fatma Yildirim v. Austria*, note 35, at para. 7.2. See also *K.L. v. Peru*, HRC, Communication No. 1153/2003, UN Doc. CCPR/C/85/D/1153 (2005), at para. 5.2 (Human Rights Committee).

61. *A.S. v. Hungary*, CEDAW, Communication No. 4/2004, UN Doc. CEDAW/C/36/D/4/2004 (2006), at para. 10.3 (Women's Committee); *Şahide Goekce v. Austria*, note 35, at paras. 7.5, 11.3; *Fatma Yildirim v. Austria*, note 35, at paras. 7.5, 11.2.

62. Optional Protocol, art. 4(1).

63. *A.T. v. Hungary*, note 35.

64. Ibid. at para. 3.1.

65. Ibid., at para. 8.4.

66. Ibid.

67. Ibid., at para. 8.3.

68. *Cristina Muñoz-Vargas y Sainz de Vicuña v. Spain*, note 34.

69. See e.g., *E.B. v. France*, Appl. No. 43546/02, Jan. 22, 2008 (European Court of Human Rights). See generally Human Rights and Equal Opportunity Commission, *Same-Sex: Same Entitlements. National Inquiry into Discrimination Against People in Same-Sex Relationships: Financial and Work-Related Entitlements and Benefits* (Sydney: Human Rights and Equal Opportunity Commission, 2007), 87–112, http://www.humanrights.gov.au/samesex/index.html (last accessed Dec. 31, 2008).

70. Michelle O'Sullivan, "Stereotyping and Male Identification: 'Keeping Women in Their Place,'" in Christina Murray, ed., *Gender and the New South African Legal Order* (Kenwyn, South Africa: Juta, 1994), 185–201, at 190.

71. Optional Protocol, art. 4(2)(a).

72. See *Rahime Kayhan v. Turkey*, CEDAW, Communication No. 8/2005, UN Doc. CEDAW/C/34/D/8/2005 (2006) (Women's Committee).

73. Convention on the Rights of Persons with Disabilities, Dec. 13, 2006 (entered into force May 3, 2008), G.A. Res. 61/106, UN Doc. A/61/611 (2006), art. 8(1)(b).

74. Protocol to the African Charter on Human and Peoples' Rights on the Rights of Women in Africa, Sept. 13, 2000 (entered into force Nov. 25, 2005), O.A.U. Doc. CAB/LEG/66.6, reprinted in 1 *Afr. Hum. Rts. L.J.* 40, arts. 2(2), 4(2)(d), 12(1)(b). See generally Fareda Banda, *Women, Law and Human Rights: An African Perspective* (Oxford: Hart, 2005).

75. Inter-American Convention on the Prevention, Punishment and Eradication of Violence against Women, June 9, 1994 (entered into force Mar. 5, 1995), OAS/Ser.L/V/I.4 rev. (Jan 2000), reprinted in 33 *I.L.M.* 1534 (1994), arts. 6(b), 8(b).

76. Inter-American Convention on the Elimination of All Forms of Discrimination against Persons with Disabilities, June 7, 1999 (entered into force Sept. 21, 2001), AG/RES. 1608 (XXIX-O/99), art. 3(2)(c).

77. See, e.g., Women's Committee, General Recommendation No. 25; Committee on Economic, Social and Cultural Rights, General Comment No. 16.

78. See, e.g., *Petrovic v. Austria*, App. No. 20458/92, 33 Eur. H.R. Rep. 307 (1998) (Bernhardt and Spielmann JJ., dissenting) (European Court of Human Rights).

79. See, e.g., *President of the Republic of South Africa v. Hugo* 1997 (4) SA 1 (CC) (S. Afr., Constitutional Court); *Public Prosecutor v. Kota*, [1993] VUSC 8; [1980–1994] Van LR 661 (Vanuatu, Supreme Court), http://www.worldlii.org/vu/cases/VUSC/1993/8.html (accessed Dec. 31, 2008).

80. *Rahime Kayhan v. Turkey*, note 72.

81. See *Leyla Şahin v. Turkey* (*Şahin II*), Appl. No. 44774/98, Nov. 10, 2005 (Grand Chamber) (European Court of Human Rights).

82. *Rahime Kayhan v. Turkey*, note 72, at para. 7.3.

83. See Courtney W. Howland, "The Challenge of Religious Fundamentalism to the Liberty and Equality Rights of Women: An Analysis Under the United Nations Charter," *Columbia Journal of Transnational Law* 35 (1997): 271–378, at 282–324; Courtney W. Howland, "Safeguarding Women's Political Freedoms Under the ICCPR in the Face of Religious Fundamentalism," in Courtney W. Howland, ed., *Religious Fundamentalisms and the Human Rights of Women* (New York: St. Martin's Press, 1999), 93–104, at 97.

84. Optional Protocol, art. 4(2)(e).

85. *A.T. v. Hungary*, note 35, at para. 8.5.

86. Ibid.

87. See, e.g., *R. v. Lavallee*, [1990] 1 S.C.R. 852 (Can., Supreme Court), at paras. 48, 52, 58.

88. *Haines v. Leves*, (1987) 8 N.S.W.L.R. 442 (Street C.J.) (Austl., Court of Appeal of New South Wales).

89. Ibid., at 457.

90. *Leves v. Haines*, (1986) E.O.C. 92–167 (Austl., Equal Opportunity Tribunal of New South Wales), excerpted in Jocelynne A. Scutt, *Women and the Law: Commentary and Materials* (Sydney: Law Book, 1990), 70.

91. Optional Protocol, art. 4(2)(b).

92. Donna J. Sullivan, "Commentary on the Optional Protocol to the Convention on the Elimination of All Forms of Discrimination Against Women," in Inter-American Institute of Human Rights, ed., *Optional Protocol: Convention on the Elimination of All Forms of Discrimination Against Women* (San José: Inter-American Institute of Human Rights, 2000), 31–107, at 53.

93. *Cristina Muñoz-Vargas y Sainz de Vicuña v. Spain*, note 34, at paras. 11.3–11.7.

94. Ibid., at paras. 12.1–12.2.

95. Ibid., at para. 12.2.

96. Ibid.

97. Ibid., at paras. 13.5 and 13.8.

98. Ibid., at para. 13.7.

99. Ibid., at para. 13.9.

100. Ibid.

101. Women's Committee, General Recommendation No. 25, at paras. 6–7.

102. Optional Protocol, art. 4(2)(c).

103. Ibid., art. 4(2)(d).

104. Sullivan, note 92, at 53.

105. Ibid., at 54.

106. *President of the Republic of South Africa v. Hugo*, note 79.

107. *R. v. Ewanchuk*, [1999] 1 S.C.R. 330 (L'Heureux-Dubé J., concurring) (Can., Supreme Court).

108. *Morales de Sierra v. Guatemala*, Case 11.625, Inter-Am. C.H.R., Report No. 4/01, OEA/Ser.L/V/II.111, doc. 20 rev. (2001) (Inter-American Commission on Human Rights).

109. See, e.g., Katarina Tomaševski, *Human Rights and Poverty Reduction: Girls' Education Through a Human Rights Lens: What Can Be Done Differently, What Can Be Made Better* (London: Overseas Development Institute, 2005) (citations omitted), http://www.odi.org.uk/rights/Meeting%20Series/GirlsEducation.pdf (accessed Dec. 31, 2008), 3.

110. See, e.g., Kay and Jackson, note 42.

111. See, e.g., Joan C. Williams and Elizabeth S. Westfall, "Deconstructing the Maternal Wall: Strategies for Vindicating the Civil Rights of 'Carers' in the Workplace," *Duke Journal of Gender Law & Policy* 13 (2006): 31–53.

112. See, e.g., Susan T. Fiske et al., "Social Science Research on Trial: Use of Sex Stereotyping Research in *Price Waterhouse* v. *Hopkins*," *American Psychologist* 46 (1991): 1049–60; American Psychological Association, "In the Supreme Court of the United States: *Price Waterhouse v. Ann B. Hopkins*; Amicus Curiae Brief for the American Psychological Association," *American Psychologist* 46 (1991): 1061–70.

113. See, e.g., Williams and Westfall, note 111.

114. *Price Waterhouse v. Hopkins*, 490 U.S. 228 (1989) (U.S., Supreme Court).

115. Ibid., at 256 (Brennan J.).

116. See *R. v. Birmingham City Council*, [1989] 2 W.L.R. 520 (U.K., House of Lords).

117. See, e.g., *Haines v. Leves*, note 88.

118. See, e.g., ibid.; *Jex-Blake v. Senatus of the University of Edinburgh*, (1873) 11 M. 784 (U.K., Court of Session), summarized in Albie Sachs and Joan Hoff Wilson, *Sexism and the Law: A Study of Male Beliefs and Legal Bias in Britain and the United States* (New York: The Free Press, 1979), 14–17.

119. Optional Protocol, art. 5(1).

120. See *Minister of Health & Others v. Treatment Action Campaign & Others (No. 2)* 2002 (5) SA 721, 2002 (10) BCLR 1033 (S. Afr., Constitutional Court).

121. See Cynthia Eyakuze et al., "From PMTCT to a More Comprehensive AIDS Response for Women: A Much-Needed Shift," *Developing World Bioethics* 8 (2008): 33–42.

122. See Jaya Sagade, *Child Marriage in India: Social-Legal and Human Rights Dimensions* (New Delhi: Oxford University Press, 2005); UNICEF, *Early Marriage: Child Spouses* (Florence: UNICEF Innocenti Research Centre, 2001).

123. See Nadine Dostrovsky, Rebecca J. Cook and Michaël Gagnon, *Annotated Bibliography on Comparative and International Law Relating to Forced Marriage* (Ottawa: Department of Justice, Canada, 2007), http://www.justice.gc.ca/eng/pi/pad-rpad/rep-rap/mar/mar.pdf (accessed Dec. 31, 2008).

124. See, e.g., *Siddique v. State*, Crl. Appeal No. 170/2000 (2002) 4 C.H.R.L.D. 145 (Pakistan, Lahore High Court). See also Lynn Welchman and Sara Hossain, eds., *"Honour": Crimes, Paradigms and Violence against Women* (London: Zed Books, 2005).

125. Optional Protocol, art. 7.

126. Ibid., art. 7(3).

127. *A.T. v. Hungary*, note 35, at para. 9.6; *A.S. v. Hungary*, note 61, at para. 11.5.

128. See, e.g., *A.S. v. Hungary*, note 61, at para. 11.5. See also *X and Y v. The Netherlands*, App. No. 8978/80, 91 Eur. Ct. H.R. (ser. A), 8 Eur. H.R. Rep. 235 (1985) (European Court of Human Rights); *Airey v. Ireland*, App. No. 6289/73, 32 Eur. Ct. H.R. (ser. A), 2 Eur. H.R. Rep. 305 (1979) (European Court of Human Rights).

129. See, e.g., *A.T. v. Hungary*, note 35, at para. 9.6.

130. See Women's Convention, art. 23.

131. See Optional Protocol, art. 7(5).

132. See *A.T. v. Hungary*, note 35; *Şahide Goekce v. Austria*, note 35; *Fatma Yildirim v. Austria*, note 35.

133. *Cristina Muñoz-Vargas y Sainz de Vicuña v. Spain*, note 34.

134. *A.T. v. Hungary*, note 35.

135. Ibid., at para. 9.4 (citations omitted).

136. Ibid., at para. 9.3.

137. Ibid., at para. 9.4.

138. Ibid.

139. See Women's Committee, General Recommendation No. 19, at para. 7.

140. See Optional Protocol, arts. 8–10.

141. See ibid., art. 10.

142. Maria Regina Tavares da Silva and Yolanda Ferrer Gómez, "The Juárez Murders and the Inquiry Procedure," in Schöpp-Schilling and Flinterman, eds., note 4, 299–309, at 299. See also Sullivan, note 92, at 74–75.

143. Tavares da Silva and Ferrer Gómez, note 142, at 299–300.

144. Ibid., at 300 note 2. See also Sullivan, note 92, at 73.

145. Tavares da Silva and Ferrer Gómez, note 142, at 300. See also Sullivan, note 92, at 73–74.

146. Tavares da Silva and Ferrer Gómez, note 142, at 300 note 3.

147. Optional Protocol, arts. 8(2), 8(5).

148. Ibid., art. 8(3).

149. Ibid. art. 9.

150. See Ciudad Juárez inquiry, note 35.

151. See Optional Protocol, art. 8(1).

152. See notes 106–18 and accompanying text.

153. See Amnesty International, *Safe Schools: Every Girl's Right* (London: Amnesty International Publications, 2008), 19.

154. See, e.g., *Lloyd Chaduka and Morgenster College v. Enita Mandizvidza*, Judg-

ment No. SC 114/2001, Civil Appeal No. 298/2000 (Zimb., Supreme Court), summarized in Kibrom Isaac, *Legal Grounds: Reproductive and Sexual Rights in African Commonwealth Courts* (New York: Center for Reproductive Rights and the International Reproductive and Sexual Health Law Programme, University of Toronto, 2005), 60; *Mfolo and Others v. Minister of Education, Bophuthatswana* [1992] (3) SALR 181, [1994] 1 BCLR 136 (S. Afr., Supreme Court, Bophuthatswana and General Division), summarized in Isaac, ibid., 59; *Student Representative Council of Molepolole College of Education v. Attorney General,* (Civil Appeal No. 13 of 1994) [1995] B.W.C.A. 17 (Bots., Court of Appeal), summarized in Isaac, ibid., 58; *Mónica Carabantes Galleguillos v. Chile,* Case 12.046, Inter-Am. C.H.R., Report No. 33/02, OEA/Ser.L/V/II.117, doc. 1 rev. 1 (2003) (Inter-American Commission on Human Rights).

155. See generally Silvia Pimentel, "Education and Legal Literacy," in Schöpp-Schilling and Flinterman, eds., note 4, 90–103.

156. Optional Protocol, art. 8.

157. Women's Committee, General Recommendation No. 25, at paras. 6–7.

158. Raday, note 4, at 71, 74.

159. *Bradwell v. Illinois,* 83 U.S. (16 Wall.) 130 (1872) (U.S., Supreme Court) (Bradley J., concurring).

160. *President of the Republic of South Africa v. Hugo,* note 79.

161. *Petrovic v. Austria,* note 78.

162. *Morales de Sierra v. Guatemala,* note 108.

163. Optional Protocol, art. 8(3).

164. Ibid.

165. Ibid., art. 9.

166. Tavares da Silva and Ferrer Gómez, note 142, at 303.

167. Ciudad Juárez inquiry, note 35.

168. Inter American Commission on Human Rights, Rapporteur on the Rights of Women (IACHR), *The Situation of the Rights of Women in Ciudad Juárez, Mexico: The Right to Be Free from Violence and Discrimination,* OEA/Ser.L/V/II.117, doc. 44 (2003).

169. See Amnesty International, *Mexico. Intolerable Killings: 10 Years of Abductions and Murders of Women in Ciudad Juárez and Chihuahua,* AI Index: AMR 41/026/2003.

170. See Human Rights Council, *Civil and Political Rights, Including Questions of: Disappearances and Summary Executions; Visit to Mexico,* UN Doc. E/CN.4/2000/3/ Add.3 (1999) (prepared by Special Rapporteur on extrajudicial, summary or arbitrary executions, Ms. Asma Jahangir); Human Rights Council, *Civil and Political Rights, Including Questions of: Independence of the Judiciary, Administration of Justice, Impunity; Report on the Mission to Mexico,* UN Doc. E/CN.4/2002/72/ Add.1 (2002) (prepared by Special Rapporteur on the independence of judges and lawyers, Dato'Param Cumaraswamy). See also Human Rights Council, *Integration of the Human Rights of Women and a Gender Perspective: Violence against Women; Mission to Mexico,* UN Doc. E/CN.4/2006/061/Add.4 (2006) (prepared by Special Rapporteur on Violence against Women, Its Causes and Consequences, Ms., Yakin Ertürk).

171. See *Esmeralda Herrera Monreal v. Mexico,* Case 282/02, Inter-Am. C.H.R., Report No. 17/05, OEA/Ser.L/V/II.124, doc. 5 (2005); *Claudia Ivette González v. Mexico,* Case 281/02, Inter-Am. C.H.R., Report No. 16/05, OEA/Ser.L/V/ II.124, doc. 5 (2005); *Inés Fernández Ortega et al. v. Mexico,* Case 540–04, Inter-Am. C.H.R., Report No. 94/06, OEA/Ser.L/V/II.127, doc. 4 rev. 1 (2007);

Laura Berenice Ramos Monárrez v. Mexico, Case 283/02, Inter-Am. C.H.R., Report No. 18/05, OEA/Ser.L/V/II.124, doc. 5 (2005); *María Isabel Véliz Franco v. Guatemala,* Case 95–04, Inter-Am. C.H.R., Report No. 92/06, OEA/Ser.L/V/II.127, doc. 4 rev. 1 (2007); *Paloma Angélica Escobar Ledesma et al. v. Mexico,* Case 1175–03, Inter-Am. C.H.R., Report No. 32/06, OEA/Ser.L/V/II.127, doc. 4 rev. 1 (2007); *Silvia Arce et al. v. Mexico,* Case 1176–03, Inter-Am. C.H.R., Report No. 31/06, OEA/Ser.L/V/II.127, doc. 4 rev. 1 (2007); *Valentina Rosendo Cantú et al. v. Mexico,* Case 972–03, Inter-Am. C.H.R., Report No. 93/06, OEA/Ser.L/V/II.127, doc. 4 rev. 1 (2007) (Inter-American Commission on Human Rights).

172. See *Campo Algodonero: Claudia Ivette González, Esmeralda Herrera Monreal, and Laura Berenice Ramos Monárrez v. Mexico,* Cases 12.496, 12.497 and 12.498 (pending, Inter-American Court on Human Rights). For a copy of the application filed by the Inter-American Commission on Human Rights on Nov. 4, 2007, see http://www.cidh.org/demandas/12.496–7–8%20Campo%20Algodonero%20Mexico%204%20noviembre%202007%20ENG.pdf (last accessed Dec. 31, 2008).

173. See Women's Committee, Consideration of Reports Submitted by States Parties Under Article 18 of the Convention on the Elimination of All Forms of Discrimination against Women; Sixth Periodic Report of State Parties: Mexico, UN Doc. CEDAW/C/MEX/6 (2006); Women's Committee, Concluding Comments: Mexico, UN Doc. CEDAW/C/MEX/CO/6/CRP.1 (2006).

174. Ciudad Juárez inquiry, note 35, at paras. 36, 61, 73. See also Amnesty International, note 169, at 25.

175. See Ciudad Juárez inquiry, note 35, at para. 36; Deborah M. Weissman, "The Political Economy of Violence: Toward an Understanding of the Gender-Based Murders of Ciudad Juárez," *North Carolina Journal of International Law and Commercial Regulation* 30 (2004–2005): 795–868, at 796.

176. Ciudad Juárez inquiry, note 35, at paras. 37, 61.

177. Ibid., at para. 73.

178. Ibid., at paras. 38, 63.

179. Ibid., at paras. 6, 37, 39, 43, 87, 96–97, 133; IACHR, note 168, at para. 33; Amnesty International, note 169, at 12.

180. See, e.g., Melissa W. Wright, "The Dialectics of Still Life: Murder, Women, and Maquiladoras" *Public Culture* 11 (1999): 453–73, reprinted in Jean Comaroff and John L. Comaroff, eds., *Millennial Capitalism and the Culture of Neoliberalism* (Durham, N.C.: Duke University Press, 2001), 125–46.

181. See, e.g., IACHR, note 168, at para. 43.

182. Ciudad Juárez inquiry, note 35, at para. 66.

183. Amnesty International, note 169, at 25.

184. Shae Garwood, "Working to Death: Gender, Labour, and Violence in Ciudad Juárez, Mexico" *Peace, Conflict and Development: An Interdisciplinary Journal* 2 (2002): 1–23, at 22, http://www.peacestudiesjournal.org.uk/docs/working2.pdf (accessed Dec. 31, 2008).

185. Amnesty International, note 169, at 29.

186. See Ciudad Juárez inquiry, note 35, at paras. 40, 87–91, 111–50. See also IACHR, note 168, at para. 70.

187. Ciudad Juárez inquiry, note 35, at para. 67. See also IACHR, note 168, at paras. 4, 125.

188. Ciudad Juárez inquiry, note 35, at paras. 50–60.

189. Declaration on the Elimination of Violence against Women, Feb. 23,

1994, G.A. Res. 48/104, UN G.A.O.R., 11th Sess., Supp. No. 49 at 217, UN Doc. A/48/49 (1993), cited in Ciudad Juárez inquiry, note 35, at para. 259.

190. Women's Committee, General Recommendation No. 19, cited in Ciudad Juárez inquiry, note 35.

191. Ciudad Juárez inquiry, note 35, at para. 36.

192. Ibid., at para. 159.

193. Ibid.

194. Ibid., at para. 261.

195. Ibid., at para. 55.

196. Ibid., at para. 57.

197. Ibid., at paras. 263–94.

198. Ibid., at para. 287.

199. *Campo Algodonero: Claudia Ivette González, Esmeralda Herrera Monreal, and Laura Berenice Ramos Monárrez v. Mexico*, Cases 12.496, 12.497 and 12.498 (Inter-American Court of Human Rights, pending as of Dec. 31, 2008).

200. Simone Cusack, Rebecca J. Cook, Viviana Krsticevic, and Vanessa Coria, *Amicus Curiae Submission to the Inter-American Court of Human Rights in the Case of Campo Algodonero: Claudia Ivette González, Esmeralda Herrera Monreal, and Laura Berenice Ramos Monárrez, Cases Nos. 12.496, 12.497 and 12.498 Against the United Mexican States* (Dec. 3, 2008), http://www.law.utoronto.ca/documents/repro-health/BriefMexicoCiudadJuarez2008English.pdf (English), http://www.law.utoronto.ca/documents/reprohealth/BriefMexicoCiudadJuarez2008Espanol.pdf (Spanish) (accessed Dec. 31, 2008).

201. *Ciudad Juárez inquiry*, note 35, at para. 261.

202. Ibid., at para. 57.

203. Ibid., at para. 25.

204. Ibid., at para. 67.

205. See generally Wright, note 180, 125–46 (discussing the concept of the "disposable" woman).

206. Human Rights Council, *Civil and Political Rights, Including Questions of: Disappearances and Summary Executions; Visit to Mexico*, note 170, at para. 89 [emphasis added].

207. Civil Code of the State of Chihuahua (as in effect in 2001), arts. 151, 170.

208. See *Morales de Sierra v. Guatemala*, note 108, at para. 44.

209. See IACHR, note 168, at paras. 4, 81, and 135. See also IACHR, *Access to Justice for Women Victims of Violence in the Americas*, OEA/Ser.L/V/II. doc. 68 (2007), at para. 20.

210. Amnesty International, note 169, at 7.

211. See Wright, note 180, at 129 (citation omitted).

212. See Debbie Nathan, "The Juárez Murders," *Amnesty International Magazine* 29, 1 (2003), http://www.amnestyusa.org/amnestynow/juarez.html (accessed Dec. 31, 2008).

213. See, e.g., Wright, note 180, at 137; Jessica Livingston, "Murder in Juárez: Gender, Sexual Violence, and the Global Assembly Line," *Frontiers: A Journal of Women's Studies* 25 (2004): 59–76, at 61–62.

214. See, e.g., Weissman, note 175, at 817–18; Livingston, note 213.

215. Ciudad Juárez inquiry, note 35, at paras. 54–55.

Chapter 6. Moving Forward with the Elimination of Gender Stereotyping

1. See, e.g., Maryann Valiulis, Aoife O'Driscoll, and Jennifer Redmond, *An Introduction to Gender Equality Issues in the Marketing and Design of Goods for Children* (Dublin: Equality Authority, 2007), http://www.equality.ie/getFile. asp?FC_ID=417&docID=704 (accessed Dec. 31, 2008); Maurice Devlin, *Inequality and the Stereotyping of Young People* (Dublin: Equality Authority and National Youth Council of Ireland, 2006), http://www.equality.ie/getFile. asp?FC_ID=244&docID=528 (accessed Dec. 31, 2008); *Stereotyping of Young People: Resource Pack* (Dublin: Equality Authority and National Youth Council of Ireland, 2008), http://www.equality.ie/getFile.asp?FC_ID=452&docID=728 (accessed Dec. 31, 2008).

2. See, e.g., Convention on the Elimination of All Forms of Discrimination against Women, Dec. 18, 1979 (entered into force Sept. 3, 1981), 1249 U.N.T.S. 13, reprinted in 19 *I.L.M.* 33 (1980), arts. 2(f), 5(a), 10(c) ("Women's Convention"); Convention on the Rights of Persons with Disabilities, Dec. 13, 2006 (entered into force May 3, 2008), G.A. Res. 61/106, UN Doc. A/61/611 (2006), art. 8(1)(b); Protocol to the African Charter on Human and Peoples' Rights on the Rights of Women in Africa, Sept. 13, 2000 (entered into force Nov. 25, 2005), O.A.U. Doc. CAB/LEG/66.6, reprinted in 1 *Afr. Hum. Rts. L.J.* 40, arts. 2(2), 4(2)(d), 12(1)(b); Inter-American Convention on the Prevention, Punishment and Eradication of Violence against Women, June 9, 1994 (entered into force Mar. 5, 1995), OAS/Ser.L/V/I.4 rev. (Jan 2000), reprinted in 33 *I.L.M.* 1534 (1994), arts. 6(b), 8(b); Inter-American Convention on the Elimination of All Forms of Discrimination Against Persons with Disabilities, June 7, 1999 (entered into force Sept. 21, 2001), AG/RES. 1608 (XXIX-O/99), art. 3(2)(c).

3. See, e.g., *R. v. Ewanchuk*, [1999] 1 S.C.R. 330 (Can., Supreme Court); *President of the Republic of South Africa v. Hugo* 1997 (4) SA 1 (CC) (S. Afr., Constitutional Court); *Petrovic v. Austria*, App. No. 20458/92, 33 Eur. H.R. Rep. 307 (1998) (European Court of Human Rights) (Bernhardt and Spielmann JJ., dissenting).

4. See, e.g., *Morales de Sierra v. Guatemala,* Case 11.625, Inter-Am. C.H.R., Report No. 4/01, OEA/Ser.L/V/II.111, doc. 20 rev. (2001) (Inter-American Commission on Human Rights); *Public Prosecutor v. Kota,* [1993] VUSC 8; [1980–1994] Van LR 661 (Vanuatu, Supreme Court), http://www.worldlii.org/ vu/cases/VUSC/1993/8.html; *State v. Felipe Bechu,* [1999] FJMC 3; Criminal Case No. 79/94 (1999) (Fiji, First Class Magistrate's Court, Levuka), http:// www.worldlii.org/fj/cases/FJMC/1999/3.html.

5. See, e.g., Women's Committee, General Recommendation No. 25: Article 4, Paragraph 1, of the Convention on the Elimination of All Forms of Discrimination against Women, on Temporary Special Measures, UN Doc. A/59/38 (2004), at paras. 6–7 ("General Recommendation No. 25"); Committee on Economic, Social and Cultural Rights, General Comment No. 16: The Equal Rights of Men and Women to the Enjoyment of All Economic, Social and Cultural Rights, UN Doc. E/C.12/2005/4 (2005), at para. 19.

6. See Peter Glick and Susan T. Fiske, "Sex Discrimination: The Psychological Approach," in Faye J. Crosby, Margaret S. Stockdale, and S. Ann Ropp, eds., *Sex Discrimination in the Workplace: Multidisciplinary Perspectives* (Malden, Mass.: Blackwell, 2007), 155–88.

7. See Carole R. McCann and Seung-Kyung Kim, "Introduction," in Carole

R. McCann and Seung-Kyung Kim, eds., *Feminist Theory Reader: Local and Global Perspectives* (New York: Routledge, 2003), 12–23.

8. See, e.g., *1999 World Survey on the Role of Women in Development* (New York: United Nations, 1999), ix, quoted in Women's Committee, General Recommendation No. 25, at para. 7.

9. See generally Adrien Katherine Wing, ed., *Critical Race Feminism: A Reader*, 2nd ed. (New York: New York University Press, 2003).

10. See Women's Convention, art. 4(1).

11. See, e.g., Joan C. Williams and Stephanie Bornstein, "The Evolution of 'FRED': Family Responsibilities Discrimination and Developments in the Law of Stereotyping and Implicit Bias," *Hastings Law Journal* 59 (2008): 1311–58; Joan C. Williams and Elizabeth S. Westfall, "Deconstructing the Maternal Wall: Strategies for Vindicating the Civil Rights of 'Carers' in the Workplace," *Duke Journal of Gender Law & Policy* 13 (2006): 31–53.

12. See American Psychological Association, "In the Supreme Court of the United States: *Price Waterhouse v. Ann B. Hopkins*; Amicus Curiae Brief for the American Psychological Association," *American Psychologist* 46 (1991): 1061–70.

13. See Michelle O'Sullivan, "Stereotyping and Male Identification: 'Keeping Women in Their Place,'" in Christina Murray, ed., *Gender and the New South African Legal Order* (Kenwyn, South Africa: Juta, 1994), 185–201.

14. See, e.g., *R v. Ewanchuk*, note 3.

15. See, e.g., *Morales de Sierra v. Guatemala*, note 4.

16. See Women's Convention, arts. 1, 2(f), 3.

17. See Diane N. Ruble and Thomas L. Ruble, "Sex Stereotypes," in Arthur G. Miller, ed., *In the Eye of the Beholder: Contemporary Issues in Stereotyping* (New York: Praeger, 1982), 188–252; Sally Engle Merry, *Human Rights and Gender Violence: Translating International Law into Local Justice* (Chicago: University of Chicago Press, 2006), 75.

18. Roger Craig Green, "Equal Protection and the Status of Stereotypes," *Yale Law Journal* 108 (1998–1999): 1885–92, at 1887.

19. See, e.g., *Gonzales v. Carhart*, 550 U.S. 124 (2007), 127 S. Ct. 1610 (2007) (U.S. Supreme Court).

20. See, e.g., *Morales de Sierra v. Guatemala*, note 4.

21. See, e.g., *Cristina Muñoz-Vargas y Sainz de Vicuña v. Spain*, CEDAW, Communication No. 7/2005, UN Doc. CEDAW/C/39/D/7/2005 (2007) (Women's Committee) (majority and concurring opinions).

22. See, e.g., *Petrovic v. Austria*, note 3 (majority and concurring opinions).

23. See Monica Biernat and Diane Kobrynowicz, "A Shifting Standards Perspective on the Complexity of Gender Stereotypes and Gender Stereotyping," in William B. Swann, Jr., Judith H. Langlois, and Lucia Albino Gilbert, eds., *Sexism and Stereotypes in Modern Society: The Gender Science of Janet Taylor Spence* (Washington, D.C.: American Psychological Association, 1999), 75–106, at 78.

24. Savitri Goonesekere, "Universalizing Women's Human Rights Through CEDAW," in Hanna Beate Schöpp-Schilling, ed., Cees Flinterman, assoc. ed., *The Circle of Empowerment: Twenty-Five Years of the UN Committee on the Elimination of Discrimination Against Women* (New York: Feminist Press, 2007), 52–67, at 64.

25. Ibid.

26. See Women's Convention, art. 22.

27. See, e.g., L.S. Groenman et al., *Het Vrouwenverdrag in Nederland anno 1997* (Den Haag: Ministerie van SZW, 1997), discussed in Rikki Holtmaat, *Towards Different Law and Public Policy: The Significance of Article 5a CEDAW for the Elimi-*

nation of Structural Gender Discrimination (The Hague: Reed Business Information, 2004), 53–57, 133–60.

28. See Jennifer Nedelsky, "Embodied Diversity and the Challenges to Law," *McGill Law Journal* 42 (1997): 91–118, at 107.

29. Ibid.

30. See Katharine T. Bartlett, "Feminist Legal Methods," *Harvard Law Review* 103 (1989–1990): 829–88, at 866.

Select Bibliography on Gender Stereotyping

American Psychological Association. "In the Supreme Court of the United States: *Price Waterhouse v. Ann B. Hopkins.* Amicus Curiae Brief for the American Psychological Association." *American Psychologist* 46 (1991): 1061–70.

Amour, Jody. "Stereotypes and Prejudice: Helping Legal Decisionmakers Break the Prejudice Habit." *California Law Review* 83 (1995): 733–72.

Appiah, Kwame Anthony. "Stereotypes and the Shaping of Identity." *California Law Review* 88 (2000): 41–54.

———. "Identity, Authenticity, Survival: Multicultural Societies and Social Reproduction." In Amy Gutmann, ed., *Multiculturalism: Examining the Politics of Recognition.* Princeton, N.J.: Princeton University Press, 1994. 149–64.

Ashmore, Richard D., and Frances K. Del Boca. "Sex Stereotypes and Implicit Personality Theory: Toward a Cognitive-Social Psychological Conceptualization." *Sex Roles* 5 (1979): 219–48.

Bartlett, Katharine T. "Only Girls Wear Barrettes: Dress and Appearance Standards, Community Norms, and Workplace Equality." *Michigan Law Review* 92 (1993–1994): 2541–82.

Basow, Susan A. *Gender Stereotypes and Roles.* 3rd ed. Pacific Grove, Calif.: Brooks/Cole, 1992.

Bonthuys, Elsje. "Women's Sexuality in the South African Constitution." *Feminist Legal Studies* 14 (2006): 391–406.

Borgida, Eugene, Corrie Hunt, and Anita Kim. "On the Use of Gender Stereotyping Research in Sex Discrimination Litigation." *Journal of Law and Policy* 13 (2005): 613–28.

Burgess, Diana, and Eugene Borgida. "Who Women Are, Who Women Should Be: Descriptive and Prescriptive Gender Stereotyping in Sex Discrimination." *Psychology, Public Policy, and Law* 5 (1999): 665–92.

Case, Mary Anne. "'The Very Stereotype the Law Condemns': Constitutional Sex Discrimination Law as a Quest for Perfect Proxies." *Cornell Law Review* 85 (1999–2000): 1447–91.

Cava, Anita. "Taking Judicial Notice of Sexual Stereotyping." *Arkansas Law Review* 43 (1990): 27–56.

Cho, Sumi K. "Converging Stereotypes in Racialized Sexual Harassment: Where the Model Minority Meets Suzie Wong." *Journal of Gender, Race & Justice* 1 (1997): 177–212.

Cook, Rebecca J., and Susannah Howard. "Accommodating Women's Differences under the Women's Anti-Discrimination Convention." *Emory Law Journal* 56 (2007): 1039–91.

Costrich, Norma, et al. "When Stereotypes Hurt: Three Studies of Penalties for Sex-Role Reversals." *Journal of Experimental Social Psychology* 11 (1975): 520–30.

Eissa, Dahlia. "Constructing the Notion of Male Superiority over Women in Islam: The Influence of Sex and Gender Stereotyping in the Interpretation of the Qur'an and the Implications for a Modernist Exegesis of Rights." WLUML Occasional Paper 11. London: Women Living Under Muslim Laws, 1999; http://www.wluml.org/english/pubs/rtf/occpaper/OCP-11.rtf.

Ewan, Stuart, and Elizabeth Ewan. *Typecasting: On the Arts and Sciences of Human Inequality; A History of Dominant Ideas.* New York: Steven Stories Press, 2006.

Fenton, Zanita E. "Domestic Violence in Black and White: Racialized Gender Stereotypes in Gender Violence." *Columbia Journal of Gender & Law* 8 (1998–99): 1–66.

Fiske, Susan T., et al. "Social Science Research on Trial: Use of Sex Stereotyping Research in *Price Waterhouse v. Hopkins.*" *American Psychologist* 46 (1991): 1049–60.

Franks, Violet, and Esther D. Rothblum, eds. *The Stereotyping of Women: Its Effects on Mental Health.* New York: Springer, 1983.

Gans, David H. "Stereotyping and Difference: *Planned Parenthood v. Casey* and the Future of Sex Discrimination Law." *Yale Law Journal* 104 (1994–1995): 1875–1906.

Glick, Peter, and Susan T. Fiske. "An Ambivalent Alliance: Hostile and Benevolent Sexism as Complementary Justifications of Gender Inequality." *American Psychologist* 56 (2001): 109–18.

———. "Sex Discrimination: The Psychological Approach." In Faye J. Crosby, Margaret S. Stockdale, and S. Ann Ropp, eds., *Sex Discrimination in the Workplace: Multidisciplinary Perspectives.* Malden, Mass.: Blackwell, 2007. 155–88.

Green, Roger Craig. "Equal Protection and the Status of Stereotypes." *Yale Law Journal* 108 (1998–1999): 1885–92.

Hamilton, David L, ed. *Cognitive Processes in Stereotyping and Intergroup Behaviour.* Hillsdale, N.J.: Erlbaum, 1981.

Heilman, Madeline E. "Description and Prescription: How Gender Stereotypes Prevent Women's Ascent up the Organizational Ladder." *Journal of Social Issues* 57 (2001): 657–74.

Holtmaat, Rikki. *Towards Different Law and Public Policy: The Significance of Article 5a CEDAW for the Elimination of Structural Gender Discrimination.* The Hague: Reed Business Information, 2004.

———. "Preventing Violence Against Women: The Due Diligence Standard with Respect to the Obligation to Banish Gender Stereotypes on the Grounds of Article 5(a) of the CEDAW Convention." In Carin Benninger-Budel, ed., *Due Diligence and Its Application to Protect Women from Violence.* Leiden: Nijhoff, 2008. 63–89.

Kende, Mark S. "Gender Stereotypes in South African and American Constitutional Law: The Advantages of a Pragmatic Approach to Equality and Transformation." *South African Law Journal* 117 (2000): 745–70.

Kiyoko, Kinjo. "Article 5: Elimination of the Discriminatory Customs and Practices, Stereotyped Notions of the Attributes and Roles of Women and Men or the Superiority of Either Sex." In Japanese Association of International Women's Rights, *Convention on the Elimination of All Forms of Discrimination Against Women: A Commentary.* Tokyo: Shogakusya, 1995. 114–27.

Krieger, Linda Hamilton. "The Content of Our Categories: A Cognitive Bias Approach to Discrimination and Equal Employment Opportunity." *Stanford Law Review* 47 (1995): 1161–248.

L'Heureux-Dubé, The Honourable Madame Justice Claire. "Beyond the Myths:

Equality, Impartiality, and Justice." *Journal of Social Distress and the Homeless* 10 (2001): 87–104.

Lippmann, Walter. *Public Opinion.* 1922. Reprint New York: Macmillan, 1957.

Mack, Kathy. "*B v. R:* Negative Stereotypes and Women's Credibility." *Feminist Legal Studies* 2 (1994): 183–94.

Macrae, C. Neil, Charles Stangor, and Miles Hewstone, eds. *Stereotypes and Stereotyping.* New York: Guilford Press, 1996.

Meyerson, Denise. "Does the Constitutional Court of South Africa Take Rights Seriously? The Case of *S. v. Jordan.*" *Acta Juridica* (2004): 138–54.

Miller, Arthur G., ed. *In the Eye of the Beholder: Contemporary Issues in Stereotyping.* New York: Praeger, 1982.

Moreau, Sophia R. "The Wrongs of Unequal Treatment." *University of Toronto Law Journal* 54 (2004): 291–326.

Moreau, Sophia Reibetanz. "Equality Rights and the Relevance of Comparator Groups." *Journal of Law & Equality* 5 (2006): 81–96.

O'Sullivan, Michelle. "Stereotyping and Male Identification: 'Keeping Women in Their Place.'" In Christina Murray, ed., *Gender and the New South African Legal Order.* Kenwyn, South Africa: Juta, 1994. 185–201.

Oakes, Penelope J., S. Alexander Haslam, and John C. Turner. *Stereotyping and Social Reality.* Oxford: Blackwell, 1994.

Pieterse, Marius. "Stereotypes, Sameness, Difference and Human Rights: Catch 22?" *South African Public Law* 15 (2001): 93–121.

Post, Robert. "Prejudicial Appearances: The Logic of American Antidiscrimination Law." *California Law Review* 88 (2000): 1–40.

———. "Response to Commentators." *California Law Review* 88 (2000): 119–26.

Raday, Frances. "Culture, Religion, and CEDAW's Article 5(a)." In Hanna Beate Schöpp-Schilling, ed., Cees Flinterman, assoc. ed., *The Circle of Empowerment: Twenty-Five Years of the UN Committee on the Elimination of Discrimination Against Women.* New York: Feminist Press, 2007. 68–85.

Rhode, Deborah L., and Joan C. Williams. "Legal Perspectives on Employment Discrimination." In Faye J. Crosby, Margaret S. Stockdale, and S. Ann Ropp, eds., *Sex Discrimination in the Workplace: Multidisciplinary Perspectives.* Malden, Mass.: Blackwell, 2007. 235–70.

Ruble, Thomas L., Renae Cohen, and Diane N. Ruble. "Sex Stereotypes: Occupational Barriers for Women." *American Behavioral Scientist* 27 (1984): 339–56.

Sachs, Albie, and Joan Hoff Wilson. *Sexism and the Law: A Study of Male Beliefs and Legal Bias in Britain and the United States.* New York: Free Press, 1979.

Scutt, Jocelynne A. *Women and the Law: Commentary and Materials.* Sydney: Law Book, 1990. 50–71.

Siegel, Reva B. "The New Politics of Abortion: An Equality Analysis of Woman-Protective Abortion Restrictions." *University of Illinois Law Review* (2007): 991–1054.

Stangor, Charles, ed. *Stereotypes and Prejudice: Essential Readings.* Philadelphia: Psychology Press, 2000.

Swann, William B., Jr., Judith H. Langlois, and Lucia Albino Gilbert, eds. *Sexism and Stereotypes in Modern Society: The Gender Science of Janet Taylor Spence.* Washington, D.C.: American Psychological Association, 1999.

Symposium. "Makeup, Identity Performance and Discrimination." *Duke Journal of Gender Law & Policy* 14 (2007).

Widiss, Deborah A., Elizabeth L. Rosenblatt, and Douglas NeJaime. "Exposing

Sex Stereotypes in Recent Same-Sex Marriage Jurisprudence." *Harvard Journal of Law & Gender* 30 (2007): 461–505.

Williams, Joan C. "*Hibbs* as a Federalism Case; *Hibbs* as a Maternal Wall Case." *University of Cincinnati Law Review* 73 (2004–2005): 365–98.

———. "Deconstructing Gender." *Michigan Law Review* 87 (1988–1989): 797–845.

Williams, Joan C., and Stephanie Bornstein. "The Evolution of 'FRED': Family Responsibilities Discrimination and Developments in the Law of Stereotyping and Implicit Bias." *Hastings Law Journal* 59 (2008): 1311–58.

Williams, Joan C., and Nancy Segal. "Beyond the Maternal Wall: Relief for Family Caregivers Who Are Discriminated Against on the Job." *Harvard Women's Law Journal* 26 (2003): 77–162.

Williams, Joan C., and Elizabeth S. Westfall. "Deconstructing the Maternal Wall: Strategies for Vindicating the Civil Rights of 'Carers' in the Workplace." *Duke Journal of Gender Law & Policy* 13 (2006): 31–53.

Annotated List of Websites

While not exhaustive, the following annotated list of Web sites contains domestic legislation, treaties, transnational case law, and other jurisprudence relevant to women's rights. The annotations and URLs are current as of December 2008.

A DIGEST OF CASE LAW ON THE HUMAN RIGHTS OF WOMEN
(ASIA PACIFIC)
http://www.apwld.org/pb_adigest.htm
This site provides access to a digest, published by Asia Pacific Forum on Women Law and Development, of women's rights cases from the Asia Pacific region.

AFRICAN COMMISSION ON HUMAN RIGHTS
http://www.achpr.org
This site provides the text of the basic documents pertaining to human rights in the African Union. It also contains reports related to the work of the African Commission on Human Rights. Decisions of the African Commission are soon to be added to the site.

BAYEFSKY.COM
http://www.bayefsky.com/
This site includes the human rights treaties of the United Nations human rights system. It also includes the case law of the United Nations human rights treaty monitoring bodies, as well as other relevant jurisprudence, such as General Comments, General Recommendations, and the periodic reports of States Parties and Concluding Observations.

CEDAW BENCHBOOK
http://www.cedawbenchbook.org/
This site summarizes Filipino case law related to the Women's Convention.

CENTER FOR REPRODUCTIVE RIGHTS
http://www.reproductiverights.org
This site contains summaries of transnational case law on reproductive rights.

COMMITTEE ON THE ELIMINATION OF DISCRIMINATION AGAINST WOMEN
http://www2.ohchr.org/english/bodies/cedaw/index.htm
This site is the official Website for the Women's Committee. It includes the text of the Women's Convention and its Optional Protocol. It lists those States Parties that have ratified these treaties, and notes relevant reservations and declarations. In addition, the site includes the case law and other jurisprudence of the Committee.
Individual complaints and inquiries
    http://www2.ohchr.org/english/law/jurisprudence.htm
General Recommendations
    http://www2.ohchr.org/english/bodies/cedaw/comments.htm
Concluding Observations
    http://www2.ohchr.org/english/bodies/cedaw/sessions.htm

ESCR-NET
http://www.escr-net.org/caselaw/
This site contains transnational case law on economic, social and cultural rights.

EUROPEAN COURT OF HUMAN RIGHTS
http://www.echr.coe.int
This site includes a database of case law decided by the European Court of Human Rights. It also provides access to the basic documents pertaining to the European human rights system.

HUMAN RIGHTS INDEX
http://www.universalhumanrightsindex.org/
This site includes a searchable database of documents related to the United Nations human rights system. It includes documents from human rights treaty bodies and the Special Procedures of the Human Rights Council.

INTER-AMERICAN COMMISSION ON HUMAN RIGHTS
http://www.cidh.org
This site contains the case law of the Inter-American Commission on Human Rights. It also provides the text of the basic documents pertaining to human rights in the Inter-American system. As well, it contains reports and information related to the work of the Rapporteurship on the Rights of Women.

INTER-AMERICAN COURT ON HUMAN RIGHTS
http://www.oas.org/oaspage/humanrights.htm
This site contains the case law, advisory opinions, provisional measures, and instruments of the Inter-American Court on Human Rights.

INTERIGHTS
http://www.interights.org
This site includes a database of Commonwealth and international human rights case law.

INTERNATIONAL WOMEN'S RIGHTS ACTION WATCH ASIA PACIFIC
http://www.iwraw-ap.org/protocol/case_law.htm
This site contains summaries of transnational case law related to women's rights, with an emphasis on case law relevant to the Women's Convention and its Optional Protocol.

LAWYERS' COLLECTIVE
http://www.lawyerscollective.org/
This site provides summaries of legislation and case law on women's rights, HIV/AIDS and civil rights. It is primarily concerned with India, but includes other transnational jurisprudence.

LEGAL GROUNDS: REPRODUCTIVE AND SEXUAL RIGHTS IN AFRICAN COMMONWEALTH COURTS
http://www.reproductiverights.org/pub_bo_legalgrounds.html
This site provides summaries of case law on women's rights and reproductive and sexual rights from national courts throughout African Commonwealth countries.

PACIFIC HUMAN RIGHTS LAW DIGEST
http://www.rrrt.org/assets/HR%20Law%20Digest.pdf
This document provides summaries of cases addressing international
human rights in Pacific Island courts.

ROSSRIGHTS.COM
http://www.rossrights.com/
This site is an online documentary supplement to Susan Deller Ross,
Women's Human Rights: The International and Comparative Law Casebook
(Philadelphia: University of Pennsylvania Press, 2008). It contains elec-
tronic copies of case law, instruments, and other materials featured in
the book.

UNITED NATIONS DIVISION FOR THE ADVANCEMENT OF WOMEN
http://www.un.org/womenwatch/daw
This site is a gateway to materials addressing the human rights and fundamental freedoms of women in the United Nations system.

UNITED NATIONS OFFICE OF THE HIGH COMMISSIONER FOR HUMAN
RIGHTS
http://www.ohchr.org
This site offers information on the organizational structure of the
UN human rights system. It provides access to international human
rights instruments, and includes a database of case law decided by
the international human rights treaty bodies, as well as other relevant
jurisprudence.
Committee against Torture
    http://www2.ohchr.org/english/bodies/cat/index.htm
Committee on Economic, Social and Cultural Rights
    http://www2.ohchr.org/english/bodies/cescr/index.htm
Committee on Migrant Workers
    http://www2.ohchr.org/english/bodies/cmw/index.htm
Committee on the Elimination of Discrimination against Women
    http://www2.ohchr.org/english/bodies/cedaw/index.htm
Committee on the Elimination of Racial Discrimination
    http://www2.ohchr.org/english/bodies/cerd/index.htm
Committee on the Rights of the Child
    http://www2.ohchr.org/english/bodies/crc/index.htm
Committee on the Rights of Persons with Disabilities
    http://www2.ohchr.org/english/bodies/crpd/index.htm

Human Rights Committee
  http://www2.ohchr.org/english/bodies/hrc/index.htm
Treaty Bodies Database
  http://tb.ohchr.org/default.aspx

UNIVERSITY OF MINNESOTA HUMAN RIGHTS LIBRARY
http://www.umn.edu/humanrts/
This database contains one of the most extensive collections of human
rights documents from around the world. It includes educational materials, annotated bibliographies, and international and regional human
rights instruments and jurisprudence.

WOMEN'S LINK WORLDWIDE
http://www.womenslinkworldwide.org
This site contains transnational case law on women's rights.

WORLDLII
http://www.worldlii.org/
This site contains a database of transnational legislation and case law.

Index

The Index and the Tables of Cases and Treaties, Legislation, and Other Relevant Instruments at the front of the book have been designed to complement but not repeat each other. This index does not include individual cases, treaties, or legislation, with two exceptions. The Convention on the Elimination of All Forms of Discrimination against Women and the Optional Protocol to the Convention are briefly referenced in the front tables; due to the necessity for sub-entries, detailed references are included in this Index.

Acknowledgments

The authors are grateful to many people for providing invaluable insights on different aspects of gender stereotyping, reviewing draft chapters of the book, and providing assistance with finding relevant court decisions and materials. We thank Bernard Dickens, Joanna Erdman, Reva Siegel, and the anonymous reviewer, chosen by the University of Pennsylvania Press, for reading drafts of chapters or all the chapters. Their comments and insights were invaluable and motivated us to think far more clearly or in different dimensions about the stereotyping of women. Linda Hutjens, coordinator of the Law Faculty's International Reproductive and Sexual Health Law Programme, was a constant source of support throughout the research and writing of the book. She edited each chapter in her meticulous way, giving it a distinct polish.

We are indebted to Peter Agree, Editor in Chief of the University of Pennsylvania Press, and Bert Lockwood, Editor of the Human Rights Series of the Press, for their vision and imagination about human rights books generally, and our book specifically. The research and writing of the book were greatly facilitated by a grant from the Hewlett Foundation. Nicole Gray, our program officer at the Foundation, sustained us in countless ways, contributing more than we ever could have hoped.

It is hard to imagine how we would have written this book without the assistance of our home institutions. The staff at the Bora Laskin Law Library, Faculty of Law, University of Toronto, especially John Papadopolous, Sooin Kim, Sufie Xu, and the former Law Librarian, Beatrice Tice, never tired of our requests for a copy of a court decision, an article, or a book, and their patience and perseverance in finding them never failed us. Our research assistants, Cara Davies, Karen Ensslen, Erin Hallock, and Kim Stanton, were always responding with a smile to our untimely requests for help. Simone Cusack would like to thank the Public Interest Law Clearing House (Vic) Inc, especially Mathew Tinkler, Lucy McKernan, and Catherine Symons. It would not have been possible to complete this book without PILCH's generous support, encouragement and understanding.

We are grateful to Onyema Afulukwe, Monica Arango, Clara Rita Padilla, Carolina S. Ruiz Austria, Purna Shrestha, Kibrom Isaac, and

Honey Tan Lay Ean for providing important court decisions or materials from their respective countries and regions which helped us to understand the commonality of stereotyping across jurisdictions.

Either individually or together, we were fortunate to be able to present previous drafts of chapters in different fora. Rebecca Cook presented a draft chapter at the Faculty of Law Workshop, University of Toronto, and in her courses on International Protection of Women's Rights and Reproductive and Sexual Health Law at the Law Faculty, taught in fall 2008. Simone Cusack presented a draft chapter at the Expert Group Meeting on Creating Resources for Lawyers on Litigation for Women's Human Rights Using CEDAW, organized by International Women's Rights Action Watch Asia Pacific, in December 2008.

We are grateful to the Academy on Human Rights and Humanitarian Law, Washington College of Law, American University, for the opportunity to try out some of the ideas in this book in the course, Women and International Human Rights Law, which Rebecca Cook co-taught with Elizabeth Abi Mershed in June, 2008. Elizabeth's insights and those of the guest lecturers in the course, Professors Janie Chuang, Anne Shalleck, and Claire Smearman, and Simone Cusack, on certain aspects of stereotyping, proved invaluable, as did those of the students. Our thinking also benefited enormously from discussions with countless people, too numerous to name, but certainly including Luisa Cabal, Shanthi Dairiam, Rikki Holtmaat, Susannah Howard, Julie Kay, and Nancy Northup.

We were fortunate to have the opportunity to coauthor, with Viviana Krsticevic and Vanessa Coria of the Center for Justice and International Law, an amicus brief in the *Campo Algodonero* case, which is pending before the Inter-American Court of Human Rights. This gave us an opportunity to apply some of the general ideas on stereotyping to the stereotyping of young, poor migrant women by the criminal justice system in the state of Chihuahua, Mexico.

Finally, we owe a tremendous debt of gratitude to the community of scholars whose work on stereotyping generally and stereotyping of women specifically inspired us in countless ways. As the saying goes, when you drink a glass of water you never can forget those who dug the well.